"David Drucker has one of the great technological minds in financial planning. He and Joel Bruckenstein have produced a practical road map for making your office more efficient. **Every financial planner should read it.**"

LEWIS J. ALTFEST, PH.D., CFP, CFA, PFS
President, L.J. Altfest & Co., Inc.

"In the words of the infamous Charlie Munger, **'Once in a while a real Lollapalooza comes along,' a book whose ideas or concept is a real change agent, a difference-maker.** This book illuminates a major paradigm shift in the maturing of the financial planning profession. The availability of technical infrastructure at affordable prices produces a huge leap in productivity that will change the dynamics of the profession. Through this book, Dave and Joel have made **a major contribution to the evolution of the financial planning profession.**"

RICHARD R. LEE JR., CFP, CFA
President, Lee Financial Corporation

"**Don't be intimidated by the title. This book is for every practitioner.** We are all looking for ways to improve efficiencies, enhance our bottom line, gain control of our workload, and provide great service to our clients. Drucker and Bruckenstein have researched and "test driven" many top productivity-enhancing tools. If you implement just one of the great ideas from the text, **it could save you countless hours of frustration and significant amounts of money.**"

SHERYL GARRETT, CFP
Founder and President, The Garrett Planning Network, Inc.

"The small practitioner has always had the advantages of mobility and flexibility. This book enables us to operate with the full-blown technology and support resources of the most "substantial" institutions, plus we can maintain the genuine intimacy and "response-ability" that has always been our strength. **With these tools, the small practitioner can now compete effectively with anyone, anytime, anywhere, on any level.**"

RICHARD B. WAGNER, J.D., CFP
WorthLiving LLC

"**At worst, this book will save you many hours and dollars; at best, it may save your business and your sanity.**"

NATALIE B. CHOATE, ESQ.
Estate planning attorney
Author of *Life and Death Planning for Retirement Benefits*

How to save time, big time

Opening a New Client Custodial Account

The Traditional Way

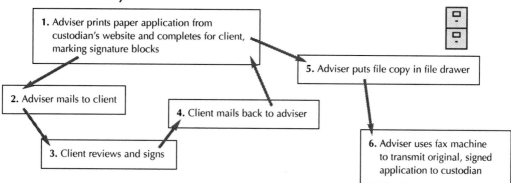

1. Relying on client's paper files for data required by application, adviser spends 60 minutes completing application
2. Adviser spends 10 minutes preparing mailing, and application reaches client in 2 days by U.S. mail
3. Client reviews, signs, and puts in outgoing mail, which is picked up the following day
4. Application takes 2 days to reach adviser by U.S. mail
5. and 6. Adviser spends 15 minutes filing and faxing document

Total days 5.0   **Total adviser-hours 1.4**

The Virtual Way

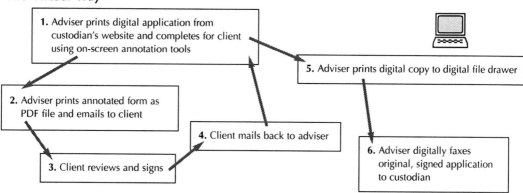

1. Relying on contact manager to gather required data, adviser spends 15 minutes completing application
2. Adviser spends 1 minute preparing PDF file, and application reaches client instantly
3. Client prints, reviews, signs, and puts in outgoing mail the same day
4. Application takes 2 days to reach adviser by U.S. mail
5. and 6. Adviser spends 5 minutes scanning and digitally filing document, then digitally faxing scanned image to custodian

Total days 2.0   **Total adviser-hours 0.4**

SAVINGS = 3 DAYS PROCESSING TIME AND 1 HOUR OF ADVISER TIME

VIRTUAL-OFFICE TOOLS
FOR A
HIGH-MARGIN
PRACTICE

Also available from
BLOOMBERG PRESS

The Investment Think Tank and *Retirement Income Redesigned*
by Harold Evensky and Deena B. Katz, eds.

Managing Concentrated Stock Wealth
by Tim Kochis

Deena Katz on Practice Management and
Deena Katz's Tools and Templates for Your Practice
by Deena B. Katz

How to Value, Buy, or Sell a Financial-Advisory Practice
by Mark C. Tibergien and Owen Dahl

Practice Made Perfect
by Mark C. Tibergien and Rebecca Pomering

Building a High-End Financial Services Practice
by Cliff Oberlin and Jill Powers

Making Referral Relationships Pay
by Thomas Grady

In Search of the Perfect Model
by Mary Rowland

The New Fiduciary Standard
by Tim Hatton, CFP, CIMA, AIF

A complete list of our titles is available at **www.bloomberg.com/books**

VIRTUAL-OFFICE TOOLS
FOR A
HIGH-MARGIN
PRACTICE

———■———

How Client-Centered Financial Advisers Can

Cut Paperwork, Overhead, and Wasted Hours

DAVID J. DRUCKER
AND JOEL P. BRUCKENSTEIN

BLOOMBERG PRESS

NEW YORK

This publication contains the authors' opinions and is designed to provide accurate and authoritative information. It is sold with the understanding that the authors, publisher, and Bloomberg L.P. are not engaged in rendering legal, accounting, investment-planning, or other professional advice. The reader should seek the services of a qualified professional for such advice; the authors, publisher, and Bloomberg L.P. cannot be held responsible for any loss incurred as a result of specific investments or planning decisions made by the reader.

First edition published 2002
5 7 9 10 8 6 4

ISBN-13: 978-1-57660-123-5

The Library of Congress has cataloged the earlier printing as follows:

Drucker, David J., 1948–
    Virtual-office tools for a high-margin practice : how client-centered
financial advisers can cut paperwork, overhead, and wasted hours / David
J. Drucker and Joel P. Bruckenstein.
        p. cm. -- (Bloomberg professional library)
    Includes bibliographical references and index.
    ISBN 1-57660-123-4 (alk. paper)
1. Financial planners. 2. Finance, Personal--Computer network
resources. 3. Internet. 4. Home-based businesses--Computer network
resources. I. Bruckenstein, Joel P., 1956– II. Title. III. Series.
    HG179.5 .D78 2002
    332.024'0068--dc21   2002006572

Acquired and edited by JARED KIELING

Book Design by LAURIE LOHNE/DESIGN IT COMMUNICATIONS

Cover design by Barbara Diez Goldenberg/Bloomberg Press. Front cover photographs by (far left) © Riley & Riley Photography, Inc./Picturesque/PictureQuest; all other images, © Corbis. Back cover illustrations © Bloomberg L.P.

In loving memory of Arthur J. Drucker

—DD

In memory of my friends Kevin Hannaford,
Tom Hobbs, and Frank Spinelli who lost their lives
on September 11, 2001

—JB

Summary of Contents

P a r t   O n e

The High-Margin Practice

P a r t   T w o

Eliminating Paper

P a r t   T h r e e

The Tools in Practice

Contents

P a r t   O n e

The High-Margin Practice

P a r t   T h r e e

The Tools in Practice

11 Making the Virtual Transition   209

12 Looking Ahead   219

Acknowledgments   222

Recommended Resources   225

Index   241

F o r e w o r d

NOT LONG AGO, I wrote an online column for about 70,000 financial advisers and asked them to tell me what they considered to be the most important issues for the future. One reply captured my attention immediately, because it drove right to the heart of what I call the Unfulfilled Promise of starting an independent business.

"There are many more issues today than fifteen years ago, when I started in this business," the adviser wrote. "Today, expenses are increasing, the cost of marketing has increased, compliance has become a monstrous headache, I spend most of my day managing employees—and at the same time, managing client expectations has become more of a burden.

"When I started my business," he continued, "my goal was to have a reasonable personal income, to spend my work days serving my clients rather than dealing with administrative issues, and to keep things simple and easy by having a small one-man shop. Now, all I want is my freedom and to go back to having fun and not having to be a slave to my business. I feel that I must either add a partner or merge my practice with another planner just in order to survive. This is not what I wanted to do.

But, I feel that I have no choice if I want to continue in this business."

Those powerful words are worth repeating: "All I want is my freedom and to go back to having fun and not having to be a slave to my business."

This is the unfulfilled promise that many financial planning practitioners grapple with every day. They started their business so that they could spend their day doing something inherently rewarding: working closely with clients. And they envisioned that eventually their company would make it possible for them to improve their personal lifestyle as well—generating an income more flexibly than is possible when you're a wage slave and allowing vacations and personal time as needed or desired, while still providing a high level of service to clients.

For most advisers, the reality is astonishingly, discouragingly different from this vision. Their business has become their life, and the things that they spend their time on are the least rewarding parts of it: administration and supervising employees and payroll, making sure the paperwork is filled out and filed properly, or case writing. The time they get to spend in front of clients seems to be threatened by a million encroaching tasks, and that flexibility and free time never seems to happen.

You have in your hands the first and only guidebook to recovering that promise and finally fulfilling it.

This book offers direct, step-by-step, practical advice on how to put a lot of those tasks that are encroaching on your life into a proverbial box and hand them to somebody else. It introduces you to a growing support structure of outside service providers who will work for you, not as employees but as outsource service providers, which means you could—as one of the coauthors actually did—create a substantial planning firm with no employees. The firm of David J. Drucker, M.B.A., CFP was listed in a recent issue of *Bloomberg Wealth Manager* as one of the top 100 wealth management firms in the country in terms of revenues. Yet Dave works out of his home four days a week and his "work" consists primarily of interacting with his clients.

This book will also give you instant access to a whole new realm of technological solutions that most advisers simply don't have the time to investigate. You have probably noticed an explosion in planning software, Web-based services, and office management tools. What you may not know is that there are paperless office solutions that are thousands of dollars less expensive than those offered by the name brands.

Joel P. Bruckenstein, CFP, is both a financial planning practitioner and a technology reviewer, a very rare combination that brings particular value to this book. You can find Joel's software reviews on Morningstar Inc.'s MorningstarAdvisor.com website, on Horsesmouth.com, and in my own *Inside Information* newsletter.

If you know of my work, you know that I've been forecasting the future of the planning profession ever since I predicted the tax shelter debacle back in mid-1986, the rise of asset management services in 1987, and the advent of life-planning services back in 1995. As I look forward today, I see the growing importance of efficiency in planning practices; in fact, I think it will be a key to survival.

But I think another key to survival is to reclaim your life and to fulfill that promise that led you into this business to begin with. You owe it to your clients to give them more of you and to begin living a focused, flexible, fulfilling life in which your company works for you instead of vice versa.

In the future the people who hire your services will want you to help them achieve this promise in their own lives. You won't be able to help them get there if you're too busy filing compliance papers or training new employees.

If you, too, want your freedom, and to go back to having fun and not having to be a slave to your business, then this book was written for you. Good luck on your journey.

BOB VERES
Editor and Publisher, *Inside Information*

Preface

MY DAUGHTER PLAYS a large role in this story, because her birth quickly led me to discover the efficiencies that are the substance of what I now call the Virtual Financial Planning Firm. I was a principal in a ten-year-old, successful financial advisory firm by the time my daughter came along. I was forty-two years old and didn't wish to shuttle the baby off to day care each morning en route to the office. So Gracey and I set up shop in a spare bedroom, she burbling softly on the floor near my feet, as her limited mobility kept her close by, and me with the rudiments of an office setup trying to do what I normally did each day—except that I was doing it from home.

If you've never tried this before, you'll find out rather quickly that you fit one of two molds. Either you're energized by the quiet, the sudden lack of interferences that devour an ordinary day at the office, and you'll perform well beyond your accustomed capacity—or the lack of social contact or self-motivation will lead you to prefer cleaning your toilet over getting any real work done. Fortunately, I fit the former mold. Intrigued by the possibilities, I started to work at home more and more, even beyond the time when my daughter's infancy required me to be there.

My makeshift office setup gradually became more sophisticated.

Joel went through a similar "transformation." After an almost twenty-year institutional brokerage career, Joel began a part-time personal financial planning practice in 1995 and transitioned in 1997 to full-time planning working out of a home office located in a New York City suburb. In late 1999, his wife raised the idea of a five-week trip to South America. Joel wanted to make the trip, but he was concerned about being away from his clients for such a long stretch. He realized that as long as he had a laptop, a telephone, and an Internet connection, anything was possible. So off he went, to both his and his clients' benefit.

The success of that trip led Joel to question his preconceived notion that he needed to be in close geographic proximity to his clients. As a result, he sold his house in New York and moved his practice to Florida, where he continues to serve his New York clients.

Many financial advisers have not seen the possibilities technology and Internet-enhanced processes hold for them, or they don't know where to begin to make them a reality. Hence, this book.

Many of the most successful players in today's financial planning industry—the fee-only and fee-based independent advisers—are stuck in a trap of their own devising. The trap is the business model created and perpetuated by industry veterans that locks its followers into a narrow blueprint for building an advisory business. The blueprint dictates that what often starts out as a sparsely furnished room housing a sole practitioner will become an ever-expanding office full of employees, each armed with a full complement of office equipment and benefit plans, as will be the new partners who are eventually added to the mix. In short, the firm's overhead will ratchet up with every client it adds.

In reality, firms of very different sizes often don't have markedly different profit margins, leading one to wonder whether any economies of scale even exist in the traditional growth model. *The 2000 FPA Financial Performance & Compensation Study of Financial Planning Practitioners* includes comparative profit and loss statements for all advisory firm respondents by size. Adding net income before taxes to total owner compensation and dividing by gross revenues, we find pre-compensation/pretax profit margins as shown in box at left. In fact, if

Firms with gross revenues	
Under $150,000	56.6%
$150,000 to $300,00	61.1%
$300,000 to $500,000	59.3%
$500,000 to $1,000,000	55.6%
Over $1,000,000	56.1%

these numbers suggest any trend at all, it might be that advisory firms experience *dis*economies of scale as they grow.

The planning industry has brilliantly transformed itself from a sales-oriented culture churning out financial plans designed to sell product into a profession that serves clients' dreams as well as their financial goals. It's perhaps ironic, then, that an industry so devoted to helping its clients change is so slow to revamp its own business practices to extract greater profitability for its owners. This inertia has fueled the urgency behind various white papers anticipating the industry's need to effect changes for its own profitable survival, most notably *The Future of the Financial Advisory Business and the Delivery of Advice to the Semi-Affluent Investor,* September 1999, and *The Future of the Financial Advisory Business Part II: Strategies for Small Businesses,* September 2000, both by Undiscovered Managers LLC under the direction of Mark P. Hurley, CEO. The survival these reports speak of will require advisers not only to increase their service offerings, but to do so with radically lower fee schedules—a challenge many firms will be ill equipped to face. To remain independent, advisers will need to do radical surgery on their business models. Just as retailing has transformed itself via the Internet, planners will have to use all the tools at their disposal to do more with less. Virtuality is one of those tools.

"But what's the deal with virtuality?" you ask. "How can a financial planning firm be virtual when its clients are real?" Obviously, a definition of *virtual* is in order. The dictionary definition you will usually find will be something like "pertaining to a device or service that is perceived as more real or concrete than it actually is." In the context of a financial advisory business, concrete things are offices, staff, face-to-face meetings, and financial plan documents. Yet all of these things have virtual counterparts that can be substituted for the "real" thing if clients will accept these substitutes without perceiving a diminution of service. If clients *will* accept virtual services, it's just possible that adopting a virtual firm business model—or at least some aspects of it—might be the key to our profitable, long-term survival in the face of new competitors with much deeper pockets than ours.

Not many years ago, a financial advisory firm with a website was a novelty. Now we perceive any business without a Web presence as a curiosity not to be taken seriously. Advisers slow to adopt new technologies are being surpassed by many of their clients' own facilities at using new digital phenomena. In this climate, we need to promote both the perception and the reality that we can operate efficiently.

What we want to demonstrate to you in this book is that virtuality isn't a process so much as it's a mentality. To see the possibilities, we must rethink each element of our workday and our work flow to discover virtual alternatives. We will give you plenty of examples in this book, starting with a look at my own practice.

For example, I am the only employee of my company, which is a "C" corporation, yet I have lots of help and delegate the major portion of every important function in my firm to someone else. I work from a home office, yet I easily attract clients with million-dollar-plus net worths. I have no file cabinets, yet I can easily locate records for clients I have served since 1987.

Powerful as all that is, this book isn't about how to transform your practice into my practice. Don't decide whether virtuality will work for you based upon whether my practice is like yours. It probably isn't. For example, you may not care to work alone or to deal with the kinds of clients I deal with. This book is about ways to create fast, efficient, virtual processes for nearly everything you do, leading not only to greater profitability, but more time for the things that are important to you besides your work. If you're caught in the trap of ratcheting costs, and you suspect the cause may be systems that are out-of-date and inefficient, let us help you adopt the virtual mentality. It may revolutionize many of the ways in which you do business.

DAVE DRUCKER

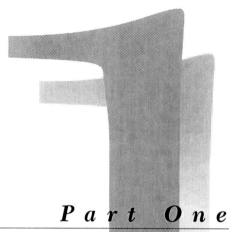

Part One

The High-Margin Practice

Chapter One

A Day in the Virtual Adviser's Life

I N THIS BOOK, many of our examples come from the story of how Dave transformed his fairly normal, mid-sized financial planning firm into an extreme virtual operation. As we have said, our goal is not to convince you to do the same. The business model you ultimately choose may result in either a small or a large firm. Our goal is to give you the benefit of the solutions Dave found, as well as some others that don't work for Dave but might work for you, and to answer the questions that you may be facing in your business:

➤ How do I get some relief from endless phone tag and phone calls with clients?

➤ It seems that I spend my whole day training employees and solving their problems instead of dealing with my important clients. What's the answer?

➤ How do I solve the problem of never being able to find anything? It seems that the older client records are the hardest to track down, whereas I need to have them at my fingertips.

➤ I feel vulnerable to the loss of significant expertise when a key employee quits with little notice. How can I better protect myself?

➤ What do I do about my inability to afford to hire an investment professional to address financial markets that seem to get more and more volatile and the new investment products that are constantly becoming available—all things that I should be evaluating for my clients?

➤ I'm just a sole practitioner at this stage, and I'm swamped with administrative work that needs to be done. What are my options for getting help, given that I probably can't keep an administrative employee busy full-time?

➤ We're running out of office space for record storage. How can I avoid paying $30 a square foot just to store paper that the SEC says we must keep, even though we seldom refer to much of it?

➤ I keep a lot of my client records on my computer but still have trouble finding them. For example, I never know whether to look under Microsoft Outlook or Word or My Documents, since the records might be in the form of a Word document, an e-mail, or something else. How can I straighten out this mess?

These questions and many more will be answered for you throughout the course of this book. For a glimpse of how you can get from where you are now to a place in which virtual processes make your business significantly more efficient and rewarding, let's take a look at Dave's practice before and after his conversion to "virtuality."

The Evolution of Sunset Financial Management, Inc. into a Virtual Financial Planning Firm

IN 1996 DAVE found himself twelve years into a partnership that had created a successful two-principal, six-employee financial planning firm in the suburbs of Washington, D.C. His and his partner's vision was to grow the firm while providing a top-level, hands-on, comprehensive, strictly fee-only financial management service. That vision represented a reasonable set of goals, which many firms are striving toward these days. The fact that the vision is elusive to so many doesn't make it wrong, but suggests that the way many advisers have gone about accomplishing it might not be the most effective.

The opportunity Dave had to change these methods came when he finally admitted he was tired—not of his partner or of his firm—but of life in Washington, D.C. He yearned for a smaller-town existence, even at the expense of breaking up an established partnership and a successful firm with a brand name, not to mention lifelong friendships in the D.C. area. His wife and he decided to move to Albuquerque, New Mexico, a destination they'd discovered on numerous Southwestern vacations. It was a location that "called" to him. It could have been anywhere.

In September 1996, he and his wife bought a home in Albuquerque and established a plan to allow eighteen months for Dave to split up his business partnership, convince his clients to work with him from afar, and finally move with an established income to the new town they would call home. He and his business partner worked with different halves of the client base, so it seemed quite logical that each would simply retain his and her own clients. It would be up to Dave to keep his half through a new, long-distance form of service. Putting a tenant in his new home for these initial eighteen months gave him the chance to plan, relate those plans to his clients, and ultimately retain his practice income.

Once Dave moved, his first inclination was to rebuild what he already knew well—a small firm with several employees—and to begin enjoying the autonomy of running the new firm without a partner. What forced him into a more creative mind-set was a need to make more money. Although Albuquerque's cost of living is far less than D.C.'s, his business projections were disheartening. When he did P&L pro formas factoring in the fixed costs he would no longer be able to share with a partner plus the added travel expenses he expected to incur, he was starting to have second thoughts about what he had done.

Dave played with his spreadsheet, making changes around the edges—slightly fewer hours of employee time here, a few more new clients there—and figured maybe he could retain as much as 75 percent of the net compensation he'd enjoyed in his former partnership. The only way to do that, it turned out, was to find easier and cheaper ways of operating without compromising client service and without putting his income at risk. His business model and its cost structure underwent radical surgery. The totality of the alternatives he discovered is what we will discuss as the Virtual Financial Planning Firm.

A Day in the Life

TO GIVE YOU a quick idea of what a virtual financial planning firm looks like, here's Dave's daily routine at Sunset Financial Management, Inc., his one-man, financial advisory "C" corporation in Albuquerque, New Mexico, serving forty-five high-net-worth clients located throughout the United States with assets under management of approximately $60 million:

7:00 A.M.: Check calendar and to-do list for current appointments and/or high-priority tasks.

7:15 A.M.: Read the *Wall Street Journal* online at online.wsj.com with breakfast and a cup of coffee.

7:45 A.M.–9:45 A.M.: Block out time for highest priority item of the day, in this case, final preparations for a client's annual update meeting. This is the one project that Dave wants to start and finish in one sitting with no interruptions. E-mail remains off and the voice-mail system catches any calls.

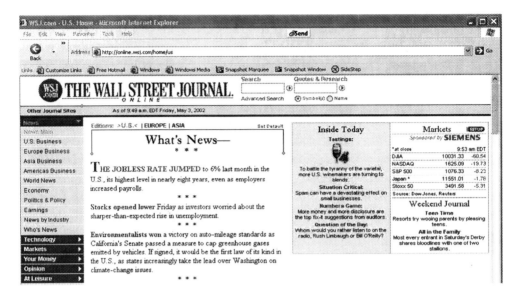

The Wall Street Journal Online

9:45 A.M.: Check e-mail and voice-mail for high-priority, client-oriented tasks. There are three client e-mails requiring an expedited response. At the time of receipt of these clients' e-mails, Dave personally and immediately answers each one saying the client can expect a response to his request shortly.

9:45 A.M.–10:00 A.M.: Set up three action items corresponding to the three client e-mails just identified:

➤ **Client 1** has requested a duplicate Schwab statement for the prior month. *Action:* E-mail a virtual account administrator in Rockville, Maryland, to whom the task is assigned and save the e-mail in Sunset's "Text Archival System" (TAS). If the client is computerized, the virtual account administrator will send a report to the client as a "PDF" (portable document file) file obtained from the monthly CD-ROM sent by Schwab to Sunset and to the virtual assistants whom it has authorized to receive duplicate CD-ROMs. If client is not computerized, virtual account administrator will mail a paper copy of the report to the client with Dave's business card attached. She will then e-mail Dave to say the task is "Done" and his original e-mail to her will be merged with her response and moved to client's section of TAS. Because a report identical to the one that was sent to the client can be accessed at any time in the future from the Schwab CD-ROM, it isn't necessary to make a copy for filing elsewhere.

➤ **Client 2** has requested a research report on a mutual fund recently purchased for his account.

Action: E-mail task to virtual financial planner in Bethesda, Maryland, who will access report from Morningstar online. If client is computerized, planner will e-mail PDF to client and, if not, will forward report to Sunset's virtual administrative assistant in Akron, Ohio, for mailing to the client with signed cover note on Sunset stationary. Because report will change in the future and it is therefore necessary to take a "snapshot" of the report sent to the client for later reference (such as during a phone call from the client to discuss the report), virtual planner will "print" the report to PaperPort, the software system by Visioneer Inc. that Sunset uses as its "Graphical Archival System" (GAS), and then planner will e-mail a PaperPort file of the scanned report image to Dave when indicating the task is done. Dave will import the file to Sunset's GAS as a permanent record of what was sent to the client along with any accompanying written communications.

➤ **Client 3** needs advice that requires a review of his financial planning file. The client's financial planning numbers, which evolve continuously with his life changes, are maintained in an Excel spreadsheet-based system called Integrate2000 by PlanWare, Inc. Dave periodically uploads current copies of client spreadsheets to his secure website to be accessed by his virtual planner.

Action: Sunset's virtual planner is assigned the analytical task required to answer the client's question; he performs it, revises the spreadsheet which Dave downloads to replace the prior version on Sunset's server, and recommends the advice to be given to the client. Dave reviews that recommendation, modifies it as necessary, and e-mails or calls the client. The e-mail is moved to the client's folder within Sunset's TAS. If the client is called, then Dave writes up notes of the client conversation and archives them to the TAS. If the client is to receive any printouts from his planning software to illustrate Dave's advice, then copies are printed to Sunset's GAS to complete the historical record of this client exchange.

10:00 A.M.–10:30 A.M.: Scan client cash balances via "Money Balances" report created by Centerpiece software system, updated and then downloaded to Sunset's server at 3:00 A.M. each morning by Sunset's virtual reporting company in southern California. Dave notes balances that appear too high or too low vis-à-vis clients' known cash preferences or needs and e-mails virtual trading firm in Atlanta, Georgia, to take appropriate action. Virtual trader will either invest excess monies or free up idle cash needed for scheduled distributions to client. Aside from account modifications required by Dave's cash balance reviews, virtual trader keeps each client's account invested on a continuous basis according to asset allocation, liquidity, and investment selection guidelines maintained in a spreadsheet which Dave updates and provides to the virtual trader monthly.

Trade orders for trades initiated by the virtual trader are faxed to Sunset daily. The faxes are received as e-mails via eFax Plus, a service of eFax.com used by Sunset because it makes possible the receipt of faxes anywhere in the world where e-mail can be received. Appropriate authorizations are added to the transmitted trade order images viewed using eFax.com's free eFax Messenger software, and the images are then printed to and archived in Sunset's GAS.

10:30 A.M.–11:30 A.M.: Exercise break. High priority is given to exercise that could take the form of walking Sunset's three canine mascots alongside the nearby arroyo or mountain biking in the nearby Sandia foothills.

11:30 A.M.–11:35 A.M.: Sunset administrative chore. A tickler reminds Dave to upload his payroll requirements (salary and tax withholding) to Wells Fargo Payroll

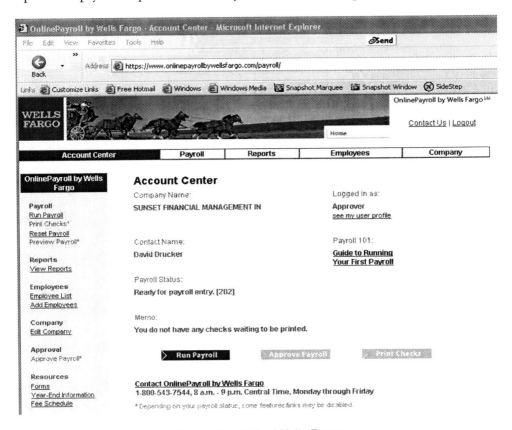

Online Payroll by Wells Fargo

Online. Wells Fargo pays all of Sunset's withholding and other payroll taxes to the proper local and federal tax authorities

11:35 A.M.–11:50 A.M.: Prospect calls by phone to say he wants to sign up and is ready to move his Merrill Lynch accounts to Charles Schwab & Co. for inclusion within Sunset's master account. The necessary information recorded on this prospect in Sunset's TAS is e-mailed to virtual account administrator to be used in setting up new client account and a new task is created within the TAS.

11:50 A.M.–12:30 P.M.: Over lunch, Dave scans e-mails from financial planning journals listing new articles published online that might pertain to client issues. Articles of interest are downloaded to his Samsung SPH-I300 combination Sprint PCS phone and Palm hand-held computer for later reading.

12:30 P.M.–1:30 P.M.: Client annual update meeting. Dave meets East Coast client online using WebEx Meeting Center, a service of WebEx Communications, Inc. The client and Dave talk to each other via their computer microphones and speakers while viewing a PowerPoint presentation each can see on his computer monitor. Similar meetings are often conducted with noncomputerized clients by mailing them printouts of the PowerPoint presentation in advance and conducting the meeting by telephone at an appointed time.

Samsung SPH-I300

1:30 P.M.–2:30 P.M.: More Sunset administrative tasks. Client proxies are voted online at www.proxyvote.com. One- to two-page copies of proxy voting form and supporting materials are printed and saved to Sunset's GAS. Drucker takes continuing education exam at www.bloomberg.com and prints certificate of completion to Sunset GAS continuing education folder for use in biannual accounting to Certified Financial Planner Board of Standards and National Association of Personal Financial Advisors. A broadcast e-mail is sent to an e-mail grouping of all virtual assistants informing them of a client's e-mail address change. An article that Dave wants to send to a computerless client he stuffs in an envelope that is automatically formatted with "to" and "from" addresses and printed with correct postage from Sunset's online account at www.stamps.com.

2:30 P.M.–3:00 P.M.: Responding to a tickler, Dave calls several non-computerized clients to chat and maintain frequency of personal communication.

3:00 P.M.: Quitting time.

One thing that may be puzzling to you, aside from the obvious virtual quality of almost every action taken during the day, is the lack of a centralized, network system by which to share information and manage work flow with virtual work partners (VWPs). This is a deliberate choice that will be discussed in detail in Chapter 9, which covers the pros and cons of centralized versus decentralized systems of information-sharing with VWPs. Either approach may work for you.

Important to note here is the radical difference between the systems used in a virtual financial planning firm and those used in a traditional firm. The trademarks of such an office are:

➤ Its ample support system, yet the lack of payroll employees
➤ Its almost total absence of paper or time wasted looking for client information
➤ The portability of its various information and operating systems
➤ The time that is blended into each day for personal needs, including capping the length of the workday to permit time for family and pets

If these are changes you would like to be able to make to your practice and your life, read on.

C h a p t e r   T w o

The Traditional vs. the Virtual Financial Advisory Firm

T HE FINANCIAL PLANNING INDUSTRY started in the 1970s, discovered it had evolutionary choices in the 1980s, and began to reach a level of profession- alism in the 1990s. Along the way, it adopted a bias that has characterized U.S. business in general: large is better than small. Growing larger as a business has long been prized not only as the means to financial success but also for lending the *aura* of success. "Large trumps small" is institutionalized in U.S. business thinking through such dichotomies as the Nasdaq, traditionally the market in which common equity shares of developing companies are traded, versus the New York Stock Exchange, reserved for businesses that have clearly "made it."

Granted, the professions, among which financial planning can be counted, are different. The country doctor can achieve respectability alongside the multidoctor practice operating in the larger town nearby. But respectability and financial success are two different things. Most of us want both. So the traditional financial planning firm has typically evolved from just its founder into a larger business with the goal of achieving more legitimacy and greater economic gain. Until the mid-1990s, there probably weren't many observers of the U.S. business scene who would question this approach.

Rapidly advancing technology in general, and the Internet in particular, has changed all of that. Financial planning firm owners who wish to run practices rather than grow multiprofessional offices can reap financial rewards much closer to those of larger firm operators with much less aggravation ... *if* they master the concept of virtuality and the technology that supports it.

Most small businesses begin with an individual who has a talent and/or a passion that he thinks is bankable and starts a business to prove it. In the case of planning practices, the founder may or may not have had any training in business administration, but he is familiar with some of the skills needed to get a warm body that will pay for his financial counsel into an office. That's where it begins for most of us.

A big step in our firm's evolution comes with the hiring of the first employee. This decision is made when the owner realizes that the client base has grown to such an extent that support is needed, and this is accompanied by the other sobering reality of having a financial obligation to someone other than himself. The existence of even one employee shifts the owner's planning for and thinking about his business radically, because it only takes one hire to set into motion a host of federal regulations telling the owner what he can and can't do with any benefit plans or company policies that affect his employee.

Nevertheless, if the founder uses his employee wisely, his business will grow and he will acquire more employees. If he acquires some business management skills, his own compensation can grow, too—or not. As was noted in the preface, the economics of owner compensation for many firms don't necessarily improve with the expansion of the firm. It seems that, as an industry, we've learned how to grow the top line, but we haven't been effective at containing costs.

If the upward march continues, the owner eventually has a large staff and perhaps several partners. He finds he's not earning an income he can brag about, but he's still doing well, making enough to support his family in some measure of style, and if he's not the highest earner on his block, he may at least have the most impressive occupation. He handles people's money. And he's so good at it that he's managed to build a firm with a presence in his hometown. He's a recognizable brand, which brings with it prestige and even the presumption that he must be financially successful.

His life resembles that of small business owners in most other fields. He works long hours, usually longer than those of his staff, and he spends far less time with his family than he would like, but the promise of even greater financial reward if he can just serve a few more clients is addictive. He rationalizes to himself that he's come too far up the growth curve to get off now because the biggest reward comes later—when he sells his company. "You can't sell a small practice," he's been told, "but you will someday get the big bucks for your company if you continue to build it." A caring friend might put this in perspective for him by saying "Let us understand this … you're working harder than you want to, you can't remember your kids' names, you make decent money but don't feel it quite adequately compensates you for all your hard work, yet you continue on this treadmill because a big reward will come someday when you cash out?"

The irony of this is that our financial planner/business owner is violating one of the most cherished precepts passed on to clients: diversify your holdings and never keep too much money invested solely in the stock of the company you work for. Likewise we tell clients that asset allocation will protect them when the economy is in its valley rather than at its peak. But small business economics make it extremely difficult for us to adhere to the principles we espouse. As we hire more people, we need more capital. An employee is worthless unless we can give him an office, a computer, a telephone, and a decent enough compensation package to ensure that we get a reasonable return on the investment we will make in his training.

The Roles of Time and Space

WHERE IS THE SOLUTION to this imperfect business model? Just as technological advances in the United States gave revolutionary new options to all kinds of businesses formerly trapped in a one-dimensional growth scenario, they have done the same for financial advisers. Advisers just need to wake up and realize they have choices. Time and space are our costliest commodities. To the extent that we can cut out unnecessary expenditures on either, we can begin to control our bottom line and do more with less.

We buy other people's time to leverage our own efforts. In the traditional firm, these other people are employees. They need time to learn their jobs, do their jobs, and take time off from their jobs. All these activities represent costs to us, the owners. The less employee time we use, the lower our costs.

Anything we do to lower costs or, conversely, to raise profits, gives us more time choices of our own. We can work as hard as we did before and pocket the difference as higher compensation. Or, we can forgo the extra compensation and use the time we've saved to have lives apart from our work—lives spent with families, in pursuit of hobbies, or community service—whatever turns us on.

Space works the same way and, as a cost element, it's inextricably bound up with time because employees require space. They need offices (or cubicles). An office suite needs common space as well, increasing with the number of bodies it houses so that people feel comfortable, professional, and productive. Spatial needs attach also to the "matter" that is a by-product of financial planning:

records. We all keep employee records, accounting records, regulatory records, and, not least, client records. Most planners I know, when in the market for larger offices, factor into their spatial needs more room for files. Record keeping in the traditional firm is done with paper, the inevitable proliferation of which increases the time necessary to retrieve important information and respond quickly to clients, regulators, and others.

So we have the picture of a traditional financial planning practice that starts out with a solo operator barely able to feed his family and develops after five or ten years into a small firm that challenges its owner with employment and other management issues as well as the need to more effectively balance all the elements of his life. The money's better, but he has new claims on his time. When he started the firm, he worked twelve hours a day—two on client work and ten on marketing and systems development. Now, he still works twelve hours a day—six on client work and six sorting out employee issues and dealing with other administrative hassles he wishes he could afford an office manager to handle for him. How do we get him off this treadmill and allow him to rejoin the human race?

The Virtual Financial Planning Firm

LET'S START BY DISTINGUISHING between two very basic concepts, "virtual" and "paperless." "Virtual" is variously defined as "simulated," "performing the functions of something that isn't really there," or "the opposite of real or physical." Each of these describes an aspect of the change we're talking about making in going from a traditional to a virtual planning firm. We want to replace physical elements of the traditional financial planning firm with something else that still does the job but takes up less time and space. In future chapters, we'll talk about virtual workers, for example. If we no longer have a secretary on our staff but, instead, a virtual assistant, then we still have someone doing the work of a secretary, but he's not an employee. He's instead a "simulated" secretary. He's real, but his reality doesn't exist in our space because he has his own space. He performs the functions of a secretary but he's not "really there," to refer to our earlier definition.

"Paperless," on the other hand, refers to the use of computers and other electronic media to record, convey, store, and retrieve information. As will be elaborated on in the next chapter, the concept of a paperless office has less to do with eliminating paper than it does with redefining how you will handle information. To create a truly paperless office, you will need to adopt a "paperless mentality."

Putting together these and a few other essential concepts, we construct our virtual financial planning firm. Like the traditional financial planning firm, the virtual firm grows and adds clients over time. But instead of adding employees to meet the needs of these clients, the owner adds more efficient processes and virtual workers. Instead of leasing more office space to house more file cabinets and more records, he collects and manages information using electronic media and systems. Instead of constantly reinvesting in his business in ways contrary to the most important lessons he teaches his clients about diversifying their wealth, he takes money out of the firm and creates with it the same kind of diversified portfolio he recommends to his clients.

When he's ready to retire, he's got the same valuable resource that all good firms develop—solid client relationships. Business valuation experts like to tell you that the only salable firm is an institutionalized firm, one that has divorced its clients' allegiance from its owner and transferred that allegiance to a support team. Although there may be *more* value in an institutionalized firm, it does not follow that there is *no* value in a virtual firm. The value, we contend, lies in how the firm's client relationships are transferred, not in how many people the selling firm has employed (on its payroll) to serve the client.

Identifying the Problem

IT'S NO SECRET that handling paper records is expensive. Not only does paper itself cost money, handling it also imposes many hidden as well as obvious expenses on a financial advisory practice. To get these expenses under control, you not only can take advantage of some technological processes, you can also overhaul the way you think about your documentation.

When you hear the word "paperless," do you say to yourself, "OK, so I take on the seemingly insurmountable task of scanning all of my client and other records onto electronic media … Then what?" Luckily, going paperless is much more powerful than scanning documents. You may also be wary of perceived security issues. "Once I've got all of my records copied onto electronic media, I'm supposed to just throw them away? What happens if I lose the media, or they're destroyed?" We will deal with those problems, too—everything that is needed for you to feel confident that your new paperless office is safe, even safer than one with paper.

Frequently Asked Questions about Going Paperless

Q: I would feel naked without the paper that supports my practice. In the case of some of my clients, I have important documents in all sorts of formats collected over a period of ten or more years.

A: You don't have to give up your paper any sooner than feels comfortable. Most planners who adopt paperless systems keep scanned documents for a year or more until they feel secure that (a) they've never needed to refer to the original documents because the information has been readily available on their computer, and (b) their backup systems have kept their scanned records safe and reliable.

Q: Won't it be terribly expensive to scan all of the paper in my office?

A: There are many ways to convert paper to electronic media. A larger practice with a long history may hire a specialized service to come into its offices and manage the task for a price in the five-digit range. A smaller practice or sole practitioner might hire a temporary worker at slightly more than minimum wage to carry out the purely physical job of scanning sheets of paper into the computer.

Q: How will I know where to look for the items I've scanned?

A: How do you know where to look for those documents now? In some cases you don't even know where a client's file is because more than one person in your office may be working with it. Once you have the file, you must manually sift through dozens of documents that may not have been ordered within the file according to your specifications. Wouldn't it be simpler to type a few words into your computer and see the document you want on your screen in front of you, even if someone else is also looking at it?

Suggestions for Making Your Essential Backups

ONE PREMISE OF THIS BOOK is that you can work more efficiently and more economically if you abandon your paper records. As you move to a paperless environment, you must have total confidence in the digital system you deploy. Events since September 11, 2001, are a stark reminder that disasters, both natural and manmade, present a risk to financial data. Minor disasters, like power outages and computer crashes, happen more often than we would like.

What kind of backup system—hardware, software, and scheduling routine—should we use to best protect our company data and our clients' personal data? The solution that is right for your firm will be determined by your firm's size, the amount of data to be stored, and your budget, but the keys to any successful recovery plan are regular backups and off-site storage.

Your backup schedule is at least as important as the backup hardware and software you select. Every firm should do incremental backups at least daily and full backups weekly. Ideally, copies should be transported off-site at least once a week, and at the end of each month an archive file for the month should be stored in a secure location, such as a safe-deposit box.

For small- to medium-sized firms, the best solution is usually to copy files to a portable medium and to store these media off-site. Recordable CD-R (read-only) disks and CD-RW (read-write) disks are an easy and inexpensive option. CD-R disks can hold up to 700 MB of data, CD-RW disks up to 650 MB.

DVDs are replacing CDs as the optical storage solution of choice, due to their much greater capacity (4.7 GB), but we do not recommend committing to them until a formatting standard has emerged. Different manufacturers are currently supporting different standards, meaning that a disk written on one drive cannot necessarily be read on another. Furthermore, competing standards mean lower

OnStream Tape Backup

production runs and higher prices. Drives that can read and write to DVD currently cost about four times more than CD drives, and recordable (write-once, read-only) DVD disks are about three times more expensive per gigabyte of storage.

Even smaller firms may have larger backup needs once they go paperless and the number of digital files critical to their operation increases. Dave's solution for his 4 GB or so of critical files—at least until DVDs become more feasible—is to use magnetic tape backups. This is an old technology with well-documented weaknesses, but it offers a format that can soak up a large number of files without swapping media. Dave uses an OnStream Echo tape backup device (www.onstream.com) with

Before You Buy an External Backup Device

WITH USB 2.0 and FireWire (IEEE 1394) interfaces entering the mainstream, we think external hard drives will become a compelling backup solution for small- to medium-sized businesses. Their combination of storage capacity, speed, and portability are hard to beat; and prices are reasonable. Before you rush out to buy one of these drives, though, make sure your PC is compatible with the drive you select. The original version of Windows XP, for example, supported IEEE 1394 but not USB 2.0. However, you can now download the necessary driver from the Microsoft website (www.microsoft.com). You will also need a port to plug the drive into. Unless you have a brand new computer, odds are you don't have a USB 2.0 port, and you may not have an IEEE 1394 port, either. Luckily, you can easily add ports by inserting an adapter card into your computer. One attractive choice is the Adaptec DuoConnect (www.adaptec.com), which includes multiple ports for both USB 2.0 and IEEE 1394. This card, which lists for about $100, provides three external and one internal USB 2.0 ports. You also get two external and one internal IEEE 1394 ports.

If you are in the market for a new computer, and you are planning to back up to an external hard drive, ask about USB 2.0 and IEEE 1394 ports before you buy. If the ports you want are not standard equipment, you can probably purchase them as an option.

tapes that will capture 15 GB of uncompressed files, or 30 GB of compressed files. Whereas OnStream's strength is the higher-than-average capacity of its tapes, any of the reputable tape backup drive manufacturers, such as Colorado or Seagate, provide reasonable tape backup solutions.

For those firms with larger backup needs, external hard drives are an attractive option because of their speed. With the advent of IEEE 1394 (FireWire) and USB 2.0 interfaces, external hard drives can transfer data three to eight times faster than the fastest CD-R drives now being installed in new computers. External hard drive storage is priced competitively with CD-RW, and transfer rates are up to eighteen times faster. Maxtor, a major hard drive manufacturer, produces a full line of FireWire external drives ranging in capacity from 40 GB to 160 GB. Western Digital, another major hard drive manufacturer, also offers a number of attractively priced external hard drives.

Keep in mind that if disaster strikes, the backups won't be of much use if you do not have a computer loaded with your software applications available. Large firms run fully redundant systems, or hire companies specializing in disaster recovery to back up their systems and provide emergency hardware if necessary. These services may be beyond the means of smaller firms, but with today's low hardware prices, you can come pretty close at a reasonable cost by storing a backup server off site (at a principal's house, for instance) and transferring files by portable media or over the Internet.

To answer our original question of which backup system is best for you, here's one way to look at this decision. First, figure out the size of your "critical files" versus your total files. Many people simply back up everything on their hard drives, but that method wastes backup media and time capturing program files already backed up, in effect, on their original CD-ROMs. Your critical files, such as text and image archives of notes and planning materials, will usually comprise less than 25 percent of your total file volume. Knowing the sheer volume of these files will help you determine what backup medium is ideal for you.

For example, if your practice is new and your critical files are less than 700 MB, then burning CD-ROMs is an effective and inexpensive solution. But if you have 10 GB of critical files, consider a tape or external hard drive solution (see sidebar). The point is not to be swapping backup media to complete a backup, since this requires human intervention and increases the likelihood of mistakes.

Having said this, even larger firms can identify a subset of files, usually less than 1 gigabyte in volume, that are the most critical. Consider one of the new miniature USB solutions for adding a second layer of protection for these files.

Flash Storage Devices

HERE'S A LITTLE TECHNOLOGY QUIZ for you: PCs have evolved at an astonishing pace over the past few years. What is the one PC component that has remained essentially unchanged and unimproved? If you answered the "floppy" drive, you are correct. Floppy drives—the permanent misnomer for 3½-inch diskette drives—are still where they were ten years ago, with their skimpy 1.44 MB of storage. Any single large file that the average computer user backs up can be many times that size.

Over the years, a number of substitutes appeared but never gained wide acceptance. SuperDisk drives, which can read both standard floppies and 120 MB SuperDisks, looked to be a natural successor to floppies, but PC manufacturers chose not to install them as standard equipment. Iomega's Zip drives were a hot item for a while, but they add weight when on the road, and they require a power source.

Wouldn't it be nice if there were a fast, convenient method of transferring files to a highly portable medium? Well, now there is. The products go by various names such as DiskOnKey, Micro Vault, ThumbDrive, and USBDrive, but they are all flash storage devices with a built-in USB adapter. All are tiny (about the size of a disposable lighter) and lightweight. They run off of your computer's USB port and no external power source is required.

We recently tested the 128 MB version of DiskOnKey, Sony Micro Vault, and USBDrive to see if these mini storage devices could potentially become the portable storage media of the future. We think they can.

DiskOnKey

When we plugged our DiskOnKey, manufactured by M-Systems, into a Dell Dimension 8100 desktop running Windows XP, the device was immediately recognized by the operating system and accessible for use. We then copied a few files onto the disk and tried to transfer them onto a laptop running Windows ME. The ME operating system recognized the DiskOnKey, but we had to wait a minute the first time we used it while the computer installed the necessary drivers. Once

The M-System DiskOnKey

this was accomplished, the drive performed flawlessly. We next moved to an older laptop running Windows 98. In order to use the drive with Windows 98, you must first download the proper driver from the DiskOnKey website (www.diskonkey.com). After that, the installation program walks you through the setup procedure in several minutes. Upon completion of the installation procedure, the disk worked fine.

DiskOnKey includes KeySafe, an application that allows you to create and access a password-protected secure area on the disk, called a Privacy Zone. The user can designate from 1 to 90 percent of the drive as a Privacy Zone.

At this writing, DiskOnKey is available in 8 MB, 16 MB, 32 MB, 64 MB, and 128 MB versions ranging in price from $29.99 to $149.99. Modules are color-coded by size for easy differentiation. Larger-capacity drives should be available by the time you read this.

Sony Micro Vault

These sleek, attractive modules are currently available in the following sizes: 16 MB, 32 MB, 64 MB, and 128 MB costing approximately $50 to $300. The translucent stripe down the middle of the modules is color-coded by size, so users with more than one size can differentiate between modules. We put the Sony device through the same tests as those we used for DiskOnKey, and performance was identical. No surprise here, since Micro Vault is manufactured for Sony by M-Systems, the same company that manufactures DiskOnKey. There are, however, some minor differences between the two products:

➤ DiskOnKey includes a clip and a key ring; Micro Vault does not;

➤ Windows 98 users must download DiskOnKey drivers off the Web; Sony includes the drivers on a CD;

➤ Our DiskOnKey unit came with the Security Zone software installed; Sony puts the software on its CD, allowing users to decide whether or not to install it.

The Sony Micro Vault

Micro Vaults are just making their way onto store shelves as of this writing, but we expect them to be widely available at major computer and electronic retailers by the fall of 2002.

USBDrive

Manufactured by JMTek, Inc., this was the only device available in a 1 GB version as we went to press. USBDrive is also available in 16MB, 32 MB, 64 MB, 128 MB, 256 MB, and 512 MB sizes ranging from about $40 to $600. They work seamlessly with Windows XP, and they are fine with Windows ME and Windows 98 as well. The drive comes packaged with a USB extension cable, which is helpful if your office computer's USB port is hard to access. Also included is a lanyard so you can wear the drive around your neck. As with the Sony product, Windows 98 drivers are included on a CD.

The JMTek USBDrive

Trek ThumbDrives

ThumbDrives are the smallest of these Lilliputian drives. They are available in sizes ranging from 16 MB to 512 MB. Prices start at $40 for the smallest model and top out at $580 for the 512 MB drive. ThumbDrive Secure, which enables password security protection, is available at a maximum size of 128 MB.

Did one clear favorite emerge from our trials? Not really. All of the drives we tested performed admirably. Any of them can be used as a rewritable backup medium or to transfer files from one computer to another. It is certainly possible to pack PowerPoint presentations and client reports on one of these devices, perhaps sparing you the necessity of taking a laptop on some of your off-site travels. Sole practitioners may be able to carry all of their critical files off-site nightly on a key chain!

As prices fall, you may find that these drives make excellent client gifts. Not only are they handy, you can pack information on them before distributing them.

The Trek ThumbDrive

Ultimately, the selection comes down to price, features, and availability. The USBDrive currently has a few things going for it: the lowest price, a very small size, and the largest capacity drives currently available. USBDrives ship with an extension cable, drivers, a lanyard, and a pocket clip. If you plan on purchasing multiple drives, the color-coding available from DiskOnKey and Sony Micro Vault could be a deciding factor. Those transporting sensitive data will want to confine their selection to DiskOnKey, Sony Micro Vault, or ThumbDrive Secure.

Regardless of the model you choose, we think these mini-USB drives will become an indispensable tool for transporting and backing up data. With the all-important matter of thorough, reliable backups taken care of, you can concentrate on finding better ways to work.

Common Paper Traps

An Illustration of a Recurring Problem: The Financial Plan

Consider the typical financial plan as one example of the inefficiency of using and maintaining paper records. The plan starts when you generate a questionnaire for your new client to complete by hand and return to you. In doing so, you pay a staff person to locate a template of this questionnaire, which is already printed and sitting in a file cabinet or needs to be printed from a computer file. Your employee then packages it for mailing to the client, incurring postage costs. The client eventually returns it, along with sometimes voluminous supporting materials like tax returns, insurance policies, and investment account statements. Someone in your office enters all of the information, or summaries of it, into a computer program and, after one week to six months, depending upon the scope of the plan and the responsiveness of the client, a financial plan is produced. The plan generally manifests itself as a paper document the size of which falls somewhere between a state tax return filing and the yellow pages of a small city.

The client comes back to your office for a meeting to discuss this paper document. If the client is happy with the plan and remains a client for the long term, the plan must be periodically updated, and you will have many occasions to refer to it or to those supporting materials the client provided you in the beginning of the relationship. Additionally, the client will send you updated materials in a steady stream that continues as long as he remains a client.

You will likely create a file for all of this client's paper. It might be a six-pocket accordion folder, a hanging file, or even a cardboard file box—but it's a physical location for this growing pile of paper. Every time the client calls with a question that requires you to review the materials in his file, someone must physically search for the right piece of paper, review it, and then re-file it properly so as to minimize the time necessary to find that item the next time it's needed.

The spatial and temporal costs related to the production of financial plans and storing of client information grow with the number of clients served, lacking any economy of scale. Most planners have been gathering, storing, and retrieving information in the physical confines of their offices for so long that they neither see nor question the inefficiency of doing it this way. Yet, the costs, when fully tallied, are huge.

Other Common Paper Files

How many other kinds of paper files do planners keep? Lots. Yet just about anything you've set up as a category within your office's paper filing system can be reconstituted in paperless form (by scanning it into your server for ready access). Such categories include the following:

➢ Blank forms or templates; e.g., applications for new accounts or other services of your investment custodian, employee evaluation forms, expense reimbursement forms

➢ Computer records, e.g., hardware specifications and instructions, software licenses, online agreements, service agreements, hardware and software user's guides in PDF format

➢ Continuing education documentation

➢ Paperwork connected with any separate ventures of your firm, e.g., software sales, speaking, consulting, or other sources of income besides financial planning

➢ Professional association records, e.g., committee work documentation

➢ Prospect materials, i.e., paperwork received in prospect meetings that will be kept for some period of time awaiting the prospect's decision about becoming a client of your firm

➢ Proxies, i.e., copies of signed proxies voted for client accounts

➢ Reference materials, e.g., articles on topics such as comparisons of specific classes of insurance products, third-party white papers, IRS tables

➢ Resumes of job applicants

➢ Subject files, e.g., magazine clippings on subjects of interest to your clients or subjects about which you may need information in the future, as when a specialized planning situation arises

➢ Trade orders

➢ Writing and speaking documentation (company newsletters, PowerPoint presentations, copies of articles in which principals were quoted, articles authored by principals, etc.)

➢ Your own company's records:
    Agreements with industry partners
    Documentation with investment custodians

Invoices and expense receipts
Licenses and memberships
Loan documents and amortization schedules
Marketing materials
Office insurance and benefit plan documents
Organizational paperwork (minutes, bylaws)
Pension plan documents
Personnel documents (employee records, time sheets)
Product warranties
Regulatory items (approval letters, ADVs, SEC regulations)
Strategic planning notes
Tax returns
Vendor information
Website documentation
Worksheets

A Planner's Dilemma

Kathleen Day, CFP, CFA, and owner of Kathleen Day & Associates, Inc. in Miami, Florida, employs eighteen people in her company and started tackling her paper problems around 1996. She remembers that "every time somebody wanted to find something, it was on someone else's desk or somewhere waiting to be filed. No one could find it. It was always difficult to locate things, and it seemed to me that I should be able to use technology to store and find things in a way that would enable me to travel more and delegate better. Now, I'm out of the office five to six days a month and I couldn't do without my paperless systems."

In remaining chapters, we'll see exactly how Day implemented the technology solution to her problem, and we will show you how to get from here to there—how to transform the high-maintenance processes of your traditional firm into the high-margin efficiencies of a virtual firm. You don't want to become a totally virtual firm, you say? No problem. You can choose whatever lessons you find from the chapters that follow to make your traditional firm considerably leaner and meaner, certainly more profitable, and, we hope, more personally rewarding.

Part Two

Eliminating Paper

Chapter 3 Three

Scanning Hardware That Can Do It for You

THE TECHNOLOGY THAT WILL ALLOW YOU to eliminate the paper in your office is primarily designed for converting printed and written documents into digital form. We will also tell you about storing critical information that doesn't originate or arrive as paper, such as e-mails, faxes received electronically, and online publications. Thinking globally about information and its electronic storage and retrieval is central to developing the paperless mentality.

The two central tools of the paperless office conversion are a scanner and a software product that complements your scanner by displaying and allowing you to retrieve scanned documents. The scanner receives and digitizes your paper, and the scanning software processes the image created by the scanner and places it on your monitor's screen. We will discuss a number of different hardware and software options for you to consider in this and the next chapter.

Scanners and More Scanners

SCANNERS CAN BE BROKEN DOWN into four broad categories:
1 Flatbed scanners
2 Home-office scanners
3 Workgroup scanners
4 Corporate scanners

Since you will presumably be dealing with large volumes of paper, flatbed scanners that require you to manually lay your paper flat on a glass surface one sheet at a time are not an option. Primarily very large firms employ corporate scanners, and their cost and complexity is beyond the needs of even the larger planning firms. Therefore, we will limit our comments to home-office and workgroup scanners.

Home-Office Scanners

Home-office scanners are often low-end to mid-range flatbed scanners that are either designed or modified to accept an automatic document feeder. Automatic document feeders at the lower end of the price scale typically can hold twenty-five to fifty sheets of paper and process them at roughly five pages per minute. All products in this category can handle letter-size documents, and some can handle larger paper sizes as well.

Home-office scanners are a solid entry-level solution for sole proprietors and small firms. Since home-office scanners are close cousins of consumer versions, they are generally designed for easy setup and use. The installation of a high-end scanner can require the opening of a computer housing to install a SCSI or other interface card. Many home-office scanners, on the other hand, operate via a USB connection, which means you can attach the scanner to your computer, plug it in, turn it on, and it will practically install itself. Many products in this category come packaged with utilities, optical character recognition (OCR) software, and photo editing software that is also consumer oriented and therefore easy to use. Home-office scanners are the lowest-cost practical solution for the financial planner who wants a digital input device.

Price alone needn't dictate your decision if you are convinced that your needs will exceed the capabilities of a home-office machine (although more than one might do the job). Just keep in mind that the price of the hardware will not be your only cost as you move up to higher-capacity solutions. As a general rule, the more powerful the scanner, the more complex installation and maintenance become, so figure those costs into your budget.

From a training perspective, experience tells us that many people are best served by learning to walk before they run. If you haven't done much scanning before, take a hard look at home-office solutions first. Learn and make your mistakes on a package that costs a few hundred, rather than on one costing a thousand or more dollars. Should you decide you need a more powerful scanner at a future date, your entry-level scanner won't be a total write-off. You can probably put it to work on other tasks, such as scanning the occasional photo, or assisting with desktop publishing chores.

Another option as you upgrade your hardware is to adopt a "two-tier" system. You can purchase one powerful, shared office scanner for large jobs and have an inexpensive scanner at every workstation so employees can scan shorter documents right at their desks. If you can't put the inexpensive scanner to productive use at your office, surely the spouse or kids would love to get their hands on it.

To give you some idea of what's available in this product category, take a look at the Epson Perfection 1640SU office. This unit, which was selling for a little less than $450 in the spring of 2002, is capable of produc-ing sharp, detailed images in both black and white and color. The version we tested includes an automatic document feeder capable of han-dling up to thirty sheets of paper. Although its flat bed only supports letter-size docu-ments, legal-size documents can be scanned using this document feeder. According to Epson, the 1640SU scans up to 5.5 pages per minute, and our informal tests confirmed this speed.

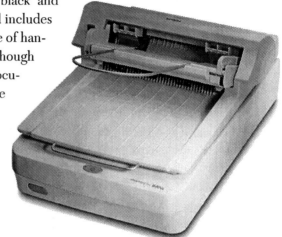

Epson scanners come with a utility called Smart Panel. Smart Panel allows you to scan, copy, scan to OCR, or scan to e-mail with a mouse click. The OCR software is

Epson Perfection 1640SU

Textbridge Pro, a capable performer (but not the latest version). Adobe PhotoDeluxe and a number of ArcSoft photo utilities round out the bundle.

Our overall impression of the Epson Perfection 1640SU scanner was quite favor-able. Whereas it is clearly not designed for daylong, nonstop scanning, it very ade-quately handles occasional scanning needs through the day. At the time of our test, the software packaged with the product was not yet optimized for Windows XP (it should be available by the time you read this), but those using an older operating system get quite a deal. We called technical support a couple of times with questions and were impressed with their service.

It's worth paying some attention to the software packaged with your scanner. OCR software and utilities can make a real difference in your productivity and sat-isfaction. If the software you need is bundled with your hardware, it can also save you hundreds of dollars, even if you choose to upgrade the software. For example,

ScanSoft's top-of-the-line OCR product, OmniPage Pro 11, costs over $500 for the full version, but upgrades cost about a quarter of that. Even if your scanner comes packaged with an old or "lite" version of a ScanSoft product, you may save hundreds of dollars by becoming eligible to purchase new versions at the upgrade price.

Workgroup Scanners

Workgroup scanners are a step up from home-office scanners. Prices in this category range from about $750 at the low end to several thousand dollars. Workgroup scanners can handle larger workloads at higher speeds, and some can do duplex (two-sided) scans. Speeds generally range from about fifteen to thirty pages per minute. Image quality is sometimes lower than the quality you get from the home-office scanners, but this is not an issue if you primarily scan text documents.

If you are in the market for a Workgroup scanner, we strongly recommend you check out the product offerings from Fujitsu. The Fujitsu ScanPartner 3091DC, which uses a SCSI interface, or its USB interface stable mate, the ScanPartner 4110CU (both at a street price of $820), can scan up to fifteen pages per minute or 7.5 duplex pages per minute. These machines are appropriate for companies scanning up to 500 pages per day.

The 4100CU/3091DC is a particularly well-designed machine. A straight paper path results in less wear and tear on the machine, as well as better scans of documents with frayed edges. With the exception of the roller and guide (which are replaceable), the unit has no moving parts, which means these scanners should have a longer useful lifecycle than competitors in this price range. And, the scan quality is excellent.

Fujitsu scanners also give you the option of using either TWAIN or ISIS drivers. ISIS drivers have a number of advantages over TWAIN drivers, including built-in page length detection and built-in image enhancement features.

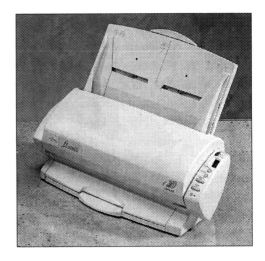

Fujitsu 4110CU Scanner

These scanners have a twenty-five-sheet automatic document feeder, but they don't include a flatbed feature. The lack of a flatbed results in a very small footprint (5″ high by 12″ wide by 6″ deep), making these machines ideal for tight workspaces.

The only thing that may be lacking is the software included with these units. As of this printing, Fujitsu was offering ScanSoft's Pagis Pro 3.0 with the 4110CU, but not with the 3091DC. Company spokesmen told us that Fujitsu believes most corporate users want to make their own software decisions, so Fujitsu generally de-emphasizes packaged software and passes on the savings to consumers. ScanAll, a basic program that allows users to scan and save images (in BMP, .TIF, JPEG, or Adobe PDF formats) is available free of charge at the company's website for those who want it.

In summary, we think the Fujitsu 4110CU/3091DC, which retails for $995 (street price should be 20 to 25 percent less) is a price/performance leader in its class. Before you buy anything else in this price range, we suggest you compare its design, scan quality, and expected lifecycle with Fujitsu's offerings and draw your own conclusions.

If you intend to scan more than 500 pages per day, you may be a candidate for a departmental scanner. While a full discussion of the product category is beyond the scope of this book, we recently took a look at the Fujitsu 4340 (list price $5,495, street price 20 to 25 percent less) to see what those willing to spend over $4,000 on a scanner can expect. What you get is speed—up to eighty images per minute ("ipm") monochrome and forty-eight ipm color, improved resolution, a daily duty cycle of up to 3,000 pages per minute, a 100-sheet capacity automatic document feeder, and the flexibility to add additional options.

Before purchasing a scanner in this price range, you may want to consult an expert about the pros and cons of various products and network compatibility issues. You should also investigate whether a few strategically placed workgroup scanners would be a better solution for your firm than one departmental scanner.

Scanners and TWAIN

IN EARLIER DAYS, it was advisable to buy the hardware of your choice and stick to using the scanning software that came with it to ensure compatibility. Since then, most software has begun featuring a TWAIN capability. TWAIN is the name of a nonprofit organization, the purpose of which is to create a public standard for linking scanning software and "image acquisition devices," or scanners. The protocols developed by TWAIN have allowed the pairing of hardware and software originating from different manufacturers.

Ten years ago in his office, Dave used strictly Visioneer products. Visioneer, Inc. is a company that practically pioneered the development and commercial success of the single-sheet-feed scanner. For $200 or less, it offered (and still offers) a scanner paired with some of the best scanning software on the market. In fact, the scanning software included so many high-end features at such a reasonable price that many users were willing to overlook the inefficiencies of being stuck with a setup that couldn't automatically feed multiple sheets of paper.

The TWAIN standard has liberated us from that. For example, Dave presently uses Paperport Deluxe—now owned by ScanSoft, Inc.—but he mates it to a Hewlett-Packard 6350 scanner, which has an automatic, multiple-sheet-feed capability.

The point is, with TWAIN you can use the scanner of your choice and pair it with your preferred scanning software, regardless of the manufacturers of these two products. We take a look at your software options, and our recommendations, in the next chapter.

C h a p t e r Four

The Best Scanning Software
for Financial Planners

NOW THAT YOU'VE GOT your scanning hardware lined up, what features should you be looking for in your software? To illustrate the must-have features of scanning software, we'll first look at examples from Dave's favorite product, PaperPort Deluxe, followed by a detailed review of PaperPort. Later in the chapter, we'll review several other scanning software options that may be more appropriate than PaperPort for firms larger than Dave's sole-practitioner setup.

Your scanning software will typically show you a folder layout and a desktop with thumbnail versions of each of the documents you've scanned into it. The folders, or categories for "filing" the documents you've scanned, might look something like those shown on the following page, with the area on the right showing what is inside the folder highlighted or opened on the left.

Essential Features

IDEALLY, THE SCANNING SOFTWARE YOU SELECT will have most or all of the following features. Let's take these one at a time:

➢ A simulated desktop
➢ Unlimited nesting folders
➢ Rapid search capability
➢ Manual OCR capability
➢ Automatic OCR and indexing capability
➢ Annotation capability
➢ Regulatory compliance capability

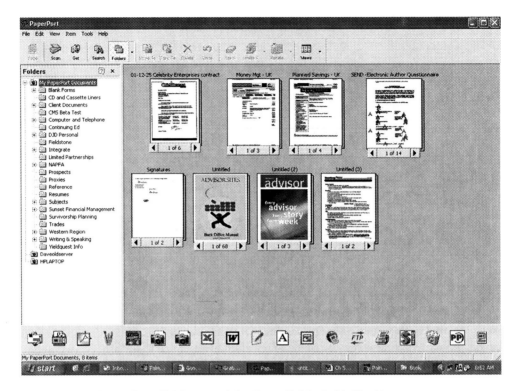

PaperPort Folders and the Root Folder's Unfiled Images

A Simulated Desktop

A simulated desktop is nothing more than the convention used in many Microsoft and Apple programs to create an analogy that an office worker will understand. It harkens back to precomputer days when one would grab a batch of files with which he intended to work and put them on his desk off to one side, leaving the majority of his desktop free for opening a single file and viewing its contents.

In most software products, a vertical strip on the left side of your monitor screen will show a list of file folders by name. In PaperPort, this area is called the Folder Pane. The large area of your screen to the right of this vertical strip is a work area. Clicking on a file folder and, subsequently, on a file within the folder on the left side of the screen will display the file's contents on the desktop portion to the right.

There are two forms of display your software should offer: thumbnail view and page view. A thumbnail view shows you small images of each document within a folder, arranged row by row and column by column across your desktop. The view is too small to allow you to read the type on the scanned page, but it's useful in allowing you to locate a document quickly. Using thumbnail views, you can tell the difference, for example, between a client's tax return and an estate planning document. A page view results when you enlarge a thumbnail view of a single scanned image. The page view shows you the scanned document at actual size, so you can read its contents.

Unlimited Nesting Folders

Your software should also give you the ability to create an unlimited number of nesting folders. This simply means folders within folders, or a hierarchy of folders. For example, you might have a main folder named for your company, within which are folders for operational categories such as Accounting, within each of which, in turn, are subfolders such as records by calendar year.

Rapid Search Capability

Perhaps the most essential feature of any software you use to archive important records is the ability to retrieve information quickly. It's doubly important when you

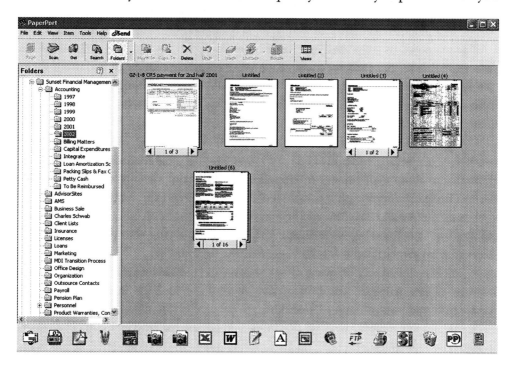

Nested Folders

have a client on the phone. The client will perceive that he is receiving a higher level of service if his questions are answered immediately, and you will probably avoid a lot of phone tag. When the needed information is somewhere in your scanning software, you'd like to be able to find it in as much time as it takes to ask the client about his golf game, and definitely faster than the old way of asking someone in your office to fetch the file because you are on the phone.

Let's say the client calls up and asks you if you think any portion of his $25,000 in medical expenses this year will be deductible from his taxable income. To answer the question, you want to review his most recent tax return, which you've scanned into a folder named for the client. That folder and its subfolders contain various records collected over a period of ten years—maybe 150 different scanned items.

Your software should give you at least a couple of options for finding this document quickly. Almost any scanning software will allow you a choice of how you name a scanned image. Dave likes to create a name for each image beginning with a date convention of year-month-day. The client's tax return image might have a name starting with "01-12-31" followed by "federal return." By naming everything in this manner, when we tell the software to arrange the files by name (i.e., sort them side by side in alphanumeric order), it will give us what amounts to a chronological array.

Dave chooses to keep multiple years' images in one folder per client, although you could divide them into separate folders by calendar year or by planning function, such as Estate Planning, and Retirement Planning. It's simple to create and name a new folder, whether a main folder such as one for a new client, or a subfolder under an existing client's main folder.

Using Dave's system of one main folder per client to hold all of that client's documents, a tax return with 12-31 in its name can be located quickly by scrolling through the thumbnail images in the client's folder and visually scouting out the desired image. Using the thumbnail view, you would read the image titles, moving your eyes across and then down the desktop until you find the tax return you're looking for. This is analogous to flipping through a paper file system that has its file folders, or pages within a folder, arranged latest on top.

When the document we want is not so easy to find this way, the digital search features of our software come into play. A digital search is done either of two ways—title searches or content searches.

A title search is performed on the titles (file names) of the documents included in a given folder (or hierarchy of folders). Using our example, we would tell our software we want to search for all images in this client's folder titled 12-31. It would return anything with that group of characters in the title. The one or more

December 31 files that are returned probably contain all of the client's tax returns for the respective year, plus any other scanned images dated on the last day of a prior or subsequent year. Or, we could search on the word "return" and get all of the client's tax returns and anything else with that character string in the title. We can also indicate whether we want the search operation to apply to the main client folder or to subdirectories.

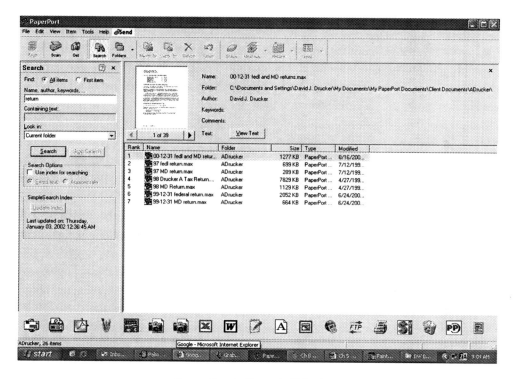

PaperPort's Search Window

Manual OCR (Optical Character Recognition) Capability

But suppose we have even less of a clear idea of what we're searching for. We just know it's a document in a particular client's folder that has something to do with a Qualified Personal Residence Trust, but we don't know exactly what we named the image. If the trust is part of the client's entire estate plan document, we might have simply named the image with the date the documents were signed plus the title Estate Plan. This is when another required feature—the automatic OCR and indexing capability—comes in. It will be the OCR capability that allows us to search by content, as opposed to searching by title.

"OCR" stands for Optical Character Recognition. This capability has been around for many years in the form of affordable, stand-alone software packages that allow the user to apply this feature to an image on his hard drive, resulting in a page of editable text. In other words, OCR software converts a picture of words back into individual characters as one would create with word processing software. Once the pictures are converted to text, that text can be operated on, i.e., edited, spell-checked, and pasted into e-mails and word processing documents.

OCR sounds wonderful, but it can take up a lot of computing time and can misread scanned words, resulting in text that must be proofread for errors. Moreover, it is not efficient to manually OCR (we use the letters here as a verb) every document within a client's folder in order to be able to search for the one that concerns a qualified personal residence trust.

Automatic OCR and Indexing Capability

We have an easier way of conducting our content search. The better scanning software, as noted above, will have an *automatic* OCR capability. This means that once a document is scanned into the client's folder and the computer senses no computing activity for a specified period of time (perhaps you've gone out to lunch), it will begin automatically OCRing the new image and creating an index of the words at the end of the conversion process. A much larger index already exists from all of the many documents you've scanned previously. The words from the new index are merely added to this existing index. Then, when you conduct a content search on a particular client folder and ask for documents with the word "qualified," the OCR process has already been done and the software should select a short list of documents, among which is the one you're looking for.

Misspellings will create the same problems in the automatic OCR process as it will in the manual OCR process, but most documents will have the word you're searching for in more than one place within the document, so chances are good that one misspelling won't completely thwart your search effort.

Annotation Capability

Make sure the scanning software you select has an annotation capability, so you can add notes to a scanned page. This means that blank forms that reside in your scanning software can be filled in using the annotation feature. A copy of the form can then be saved within the software to a category such as Expense Reimbursements in Process. Your in-house accountant would be alerted to the expense form by internal e-mail, would process the payment, would use annotation features to mark the form "paid" and would move the form within your scanning software to a Bills Paid category. Because the scanning program is on your network available to those employees to whom you've given the necessary permissions, they can review and work with this expense documentation at any stage along the way without anyone searching through paper files for the information. If you outsource your accounting and operate in a decentralized mode (see Chapter 9 for a discussion of decentralized versus centralized treatments of Virtual Work Partners), then your accountant can also join your network and secure the same permissions to review your scanned documents.

The annotation feature of scanning software can come in very handy in other ways by eliminating the need for various special-purpose software products. For example, have you spent money on software designed specifically to assist you in creating and maintaining your firm's ADV? With a scanning product having annotation features, you can eliminate the need for that product. Just scan in a blank ADV form and file it in the Blank Forms subdirectory of your scanning software. Make a copy of this form within your software (i.e., copy the form from its subdirectory to the main desktop of your software, leaving the blank copy in the subdirectory unaltered), complete it using the annotation feature, and file it by renaming and saving it in your Regulatory folder within your scanning software. The first time you do this it will take a bit of time to enter the text and format it properly. Subsequent amendments will be a snap.

Regulatory Compliance Capability

The last must-have feature in scanning software is a regulatory compliance capability. Effective May 31, 2001, the SEC issued its Final Rule on Electronic Recordkeeping by Investment Companies and Investment Advisers in Securities and Exchange Commission, Title 17, Parts 270 and 275 via amendments to rules 31a-2 and 204-2 under the Investment Company Act of 1940. The Commission's Final Rule states:

> Under revised rules 31a-2 and 204-2, funds and advisers are permitted to maintain records electronically if they establish and maintain procedures: (i) to safeguard the records from loss, alteration, or destruction, (ii) to limit access to the records to authorized personnel, the Commission, and (in the case of funds) fund directors, and (iii) to ensure that electronic copies of non-electronic originals are complete, true, and legible.[7] In response to a suggestion of one commenter, we are expanding rules 31a-2 and 204-2 to include all records that are required to be

maintained and preserved by any rule under the Investment Company or Advisers Acts ("other record keeping requirements") so that it is clear that if funds and advisers keep records electronically they must comply with the conditions of these rules.

The Commission considered requiring advisers to maintain electronic records in a completely unalterable, WORM (write-once, read-many) format, such as burning records onto a CD-ROM, but stopped short of this requirement. In footnote 7 to its Final Rule, the Commissions said:

> 7. Rules 31a-2(f)(3) and 204-2(g)(3). We requested commenters to address whether rules 31a-2 and 204-2 should require funds and advisers to preserve records in a non-rewritable, non-erasable (also known as "write once, read many," or WORM) format. Commenters concurred in our preliminary assessment, at the proposing stage, that the costs of such a requirement would be likely to outweigh the benefits (with respect to advisers and funds). Based on our consideration of costs, benefits, and other factors described in the proposing release we are not adopting such a requirement at this time.

From its rules 31a-2 and 204-2 amendments, it is clear the SEC wants records to be unalterable, but that's as much a demand on the adviser to employ prudent backup systems and restrict access to those records as it is to use a particular form of technology in initially capturing them in electronic form.

Nonetheless, there are differences in how the popular scanning software products deal with the issue of alterability. PaperPort Deluxe would appear to meet the SEC's requirements out of the box if, as said earlier, the user safeguards properly the records he creates with the software. Other, pricier products may come with an "audit trail" feature for regulatory compliance purposes. This feature typically monitors and records user access and actions vis-à-vis a scanned image to assure an SEC auditor that the document hasn't been altered. However, in light of the SEC's Final Rule, this feature and its higher price may be unnecessary for your practice.

Be aware that some states may have different interpretations of the SEC's Final Rule, or entirely different regulations regarding electronic record keeping.

PaperPort Deluxe

MANY HOME OFFICE SCANNERS on the market today come with a utility that resembles PaperPort, but looks can sometimes be deceiving. Smart Panel, the utility that comes with the Epson Perfection 1640 SU scanner, allows you to scan, copy, scan to OCR, and scan to e-mail. Sounds a lot like what PaperPort does, right? Not really. What sets PaperPort apart are its organizational tools and its reasonable price which, as of this writing, has been as little as $49 after rebate.

PaperPort "Items"

In order to understand how PaperPort works, one first must understand what PaperPort refers to as "items." Items are files that PaperPort acquires. Scanned documents generally go into PaperPort as images. This means that the document, even if it contains text exclusively, is stored as a picture file. All that the program and your scanner have done is to take a snapshot of your paper document and to store it as a graphic file. A word processor cannot read or edit such a file.

PaperPort can convert these graphics files into text files by dragging and dropping them onto the icon representing your word processor on the program's Send To bar (see graphic on the following page). PaperPort automatically OCRs the image, opens your word processor, and deposits the resulting text document in it. The PaperPort OCR software does a decent job of optical character recognition, but if the document in question is governed by securities regulations or is otherwise critical, it's best that you proofread it carefully after the OCR is complete.

Getting Objects into PaperPort

Before PaperPort can be used to organize your information, you need to move documents into the program. In PaperPort parlance, this is called "acquiring items," which can be done several different ways. The most obvious way, of course, is to scan an item into the program; but there are other ways, too. For example, if you want to easily move files (as image items, not text items) into the program, you can use one of the PaperPort virtual printers from within the originating application (as discussed in detail in Chapter 6). These virtual printers work in a manner similar to that of creating an Adobe Acrobat Portable Document Format (PDF) document. In most applications such as Microsoft Word or Excel, the user clicks on File, then Print to access the print dialog box. The dialog box contains a drop-down list of print drivers installed on the computer. Depending on the type of document being scanned, the user would select either the PaperPort (for black and white) or

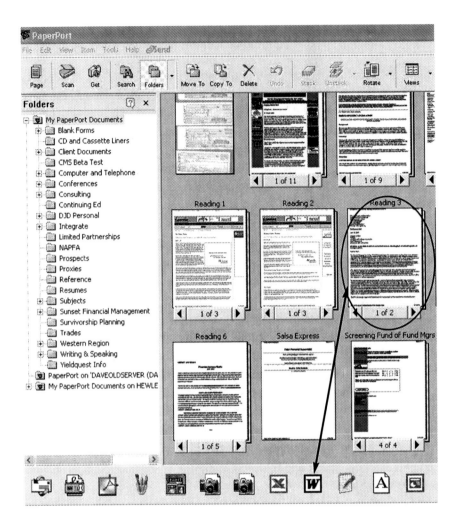

PaperPort Drag 'n Drop OCR

PaperPort Color print driver. Clicking on Print will send the files to the selected PaperPort driver, which will convert them to PaperPort image files and display the files on the PaperPort desktop.

PaperPort provides another tool that makes acquiring Web pages a breeze. From the Tools menu, select Web Capture (a check mark should appear). This action prompts PaperPort to add a Web Capture Icon to the Windows toolbar at the lower right-hand corner of your screen near the time display. You can now surf the Net to the Web page you wish to acquire. Once there, click on the little Web Capture icon and select Capture Entire Page or Capture Visible Portion. That's it; you're done. Now the Web page is on your PaperPort desktop and you can view a static image of the Web page, save it, print it, mail it, or annotate it.

Photos can usually be downloaded directly from your digital camera. Image files that reside on your hard drive in formats such as JPEG (.JPG), TIF (.TIF) or bitmap (.BMP) can be imported by clicking File, and then Import from within PaperPort.

We've Got It–Let's Do Something with It

Once an image has been acquired, it can be annotated. Any part of a page can be highlighted, sticky notes can be added, or arrows can be inserted to make important points. The ability to "mark up" documents and images from within PaperPort can save time and improve efficiency. For example, if a client sends you a trust document for review, you can save the original, make a copy within PaperPort, annotate the document, and transport it back to the client electronically.

One easy way to do this is to convert the document to Adobe .PDF format, because PDF files retain all of a document's formatting. In order to use this method,

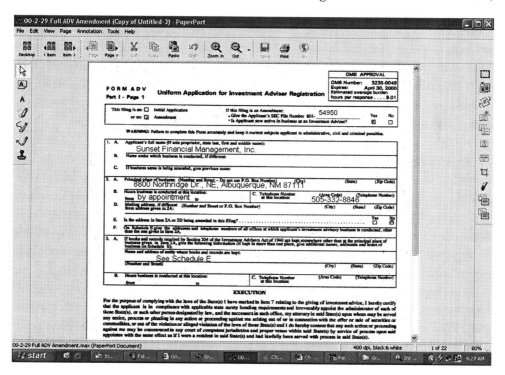

A Page from Dave's ADV Completed Using PaperPort's Annotation Features

you must have the full version of Adobe Acrobat installed on your computer. If Acrobat is installed, you can convert a PaperPort file to a PDF file by dragging and dropping it onto the Adobe Acrobat icon on the toolbar at the bottom of the page. (Important tip: Windows XP users will not be able to use Adobe Acrobat 5.0 in conjunction with PaperPort 8.0 if they use the Adobe default, or Typical, set-up. In order for the two products to work together, you must select the Adobe Custom installation, and chose to install the Adobe PDFWriter files in addition to the other default selections.)

In fact, if you use PaperPort in conjunction with Web conferencing, you can even make your annotations online in real time. Both the original and your marked-up copy are on file for future reference.

Graphics can be "stamped" onto an item, so if you receive an invoice from a vendor, you can virtually stamp it PAID with a date as you pay it. Signature lines on forms can be highlighted in any color you choose, making it easier for clients to complete forms correctly. Explanatory text can be added in the margins. Even entire forms can be scanned and filled in, as Dave does with his ADV.

PaperPort also includes image-editing tools that can perform basic photo editing chores such as cropping, rotating, enhancing, and sharpening images and removing red eye. Possible uses for this tool include prepping images for use in your firm's brochures, newsletters, and Web page. If you regularly use dedicated image-editing software such as Adobe Photoshop or Adobe Illustrator, you probably won't be impressed with PaperPort's image-editing tools, but for those without such programs who need to tweak an image once in a while, these tools work.

We've Acquired It—and Annotated It—Let's File It!

PaperPort's Folder Pane comes populated with a number of folders. The primary folder is the My PaperPort Documents folder. A number of subfolders are nested underneath this folder. Existing subfolders can be deleted and new folders can be added in much the same way you work with folders within Windows Explorer. To delete a folder, right click on it and select Delete. To insert a new folder into the main My PaperPort Documents folder, right click on it and then click on New Folder.

It is also possible to bring your computer's existing folders, network folders, and external drives into the Folder Pane. In the Folder Pane, right-click, select PaperPort Folders, click on the Add button in the dialog box, then select the folders you want to add. The advantage of populating the Folder Pane with all of your files and folders is that all of your data can now be managed through the PaperPort filing system.

Once all of your information is listed in the Folder Pane, it can be rearranged to suit your needs (the sole exception is the My PaperPort Documents folder, which will always be at the top of the list). Folders can be organized by right clicking on them, which allows them to be manipulated. Folders can also be dragged and dropped to a new location. Items on the desktop can be dragged and dropped into folders as well.

Employing the PaperPort filing system allows the user to perform some filing tricks that ease the retrieval process. For example, users can color code folders by right clicking on a folder and selecting Properties. If you routinely set up similar sub-folders for each client (Tax Returns, Performance Reports, Estate Planning), assigning a different color to each subfolder type speeds the folder browsing process.

More importantly, it is now possible to make use of PaperPort's indexing and search capabilities. PaperPort allows the user to assign properties to a file in much the same manner as has been possible for years with document files created with Microsoft applications like Word or Excel. Properties can include one's name, the author, and multiple keywords and comments. Once properties are assigned, clicking the Search button on the Command Bar, which activates the Search Pane, can run property searches.

As your file archives grow, you will want the capability to search for text in a file. That's where SimpleSearch comes in. SimpleSearch allows you to index all files in the Folder Pane by applying PaperPort's built in OCR technology to "read" and catalog all text in your filed items. Cataloging your entire collection of files can be time consuming, so PaperPort lets the user control the indexing process. It can be done for a single item or folder, as well as for a complete index. We suggest that you perform the initial indexing in stages. When we tried to index several gigabytes of PaperPort files at one time, PaperPort was unable to complete the process. When we broke the task down into several pieces, however, it worked fine. If you choose to index large quantities of information at one time, we strongly suggest doing so overnight or on a weekend.

Search results can be displayed in one of two views. The All Item view reports all items meeting the search criteria in a manner similar to a typical Windows search. The First Item view displays a thumbnail view of the first item meeting the criteria on the desktop. The thumbnail displays work fine, but if your search yields a large number of results, try to refine your search before browsing through the thumbnails. On our P4 computer, we found that up to about twenty images (some of them complex) loaded rapidly. Be prepared to wait a few minutes (or longer on an older computer) for all of the thumbnails to be displayed. Pressing F3 enables the user to scroll to subsequent results.

We find a lot to like about the PaperPort file management features. We ran a test by loading a library of presentation documents that included Microsoft Word documents, HTML pages, and PowerPoint slides into the PaperPort SimpleSearch Index, allowing the index to analyze the files without us inputting properties. We then ran a number of keyword searches and compared them with the results of a Windows Explorer search. In every case, the SimpleSearch was superior. Of course, if we had entered properties for each file as we created it, we would expect the results to be similar.

Better OCR and Better Indexing

PaperPort comes with a perfectly serviceable OCR capability, but it can be confused by busy layouts and fancy formatting, for example. If you are using OCR strictly for indexing purposes, this does not present much of a problem; however, if you need to scan and edit documents with complex formatting, Premium OCR software can be a tremendous time saver. ScanSoft, PaperPort's publisher, produces a full line of OCR products. Their current top-of-the-line product is OmniPage Pro 11, priced at $499.99. OmniPage Pro possesses a number of capabilities that PaperPort does not, including greater accuracy, semi-automatic proofing, the ability to automatically straighten crooked pages, and the ability to convert documents to and from Adobe PDF format. Other fine OCR options exist, but OmniPage Pro's long pedigree, combined with the fact that it is published by the same company as PaperPort, suggest that PaperPort users will want to put it on their short list of candidates when shopping for a high-quality OCR package.

ScanSoft's OmniPage Pro

MUCH OF THE ADDITIONAL FUNCTIONALITY supplied by high-quality OCR software like OmniPage Pro 11 used to come at the price of complexity. These days, automatic settings, templates, and wizards allow novice users to enjoy many sophisticated features without extensive training. At the same time, the presence of extensive manual controls lets power-users achieve the results they desire. We cannot possibly cover all of the convenience features built into OmniPage Pro 11, but the following eight may prove instructive.

➢ Greater scanning accuracy
➢ Direct OCR
➢ Sending an item as an e-mail attachment
➢ Better proofing

➤ Improved format retention
➤ Adobe PDF file capabilities
➤ Multilanguage support
➤ Improved HTML

Greater Scanning Accuracy

OmniPage Pro and other state-of-the-art programs supply a level of accuracy that is not available in lesser programs like the version included in PaperPort Deluxe.

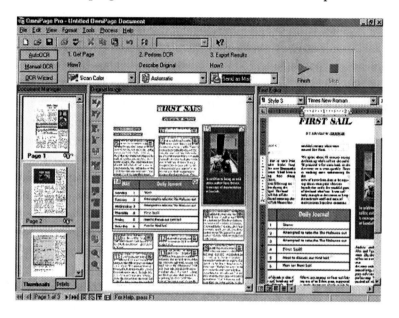

The OmniPage Pro 11 Document Window

In the automatic mode, OmniPage Pro recognizes text and complex layouts better than lesser programs. In the case of complex layouts, users can help the program along by "telling" the program what type of document (spreadsheet, table, multiple column/no tables) is being scanned. One can even divide a page into zones with different characteristics so that the program can apply the optimal processing method to each zone. For those who deal often with the same type of complex layout, a template can be created, eliminating the need to repeatedly "zone" the document being OCRed. Premium quality OCR programs also do a better job on hard-to-read documents, such as faxes or text printed on colored paper.

Direct OCR

If you spend much of your time working in an application such as Microsoft Word or Microsoft Excel, Direct OCR is a useful feature. Direct OCR allows you to access the functionality of OmniPage Pro from within the program you are using (Microsoft Word in this example). OmniPage Pro's Direct OCR is a bit more convenient to use than PaperPort's ScanDirect, because Direct OCR runs from within the native application whereas ScanDirect is a separate program that must be launched from the Windows start menu.

Before OCR operations can be performed from within a native application, a link must be created from within OmniPage Pro to enable the functionality. Some links may have been enabled during the installation process, but you may want to add or delete applications from the list. To do this, click on the Options button on the Standard Toolbar to reveal a dialog box and select the Direct OCR tab. This tab will list applications that are registered for Direct OCR, as well as unregistered applications that OmniPage Pro has also recognized. Click on the Add and Remove buttons to move applications between the two lists. If an application does not appear in either box, and you want to enable it for Direct OCR, try using the browse button to locate it and move it to the unregistered list. According to OmniPage Pro's online help, "as long as the program has a File menu and can paste text from the Clipboard, Direct OCR should work fine." (There are some exceptions, such as Microsoft Works and Microsoft Publisher, but many programs seem compliant. If you run into problems with your application, you can simply disable Direct OCR, so it's always worth a try.)

Once Direct OCR is enabled, click on File-Acquire Text to begin the OCR process. Settings can be adjusted by selecting File, then Acquire Text Settings. From a user's perspective, OmniPage Pro now operates almost seamlessly as an extension of the native program.

Sending an Item as an E-Mail Attachment

Let's say you want to e-mail a copy of a magazine article to a friend. If the article is primarily plain text, and you are using PaperPort, you could probably scan it, OCR it, and send it off as a text document. If the layout is complex, however, the above method may not work. You could still send it as a PaperPort .MAX file, but your friend would have to install the free PaperPort MiniViewer on his or her computer to access the file. As an alternative, you could convert the file to a common image format (JPEG or bitmap, for example), PaperPort Browser Viewable, or PaperPort Self-Viewing (.EXE) format. All of the above methods will work, but they have disadvantages. They consume valuable time, may entail a larger download for your friend, or may be blocked (unknown .EXE e-mail attachments can be a source of virus infection).

In the case of OmniPage Pro, there is a much higher likelihood the article will be OCRed correctly, allowing you to use the Send-As-Mail command to quickly e-mail the OCRed article.

Better Proofing

A good proofing editor allows the user to easily spot errors and correct them. Premium products are generally easy to use and offer the user customization options. For instance, OmniPage Pro users can create multiple custom dictionaries to be used with various types of documents. A financial planner specializing in estate planning might want to have one dictionary containing legal terms in use when scanning legal documents, and another dictionary containing financial terms when scanning economic reports.

Some programs now employ a form of artificial intelligence that "learns" your tendencies based on previous corrections you have made, in a fashion similar to the technique voice recognition software employs to learn your voice. OmniPage Pro calls it IntelliTrain. The more you use the feature, the more it learns about your tendencies and the better it works.

Improved Format Retention

With improved recognition, zoning, and other advanced features now available, it is often possible to control how much or how little of the original formatting is transferred to your finished product.

Adobe PDF File Capabilities

Both OmniPage Pro 11 and Abbyy FineReader Pro (discussed below) are capable of producing output in Adobe .PDF format. OmniPage Pro can open and OCR .PDF files. Once a file is loaded into OmniPage Pro, it can be saved as an ASCII (text), Excel, Framemaker, HTML, OmniPage Document, Microsoft Word, or WordPerfect file. It can also be saved as a Rich Text Format (RTF) file, which can be opened by Microsoft PowerPoint or Microsoft Publisher.

Multilanguage Support

OmniPage Pro 11 and Abbyy FineReader Pro both claim to recognize text in at least 100 languages.

Improved HTML

As the role of the Internet in our businesses and personal lives continues to expand, so does the necessity of being able to produce output in a Web-friendly format. Manufacturers of premium OCR products recognize this fact as they continue to improve their programs' HTML capabilities. This means you can start with information in graphic form and convert it to HTML format for inclusion on your company's website.

OmniPage Pro 11 costs $499.99 for the full package, or $149.99 if upgrading the OCR capability within the scanning software you already own.

There's another option with a lower price tag and a slightly different feature set: Abbyy FineReader Pro 5.0. Our comments also apply to release 6.0.

From Russia ... with OCR: Abbyy FineReader Pro

OF THE OTHER PRODUCTS WORTH CONSIDERING, one that impressed us is Abbyy FineReader Pro 5.0 (and the recent 6.0 release). The program, produced by Russian-based Abbyy House, used its own proprietary IPA (integrity, purposefulness, and

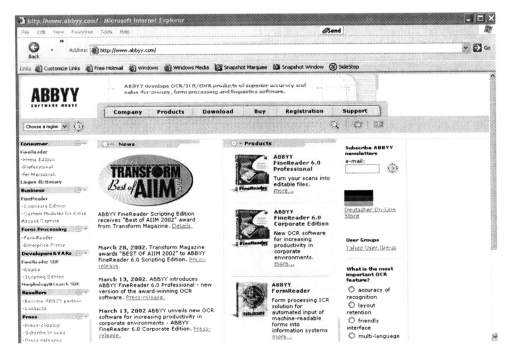

Abbyy FineReader Pro

adaptability) technology to recognize and learn both characters and layouts.

The program's feature set and overall functionality are very similar to those of OmniPage Pro 11, but Abbyy FineReader Pro stood out in a number of areas:

Language support. If you happen to do a lot of work in foreign languages, FineReader Pro may have the upper hand. Abbyy claims recognition of 176 languages, including Armenian (three dialects), Bulgarian, Crimean Tartar, Estonian, Sami (Lappish), Latvian, Russian, and Ukrainian, and can spell check in twenty-nine languages.

Layout recognition. In a number of unscientific tests, we scanned pages with difficult formatting and layouts that challenged the ability of PaperPort's OCR engine in both OmniPage Pro and FineReader Pro. FineReader Pro did at least as well and in some cases better than OmniPage Pro at reproducing the images.

Cost. For those of you new to the business, or just going out on your own, price can be an issue. If you are on a tight budget and you must purchase a full version (as opposed to an upgrade version) of a premium OCR product, Abbyy FineReader Pro's sub-$100.00 street price looks awfully attractive. Still not sure whether Abbyy FineReader is right for you? Why not download the free Try & Buy version, which offers a full functional thirty days of use (or thirty hours, whichever comes first), and form your own opinion?

We have discussed Abbyy FineReader to highlight an OCR option that offers a low price and several specialized features but, for most readers, OmniPage Pro 11 will be the appropriate choice. There are a number of reasons for our bias:

➤ We highly recommend PaperPort Deluxe for smaller operations in particular, and since ScanSoft produces both products, integration is tight

➤ It is a fine product from an established company that will meet the needs of most users

➤ Although the full version of OmniPage Pro is rather expensive, it's probably worth it; and many readers who purchase a scanner will be eligible to purchase the less expensive upgrade version

We've provided you with a number of practical reasons why buying premium OCR software could be an excellent investment for your firm, but the best one is that it can save you time. Premium OCR software automates some tasks, offers a higher degree of user control over the OCR process, and cuts down on proofing time due to its greater accuracy. Undoubtedly, you will discover additional applications for these programs as you begin to use them.

If your budget is limited and your primary goal is to reproduce your current files digitally, premium OCR software may not be a priority. If you don't need to edit your scanned images, or edit them rarely, PaperPort's OCR engine will suffice because you don't need anything close to 100 percent OCR accuracy for Simple-Search to work effectively. As you become more comfortable working digitally, however, you may want to edit image documents, cut from or paste to existing documents, or create your own forms using an existing form as a template. At that point, as you continue your quest for the fully digital environment, the allure of premium OCR software will become irresistible.

OmniForm Premium

IT SEEMS THAT FINANCIAL PROFESSIONALS and their clients spend a disproportionate amount of time dealing with forms. Whether it is an account application, a client profile, a financial planning fact finder, or a Form ADV, we just can't seem to avoid forms on a daily basis. Since we can't avoid them, we had better learn to deal with them! OmniForm Premium version 5.0 helps us to do that.

OmniForm can perform a lot of tricks. Of particular interest to financial professionals is its ability to convert paper forms to digital format for use on your computer or on the Web. One method of doing this is to scan a paper form onto your hard drive using your scanner and scanning software. Another method is to import and convert a file. Once the digital image is in OmniForm, the program is supposed to generate a form that can be filled out on your computer or on the Web. Well, it's not quite that easy. We scanned a few fairly simple forms into OmniForm Premium. They scanned in almost perfectly, and a wizard guided us through the proofreading process, but when objects needed fixing (like an adjustment to a check box), it took us a while to get things right. Other forms scanned less successfully and repairing them was a frustrating process.

We thought importing forms would work better, but that was also a mixed bag. The problem we encountered was that OmniForm could only import in .PCX or .TIF formats. We tried to work around this limitation by importing incompatible file formats to PaperPort, let PaperPort convert the file to TIF, and then move it to OmniForm. Results were uneven. Some conversions were OK, but some required major fixes.

If you want to design your own forms, mastering the basics is fairly straightforward

A Word about Forms

IT SEEMS THAT FINANCIAL PROFESSIONALS and their clients are required to fill out a never-ending list of forms. PaperPort includes FormTyper, a form digitizer. Once a form is scanned, drag and drop it onto the FormTyper icon on the Send To bar so that the program can work its magic. After the form is analyzed, you can save a blank form, edit the form, or fill in the form. As is the case with OCR software, the PaperPort form digitizer is good, but more robust solutions exist and, as you may have guessed by now, ScanSoft happens to publish one of the leading products: OmniForm Premium 5.

provided you use the supplied templates (or the additional ones on the OmniForm website) as a starting point; however, designing forms from scratch or creating elaborate designs is best left to those with graphic arts experience.

If you can use the program proficiently, the benefits are substantial. All types of elements and graphics can be added to forms. User profiles and client profiles can be stored in a database, so information does not have to be typed over and over again. Fields can be programmed with drop-down lists, and one field can be programmed to control another (e.g., if you enter a customer number in one field, the customer name field is automatically populated). Fields can perform calculations as well. Once forms are completed, they can be distributed in a number of formats, including one that is Web-ready. OmniForm supports digital signatures, possibly relieving you of the burden of storing signed original documents.

We don't think that OmniForm Premium is for everybody, because we got uneven results and because designing anything beyond basic forms takes practice. Also, the program's $699.99 price will give some advisers pause. On balance, we think that most readers would probably be better off outsourcing digital form creation; however, if you are determined to create your own digital form, or if you have an employee who possesses talent in graphic design, OmniForm is worth a try. Even if you outsource form creation, you might want a copy of OmniForm Premium so that you can take advantage of its database and form-filling capabilities.

The hardware and software required for a successful paperless operation is just the beginning. In the next chapter, we'll look at some filing systems for all the information you'll be collecting.

Storing and Retrieving Text-Based Information

UNTIL NOW WE'VE DISCUSSED only the treatment of images but haven't discussed the handling of text-based information. Almost everything worth saving for later retrieval will be in one of two forms: an image file or a text file. What's the best way to handle information that originates in text form, that is, information we create with our own word processors, such as letters, notes, and bulletins, and things that come to us in text form, such as e-mail?

E-mail is edging out the telephone as the primary means of communication between many financial advisers and their clients. Younger clients often use it because they have been educated in the computer age. But older, retired clients use it, too, because they're more likely to have had the time necessary to learn how to use a computer.

From the perspective of our legal liability, we need a record of every client communication, so if clients use e-mail more and more, our job is easier. Whereas we might once have had a phone conversation with a client that required us to create a written record after the fact, we now get an e-mail question from and supply an e-mail answer to a client, so the entire conversation is recorded first-hand. When we take notes of a phone conversation, those notes usually paraphrase, but e-mails are verbatim. In the print realm, some of the kinds of information that we used to receive in image form, such as trade publications and newsletters, now come in e-mail form as well. More and more websites send their subscribers e-mail synopses of the latest day's, week's, or month's articles, which is often information worth saving.

What's the best way to store and organize text documents and e-mail? We wouldn't use the PaperPort print driver to just "print" all of this information to our scanning desktop, because then we'd lose the rapid text-searching ability we have with text files. We need a system that handles text-based documents as capably as our scanning software handles image documents. Ideally, these two systems would be one and the same. But you may find that the needs are better met with separate packages.

For text, Dave's practice has for many years used a product that fits loosely within the category of software called PIMs, or Personal Information Managers. The software is Info Select and is developed and sold by Micro Logic, Inc. of Hackensack, New Jersey (www.miclog.com) online for $149.99. Info Select is a product that is hard to pigeonhole. It can keep your calendar, get your e-mail, house all of your client contact information, originate and store documents, create document templates, and perform many other functions. But its greatest strength is its search engine. We have found no other software that allows you to find a text-based client record as quickly as Info Select.

Its primary weakness is its rudimentary networking capabilities. In other words, it works best in a sole practitioner environment. We're about to suggest to you some alternative product solutions, but looking at Info Select's format and features first can serve as guidelines for what to look for in the software *you* choose for *your* practice.

What Info Select has in common with PaperPort, and what you should be looking for in any software you use for text or image storage and retrieval, is the nested folders feature we discussed earlier. With this structure, one can create virtually unlimited numbers of folders within folders comprising a logical pyramid of categories.

Typical categories within Dave's setup in Info Select are not unlike his categories within PaperPort. They include client folders, folders for the firm's operations, personal folders, and so on. Searches function the same way, too. A person goes to the category in which he believes the information resides, clicks on the category title, and then clicks on the search icon at the top of the screen. He then types in one or more keywords and, as he is typing, Info Select shows in a block pattern the hits or matches it has found.

Info Select almost instantaneously displays each record that contains the chosen keywords.

A program in which you collect your important text-based communications for future reference is of little value, though, unless *all* text communications are stored there. Many advisers will use a program like Microsoft Word to compose letters to clients and Microsoft Outlook to compose e-mails to clients. Those letters and e-mails will get stored in the default directories created by the originating programs unless directed elsewhere by the user. And that's precisely what you must do—reset those application defaults to make sure all communications with a client are saved in the same place. This process is fairly automatic if you use a program like Info Select, which can be a conduit for all of your e-mail as well as your main word processor. Since it contains the directories you've set up to house all of your client information, text communications of whatever type can be dragged and dropped to a client's folder.

The reason to follow a system such as the one we've outlined above is to mini-

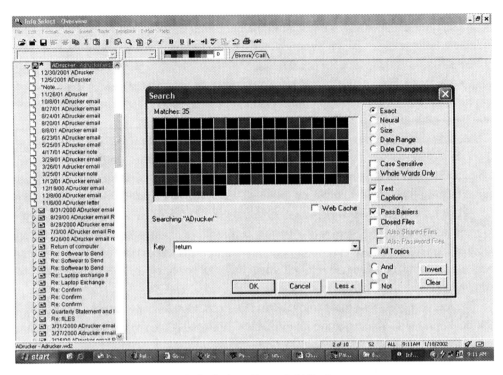

The Info Select Search Window

mize the time it takes to find any record that you may be searching for. You need to be able to find what you want the first time you look for it. Because Dave's personal system depends upon separate programs for text-based and image-based information, he has a strict set of rules about what type of information goes into which program. A tax return will always be captured as an image file and will be searched for in PaperPort. A letter or e-mail he's written to a client will always originate from Info Select and thus be stored in the client's folder there. So Dave's search time for any type of document will be minimized because he knows what program to start searching in and he's assured of finding the information the first time.

Most advisers are experiencing a shift from U.S. mail or overnight delivery services to e-mail for the transmission of communications to clients and business associates. Nowadays, the communication you need to find is just as likely to be in e-mail form as in letter form, and you'll be lucky if you can remember in what form the communication took place.

Add to this your need to keep other kinds of written communications in addition to letters and e-mails and to literally document every client transaction, retain meet-

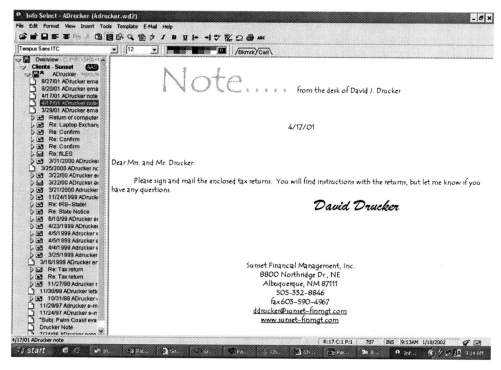

Info Select Search Results

ing notes and phone notes, and capture e-mails received from clients or from third parties concerning clients, and you can see why all of these kinds of text-based information need, above all, to reside in one location.

One Planner's Solution

IN CHAPTER 2 WE MET KATHLEEN DAY and her firm, Kathleen Day & Associates, Inc. in Miami, Florida. Day's technology solution for implementing a paperless office was to put a Visioneer sheet-fed scanner on the desk of every employee. She also has a two-sided scanner and another larger, higher-speed scanner used for larger documents. "We have a rule," Day says. "If you're an employee dealing with a document of fewer than ten pages, then you scan it yourself." Otherwise, another employee scans the document on the firm's high-speed scanner.

Day mates her Visioneer scanners to WORLDOX software, and she and her staff share all documents across their LAN. Why WORLDOX? "What I wanted was software that would allow me to create a profile of a document and later search for that document by comments or by any piece of its profile," says Day. "I save a document with the client's name; document type; 'mailed-on' date, who mailed it, who it was sent to; was it a document that required approval and who approved it; did it require a log, what type was it; who created this file, was it updated at any time; its descriptive name ('tax return for XYZ client'); and comments." Together, these notations comprise the document's profile, and Day can retrieve the document by searching on one of these notations, by visually looking for the document within a tree of folders, or by searching a folder for all documents scanned on a certain date. She can also do a simple text or keyword search across her entire archive if all else fails.

Before WORLDOX, Day relied on PaperPort Deluxe for her scanning software needs, which was an adequate solution by itself when her firm was smaller. Her number of employees had expanded to eighteen by 2001. Filing documents with PaperPort's free-form folder system didn't give Day the uniformity she needed for properly storing and retrieving documents in an office of the size to which hers had evolved.

Her son and daughter-in-law solved her problem when Kevin Day, with his background in software programming and process development, and Jo Day, with her experience working in the Phoenix, Arizona, fee-only planning firm of Keats, Connelly and Associates, Inc., saw a way to give their mom the structure she needed without a radical change to her existing systems.

"WORLDOX works in conjunction with PaperPort and other imaging solutions; the two are symbiotic," explains Kevin Day, adding, "PaperPort is one of the best user interfaces for maintaining the paper analogy, and WORLDOX allows you to keep track of the PaperPort document by way of its WORLDOX profile." Kevin and Jo Day's experience doing technology installations for financial advisory firms since 1999 at Phoenix-based Trumpet Inc. taught them that a three- to four-employee firm can manage a PaperPort file structure because only a couple of people are making decisions on where things go. With larger firms, it is nearly impossible to establish and enforce rules for filing documents in a system like PaperPort. "WORLDOX does away with folder structure and introduces the idea of profiling or categorizing a document," says Kevin. This was the new order he brought to his mom's firm—the WORLDOX/PaperPort combination.

Let's take a closer look at both WORLDOX and another scanning software product—DocuXplorer—in the following reviews.

WORLDOX

Learning from Lawyers?

If there's one thing that financial planning firms have in common with law firms, it's that they both generate large quantities of paper that must be filed, stored, and retrieved on a regular basis. Many law firms are well ahead of financial planning firms in digitization and document management, so we looked at the products law firms are using to see if financial planners could adapt these solutions to their own needs.

Three names kept cropping up in our investigations: iManage, GroupWise, and WORLDOX. Whereas iManage might be an option for large firms, and GroupWise is a possibility for firms that are committed to Novell systems, we believe WORLDOX is the one solution that can be implemented by a wide range of financial advisory firms.

WORLDOX is a corporate-strength document management system (DMS). It would be a stretch to say that setup is intuitive, but after reading the documentation, single user and small network installations appear within the capabilities of most readers. For larger installations, it would be wise to engage a consultant, not just for the installation, but also for help in creating the optimal file structure.

As we discussed earlier, one key to finding documents rapidly is good profiling, and profiling is one of WORLDOX's strong suits. WORLDOX integrates seamlessly with many commonly used applications, including Microsoft Office (with the exception of Microsoft Publisher). When a user is ready to save a file, the WORLDOX profile window appears. WORLDOX provides seven customizable fields in addition to numerous prenamed fields. The document storage system can be divided into groups (such as financial planning, investment advisory services, and our business documents), and each group can be assigned different fields. The Financial Planning group might have fields for topic (e.g., Insurance), document type (e.g., Client To-Do List),

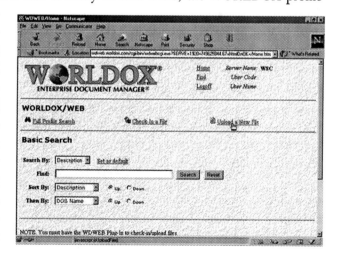

The WORLDOX Search Window

and author. Totally different fields can be assigned to the Investment group and the Business group. The administrator can equip each field with a drop-down list, which saves time, ensures uniformity, and reduces errors. The entries required to populate the drop-down lists can be made manually or imported from another program. The software can also be instructed to automatically input the document author's name.

These groups can be used to more easily control and monitor file access. If, for example, an organization requires a space for files that only firm partners are to be granted access to, it might be a good idea to assign those files to a unique group. The WORLDOX program comes with a Planning Guide, which includes advice on how to create the right filing system for your firm.

Once the profile is completed, WORLDOX automatically files the document in the proper location based on the information provided to the profiler. The downside of this system is that WORLDOX imposes its file structure on the user, but the benefits of a uniform system are substantial: every document is filed in a known location, easily accessible from within the WORLDOX system. There is less chance of user error resulting in a document being misfiled.

At this time, WORLDOX does not support extended file names (that feature will be released in an upcoming version). It does, however, allow users to input an extended name in a separate field. Should additional notes and comments be needed, the additional comments field can accommodate up to four pages of notes.

Document Retrieval

WORLDOX offers a number of ways to retrieve documents. To simplify the retrieval process, a Quick Pick selector provides access to most common search methods. If you know the extended file name, for example, you can enter it here. A number of buttons access other search features. Find Menu displays a list of Find Templates (preconfigured search screens). Direct Access is a nonindexed retrieval system that is the fastest way to find documents if you know some of the properties of the file you are looking for (client and date, for example). Favorite Files maintains a link to recently opened files so that users can access them instantly. Another button links to Favorite Folders.

Of course, WORLDOX

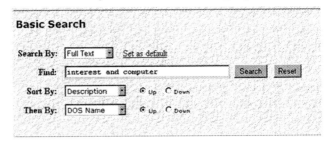

WORLDOX Search Criteria

has a powerful index search capability, powered by ISYS, a search engine that catalogs both profile information and text. It is extremely fast, flexible, and accurate.

Advantages for Network Users

Architecture. WORLDOX architecture is very appealing to networked offices. Unlike many other document management systems, WORLDOX does not require an SQL server, which can add significantly to the initial cost of implementation as well as system maintenance. Instead, WORLDOX uses cleverly designed dual database architecture. One database is a distributed database, which distributes files and folders throughout the network, saving their profile with them (in a hidden file). For full indexed search capabilities, a central database, which contains indexing information, is created on a server. The central index contains much of the same information as the distributed database, but in a different format, so that it is optimized for fast searches.

Mirroring. This feature saves a copy of each document a user edits to the local hard drive. If the network goes down, or if the user is disconnected from the network, the latest copy of the document will still be accessible, greatly reducing downtime.

Security. All conscientious planners view security as a major concern these days. WORLDOX contains predefined security classifications that can be applied when a document is saved, or anytime thereafter. Authors can define who can find, read, write, profile, or delete a file. WORLDOX's check-in/check-out feature is an easy way for owners and administrators to track who is working on what project in the office.

Document tracking. WORLDOX contains full audit capabilities, which can be customized during the installation process to reflect the firm's needs. Right-clicking on the document and selecting Audit Trail from the menu can generate an audit trail report for a document. WORLDOX displays a list of every action performed on the document along with a date. If further details about an individual action are required, you highlight the action and click the Details button. WORLDOX displays what was done, when, and by whom. Reports relating to groups of documents can be easily compiled.

The program includes DropZone, an e-mail management tool, which enables users to profile e-mail messages and drag and drop them directly into the document filing system. DropZone works with any OLE2- (object linking and embedding) and MAPI- (messaging application programming interface) compliant e-mail program.

WORLDOX supports more than 150 file formats. Many applications that are not supported can be filed in WORLDOX with modification. This would entail contacting the program's publisher, World Software Corporation, and engaging them to add code to your application so that it will launch WORLDOX when saving files. Those files could then be searched by properties.

WORLDOX/WEB

For an additional cost, firms can purchase WORLDOX/WEB, which allows users to access files over the Internet from wherever they are, assuming that they have Internet access. For organizations that employ virtual assistants or virtual planners, WORLDOX/WEB may be a necessity. If an organization's traditional employees frequently work from remote locations, or from home, adding Web capabilities to WORLDOX maintains document controls. If you feel comfortable living on the cutting edge, you could even enable clients to access many of the documents you have prepared for them directly from your server.

Price

Considering the performance, capabilities, and scalability of this product, WORLDOX is reasonably priced at $350 per license, with annual maintenance costing an additional $60. A firm with more than one employee will probably want more than one license. The more licenses it has, the more concurrent users it can have working in WORLDOX simultaneously. But the firm need not hold a separate license for every potential user; a twenty-person office might need only five to ten licenses since it's unlikely every employee would need WORLDOX at the same time.

WORLDOX/WEB has its own pricing structure based on the number of underlying WORLDOX licenses your firm has. If you hold one to five WORLDOX licenses, the additional cost for the WORLDOX/WEB is $600, then $100 per year annual maintenance; with six to twenty licenses, the cost for WORLDOX/WEB is $1,200, then $150 maintenance; and with twenty-one to fifty licenses, it's $2,300, then $300 maintenance.

So What's the Catch?

The first one is that you are purchasing a document management system, but not a document imaging system. You will need a convenient way to scan images into your system and annotate them. (One possible solution is to pair WORLDOX with PaperPort.)

Another gotcha is the way the product is marketed and documented. Since WORLDOX is a document management system, and the primary client base appears to be attorneys, most of the emphasis is placed on the program's indexing and retrieval capabilities. It was not readily apparent to us, for example, when we first tried the program, that DropZone, which the company touts as an e-mail management tool, can be used to bring almost any kind of file into WORLDOX. For those who plan to scan images, and use WORLDOX to manage them, this is a vital piece of information.

Is WORLDOX Right for You?

WORLDOX has a lot going for it. We think it is particularly attractive for those organizations that already have most of their information in a digital format (such as Microsoft Word files or PDF files) and that require a better way to index and track them. The program offers tight document tracking, good security features, scalability and a top-notch search engine at a reasonable price. For those who need to transform paper files to digital ones before filing them, WORLDOX can be paired with PaperPort or other imaging software, but you will probably have to talk with WORLDOX technical staff or a consultant to achieve optimal performance.

DocuXplorer Professional

DOCUXPLORER PROFESSIONAL is the most user-friendly "industrial strength" document management and archiving system we have come across. Unlike WORLDOX, it has image-capturing ability built in. It uses filing conventions similar to those employed by Windows Explorer and PaperPort that are intuitive and easy to understand.

All DocuXplorer files and folders reside in the Library. Inside the Library are the DX In Box, the Recycle Bin, and the Work Folder. The DX In Box is a tool designed to ease the process of moving documents and images into DocuXplorer. By setting the DX In Box as the default location for saving scanned images and files produced by Windows applications, you will make them easy to drag and drop into any DocuXplorer Folder. This is very helpful if you have a low-level employee scanning documents for you. They can do the scanning while someone else with a better understanding of the filing system does the filing.

The Work Folder can also be used to move documents into DocuXplorer. Right-clicking on a document in Windows Explorer reveals the Send To menu. Select DocuXplorer from the menu, and the document will be copied to the Work Folder. The Work Folder serves as a work flow creation tool as well. Subfolders can be created for individuals or tasks.

Cabinets typically contain a number of drawers, which store documents and

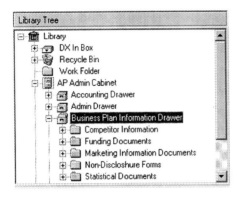

A Typical DocuXplorer Library Tree

images. The cabinet level is where index information is stored. A financial planning firm might want to create a separate cabinet for each office or each department within an office.

Drawers are where the actual document images are stored. Unlike their physical counterparts, there is no limit to the number of drawers that a virtual file cabinet can hold, so you can create a filing structure that meets your unique needs.

Folders are useful for examining a directory tree in the tree window. Their primary function is to allow users to browse through the directory tree visually. If you prefer using lots of narrowly defined folders to browse through information, as opposed to using a search function, the system can accommodate you.

Profiling and Indexing

DocuXplorer has powerful and easy-to-use profiling and indexing capabilities. When a cabinet is created, you can create an index by clicking on the Create Index Set button. Once a default index is created, it can be easily modified (the basics of this process can be mastered in about five minutes using the Getting Started Guide). Users can create an unlimited number of index sets. Each index set can contain up to twenty-five user-defined fields (five date fields, five currency fields, five integer fields, and ten character fields). The program grants the user considerable control over field properties. For example, if you are tracking clients, you might assign each client a client number. Since each client number is unique, you would use a standard field. If you had a client database that used a field to track custodians, however, you would most likely want a drop-down list. Field properties can be set with a couple of mouse clicks.

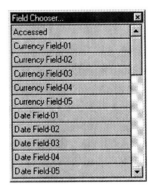

DocuXplorer
Add Fields Function

Adding fields is also simple. Right-click on an existing field heading, select Add Field, and a list of fields is displayed. Just drag and drop the desired field onto the column header bar and you have created a new field, ready to customize. Users can create multiple indices for a single cabinet. This is a useful feature if different types of documents reside in a single cabinet. Life insurance contracts could be searched under one set of criteria, while wills could be searched by a completely different set.

OCR Capabilities

DocuXplorer has an OCR engine built in. Since the OCR process takes time and considerable computer processing power, the program allows the user to create a processing queue for batch processing later. You may find it convenient to scan by day and to process the OCR queue overnight.

Annotation

DocuXplorer includes a good selection of tools to annotate images. These tools are a great client service aid. If a client asks you about a particular holding of XYZ mutual fund, you can pull up a report on your desktop, highlight the holding in question, jot down a comment on a virtual sticky note, and transmit the information electronically to your client in a matter of minutes. It's fast, clear, and documented in your permanent file. Documents, such as those created in Microsoft Word, can be annotated in their native application.

Document Retrieval

Finding documents is very simple. Click on the Find Documents button, select the cabinet you want to search, select your search criteria, and click Find Now. If you choose to search by field, drop-down lists allow you to select the index set to search by, the field to search, and the criteria. A Search All Fields option is also available. Full text searches can be performed on all indices and OCRed images, but not on computer-generated text documents.

Security

DocuXplorer's security is more than adequate for most offices. Passwords and levels of access (read/write, read only, none) can be applied at the Library level, the Cabinet level, the Drawer level, and the Folder level. At the File level, permission can be granted or denied to delete, copy, move, create documents, and create subfolders. The program does not provide full audit-log capabilities, but it will record when a file was last opened and by whom. By adding the search criteria to an index set, you can easily find out what files have been opened recently or search to see what file a particular employee has used.

Archiving

One of DocuXplorer greatest strengths is the way it handles archiving. Users can set a maximum size for each file drawer to match the size of their backup medium. If your office wants to create WORM backups to CD-ROM for compliance purposes, right click on the file drawer, select Drawer Properties, then click on the drawer tab and enter a maximum drawer size of 640 MB. You have now limited the size of the drawer to the amount of information that can be stored on a CD-ROM disk. If you wish, the program will monitor the drawer's size for you.

Backing up to CD-ROM is great for compliance purposes, but it is not a good solution for disaster recovery situations. If you would like to create daily backups to move off site, it makes more sense to back up full cabinets to a tape, removable hard drive, or mini-disc. Cabinets can be limited in the same manner as drawers so that they fit on your backup medium.

Priced at $1,295 per concurrent user (with volume discounts available), DocuXplorer Professional is a solid deal for those who want a very capable, scalable, easy-to-use product at a reasonable price.

Upgrade maintenance contracts are included for the first year. After year one, upgrade maintenance contracts cost 20 percent of the listed price. Further information is available at www.DocuXplorer.com.

Advantages
➤ Easy to use for its class of software
➤ Strong indexing features
➤ Good OCR
➤ Annotation capabilities
➤ Comprehensive: can handle images and all computer files

Disadvantages
➤ Limited audit features
➤ Can't do full text searches of Word documents

DocuXplorer Personal

IF YOU ARE A SOLE PROPRIETOR on a budget, looking for a PaperPort-like product with more robust search and retrieval features, DocuXplorer has quite a deal for you. DocuXplorer Personal, a scaled-down version of DocuXplorer Professional, is available for just $229.95. Maintenance is included for the first year and costs 20 percent of the listed price thereafter. At this price, you have to give up a bit of functionality, but the trade-off should be minimal for a one-person shop. The major limitations are (a) you are limited to one user, one file cabinet, and three index sets, and (b) there is no security and no processing queue. What remains is still a powerful program capable of unlimited drawers, unlimited folders, three index sets with up to twenty-five user-defined fields in each set, auto-collate, OCR, annotation tools, and the ability to e-mail, print, or fax from within the program. Overall, DocuXplorer Personal is quite a deal, and if your business grows, you can upgrade to the Professional version at a later date.

We still think DocuXplorer Professional is a good, reasonably priced solution for

DocuXplorer for Financial Services

DOCUXPLORER IS CURRENTLY DEVELOPING a special edition of its software for financial professionals. The Financial Services Edition will include ready-to-use index sets geared to the specific needs of the financial planning community. Index set templates should reduce setup time. Users will be able either to use a template as is, or to modify it slightly, as opposed to constructing one from scratch.

The company also plans to include an enhanced backup module that will include a run-time version of the software. This addition will allow users to retrieve documents from a backup medium using the DocuXplorer interface, even on computers that do not have a full version of DocuXplorer installed. While not essential, enhanced backup could be helpful when taking documents off site or when regulatory agencies pay you a visit.

The Financial Edition (Professional version) is scheduled for release in fall 2002. The company has told us that it will be priced at a $200 premium to the regular Professional Edition. Personal Edition users will be able to download a Financial Edition at no extra charge.

DOCUXPLORER SOFTWARE — *Document Management and Archiving Software*

DocuXplorer Version Comparison

DocuXplorer Features	DX PROFESSIONAL	D PERSONAL
Multi-user systems for workgroups	X	
Unlimited number of Cabinets can be created in a Library	X	
Security - password protection at every DocuXplorer level	X	
Batch Scanning	X	
OCR Processing Queue	X	
Image Batch Processing	X	
Searches for documents off-line on other media (i.e. CD-R)	X	
Document Check in/Check out	X	
Versioning - create an unlimited number of document versions	X	
Portability of Documents	X	
Send documents from Windows Explorer to DocuXplorer	X	
Intelligent document recognition	X	
Auto-Update and download of Maintenance Releases	X	X
Unlimited number of Drawers can be created in a Cabinet	X	X
Unlimited number of Folders can be created in a Drawer	X	X
Multiple user-defined Index Sets to profiles by document type	Unlimited	3
25 user-defined fields in an Index Set	X	X
Auto-complete Static Data Lookup List Fields	X	X
Auto-complete History Data Lookup Fields	X	X
DX In Box to monitor a designated folder on a hard drive	X	X
Heads-up Indexing	X	X
Auto-Collate	X	X
Built in Optical Character Recognition (OCR)	X	X

the small to medium-sized practice; however, single practitioners may find they can get the functionality they need at a fraction of the price with DocuXplorer Personal, PaperPort, or Executive Assistant (profiled in the next section). The two programs compared above offer a lot of bang for your buck.

Executive Assistant from CEO Image Systems

EXECUTIVE ASSISTANT IS a brand-new product from CEO Image Systems, a company with a long history of providing imaging technology to large organizations. Executive Assistant was still in the beta testing phase as we went to press, but it will

DocuXplorer Features	DocuXplorer v.5 DX PROFESSIONAL	DocuXplorer v.5 D PERSONAL
Thumbnail view of pages in a multi-page document	X	X
Manipulate multiple page document pages using drag and drop	X	X
Complete set of image document annotation tools	X	X
Documents can be printed with or without annotations	X	X
Add, print or delete pages in a multi-page document	X	X
Import any type of computer-generated file	X	X
View and edit computer-generated documents using their original source program	X	X
Full Text Search on index fields data and OCR text	X	X
Boolean index search	X	X
Group documents by field in a Folder List View	X	X
Create summary fields by group in Folder List View	X	X
Export the index data in a Folder List View to create formatted reports in Excel or HTML	X	X
E-mail document directly from DocuXplorer	X	X
Fax documents directly from DocuXplorer	X	X
Print document directly from DocuXplorer	X	X
Check database integrity	X	X
Basic and Advanced Interface modes	X	X
Recycle Bin	X	X
Single-user version		X
Single Cabinet can be created in a Library		X

be available by the time you read this. We expect that there will be a number of changes to the software before its final release, but we were sufficiently impressed to bring Executive Assistant to your attention.

Executive Assistant is divided into three modules: Scan Documents, File Documents, and View Documents. Launching the program brings up the Executive Assistant Toolbar.

The scanning applet, powered by an ISIS driver, provides a great deal of scanning flexibility. Images can be

The Executive Assistant Toolbar

scanned in TIF, JPEG, or PDF formats. Filters are available to perform tasks such as border removal, hole removal, and background removal. The program is capable of single-page scans, multi-page scans, and duplex scans, provided your hardware supports these capabilities. Before scanning, the user specifies which of the possibly unlimited number of file cabinets the documents will be filed in.

Profiling and Indexing

After the scans are completed, they reside in a queue, ready to be indexed and filed. Before you begin this process, you may want to create file folders within the cabinet and indices.

For example, you might create a cabinet named Client Records, with a folder for each client residing within it. You would then create indices for the folders. Indices would be customized based on how you intend to search for an image at a later date. For example, you might search for a client by name, Social Security number, or account number, so you would create an index for each of these. You can also create indices at the document level. One method you might want to use is document type, such as Tax Return. Values could be a description of the return, such as "Federal Income Tax Return" of a form number, such as 1040. You would want to index tax returns by year as well.

Once the indices are established, the user selects an image from the queue, types in a description, assigns values to the indices, and saves it.

Document Retrieval

Retrieving documents is easy. Click View Documents on the toolbar, type in your search criteria, hit the Process button, and the results are displayed.

OCR Capabilities

The beta version we previewed does not offer OCR capabilities. The company is currently developing Executive Assistant Premium, which will include OCR and full-text keyword searches for release at a later date.

Annotation

Executive Assistant does not include tools to annotate images. The company has not yet decided whether this feature will be included in the Premium edition. Documents, such as those created in Microsoft Word, can be annotated in their native application, however.

Security

Executive Assistant does not have security features built into the system, but this may not be much of a problem for its target audience. On a single computer, security is not a problem, and on a small network you may be able to achieve an adequate level of security by using the security features built into your operating system. (CEO Image Systems will provide help configuring your operating system's security.)

Archiving

Executive Assistant's archiving works in much the same way as DocuXplorer's does, although we did not find the process quite as intuitive. The user can set a backup size that conforms to the backup medium for CD-ROM WORM copies. The complete directory tree can be backed up for off-site storage.

Another Feature of Note

Executive Assistant offers alternative methods of organizing and indexing your files. One thing you can do is to create an HTML table of contents as your index scheme, with a hyperlink to each image. The index would then be posted to a password-protected section of your company's website, providing users with access to the images residing on your hard drive from any Web browser.

Pricing

Executive Assistant is priced at $299 per license (www.ceoimage.com). Technical support is free for the first sixty days.

Advantages
➤ Powerful scanning module
➤ Flexible and comprehensive filing system
➤ Strong indexing features
➤ Comprehensive: can handle images and all computer files

Disadvantages
➤ Limited audit features
➤ Can't do full text searches
➤ No annotation
➤ No OCR

A Word about Image Executive

MEDIUM- TO LARGER-SIZED FIRMS that like the look and feel of Executive Assistant but require a more robust product should check out Image Executive, CEO Image Systems' enterprise solution. Installations can run anywhere from a couple of thousand dollars to much more, depending on the number of users and the options desired.

So Which One Is Best?

DIRECT COMPARISONS BETWEEN these two products are difficult. At this point, we think DocuXplorer Personal is more intuitive, better documented, and easier to use, although that may change by the time CEO Image Systems releases the final version of Executive Assistant. One major annoyance with the EA product was its lack of a directory tree display within the program, so you cannot view the file structure as you create it. At the time of this writing, the company was working on a directory tree for inclusion in the final release, as well as wizards to help create a file structure. An EA tutorial will be posted on the Web. We did not review the latest improvements, but if they are properly implemented, they should go a long way toward fixing the product's greatest weakness.

With regard to features, it appears that EA offers more. There are no limits on indices, and there is a processing queue included for batch processing. We found image processing to be superior with EA, but there is a price to pay. In order to use its filtering and duplex capabilities, you need to purchase a more expensive scanner. EA worked great with our Fujitsu 4110 scanner using an ISIS driver, but the company does not recommend using the software with TWAIN drivers, the standard drivers shipped with consumer scanners. DocuXplorer, on the other hand, worked fine with our Epson 1640 SU, although admittedly without all the bells and whistles.

Even something seemingly straightforward, like pricing, can be difficult to compare. For a single user on a single machine, the comparison is straightforward: you need one license in either case, and you can shop based on whatever features are most important to you. For an office of two to five, however, comparisons become more difficult. EA might work very well in that type of setting, but in the case of

DocuXplorer, you would have to move up to the Professional version, so you would want to compare the price and features of EA or EA Premium against the price and features of DocuXplorer Professional. And keep in mind that you need one license for each concurrent user. With DocuXplorer Professional, you generally need a concurrent license whether you plan to scan or to view (although they plan to sell a view-only license soon at a reduced rate); with EA, you can view without a concurrent license.

The bottom line is that we can point you in the direction of some very good products that have impressed us, but selecting the product best suited to your needs will take some additional work on your part. Think about your needs. How many people in your office will be scanning and filing documents? Is ease of use a priority? What about OCR? Do you have years of records that need to be digitalized? If so, you will certainly want batch scanning. If you are just starting out, this feature may not be important.

Not sure what you need? Contact the companies, describe your organization's needs, and ask for their suggestions. Odds are they have existing similar customers. Obtain demo versions with documentation. Try out the software. Call technical support and ask questions. Finally, ask for a price quote based on the exact configuration you will need.

Will this process take some time? Sure it will, but it may be time well spent. We know of a number of planners (we won't mention any names, but you know who you are) who spent literally tens of thousands of dollars unnecessarily because they did not take the time to evaluate their needs, let alone compare prices and features. Armed with the information provided in this book, you will undoubtedly have a more satisfactory experience.

Chapter Five

Virtual Filing Systems

A S YOU CONVERT YOUR DOCUMENTS into digital files, you face the challenge of filing them in a format and structure that allows you to find them when you need them. We've spoken with some advisers who have "gone digital" but are not totally satisfied with the results. We've spoken with an even larger number of advisers who are hesitant to go digital because they haven't figured out the storage and retrieval puzzle yet.

Kathleen Day has been successful in her transition to a digital filing system. Day says, "Owners may think something's good for the office but not believe everyone on staff will adopt it. My people aren't given an option. I just say to them, 'Today this is how we're going to do this … I hope you like it.'" She adds, "We've never had any kind of problem with the staff's adoption of our paperless system; if you ask anyone here, they'll say they love it because they can always find stuff."

Norman Boone, owner of Boone Financial Advisors, Inc. in San Francisco, California, went through the exercise of scanning client documents several years ago, but at the time of this writing was still finding something lacking. Whereas the paper conversion may be complete, he's not sure the mental one is yet. "[A paperless office] requires behavioral changes that some of us are better at than others. My experience is that the 'heavies' will instruct their staff to use the new system, but the heavies are less likely to make the changes themselves." Boone admits, "I almost never have the filing system open [on my computer]," and says his staff hasn't completely bought into the process, either.

One of Boone's problems is that consultants who helped set up his scanning software created information categories that don't entirely make sense to him. "They're not always intuitive to me and the staff," he says, and that hampers his ability to retrieve data—at least with visual searches. The more "open-ended" kinds of search capabilities he says he doesn't use too often, which is perhaps a function of Boone's needing to take more time to learn the basic functions of his software. He would also benefit from remaking some of the information categories in his scanning software to more closely duplicate the categories he used when he maintained paper files.

Let's look at several options for virtual filing systems that could solve Boone's problems.

Windows Explorer: A Basic Model for a Scanned Document Filing System

BOONE'S SIMPLEST SOLUTION might be to base his scanned document filing system on the folder breakdown he's already created in Windows Explorer if that system of organization is working well for him and for everyone else in his firm. For example, if you have created a separate folder within Windows Explorer for each of your clients, then you might duplicate this folder system in your scanned document files, creating subfolders as necessary. Client Jones would have his own folder and perhaps a "Tax" subfolder, with further subfolders for tax returns and for supporting documents. An "Investment" subfolder might, in turn, contain subfolders for monthly statements, investment policy statements with updates, and transactions. Separate from this hierarchy of clients' folders you might create other folders for your business itself. A main folder identified with your business name could contain subfolder subjects such as "Compliance," "Articles," and "Business Documents." Your business document folder's subtopics might include business plans, corporate documents, insurance policies, financial statements, ADV filings, and income tax returns, to name a few.

Windows XP Tools for Documents Created, Not Scanned

IF YOU HAVE ADOPTED the new Microsoft XP operating system and much of your work product is created using Microsoft's Office XP or earlier versions of the Microsoft Office application suite, search efficiency can be increased by using the new Search Pane feature in Windows XP. First, you assign Document Properties to

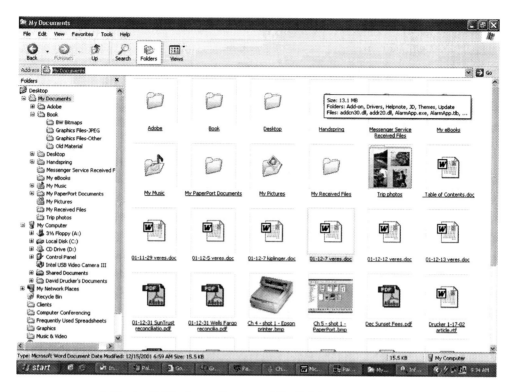

A Typical Windows Explorer File-Folder Arrangement

the documents you create with Office, such as title, author name, categories, and keywords, allowing you to find them more easily in the future. You can even make up your own, custom property names. Unfortunately, most people don't make use of these features, either because they don't know about them, or they simply forget or don't bother to use them. One solution is to set each program's preferences to automatically prompt you to assign properties for every Word, Excel, and PowerPoint document created when a file is saved for the first time.

Even with this prompt, though, setting up automatic property prompts can be a bit confusing, because the procedure is not consistent across Office applications. In Microsoft Word, select Tools, Options, then Save, and then place a check mark in the Prompt for Document Properties box. In Excel, select Tool Options, then General and then check Prompt for Workbook Properties. In PowerPoint, it's Tools, Options, then Save and Prompt for File Properties. Access properties must be set manually by clicking on File, then Database Properties.

Finally, when you have assigned properties to all of your files, the retrieval process is quick and painless. From within Microsoft Word, PowerPoint, Excel, or Access, clicking File, Search In reveals the Windows XP Search Pane. The Search In box on the Search Pane allows you to search, for example, by file type or by the likely location of the desired file on your hard drive or local area network. Of course, you can also search by regular and custom Document Properties, and you can even search for other documents right from within the Office file you're working on.

For an alternate method of searching all files on your hard drive or other storage devices recognized by Windows as additional drives, try using the search companion in Windows XP Explorer. Clicking on the search button on the toolbar exposes the Search Companion. The Companion asks you in plain English what you are looking for and it helps you narrow the search. If you intend to use this search method regularly, you should enable the Indexing Service by clicking on Change Preferences when the Search Companion displays the initial "What do you want to search for?" question. With Indexing Service enabled, Windows will regularly index your files in the background, resulting in faster search results. The Indexing Service can index documents created by Microsoft Office 95 or later—both text and HTML. Other file types can be indexed if a filter is available for them.

Windows XP stores its information in "catalogs" for fast retrieval. The Indexing Service stores document properties, such as those entered in the Properties dialog boxes. The Service also indexes document contents such as the body of word processing documents, text in an HTML document, the body of an e-mail message, and the body of newsgroup articles.

An aftermarket alternative to the Windows XP indexing process that you might find helpful if you're running earlier versions of the Microsoft operating system is FranklinCovey's OnePlace (shown at right). OnePlace is designed to provide a single, unified interface that allows you to check e-mail, surf the Web more effectively, organize your to-do list, and review your calendar.

What really makes OnePlace interesting, though, is its robust search capabilities. The first time you run OnePlace, it indexes much of the information on your hard drive and cross-references it. Notice that we said *much* of the information, not *all*. OnePlace can only index certain file types. The good news is that OnePlace does index the file types most likely to be used by most financial planning practitioners, including current versions of:

➤ Microsoft Outlook   ➤ DOS
➤ Microsoft Outlook Express   ➤ ANSI
➤ Microsoft Word   ➤ Microsoft Excel

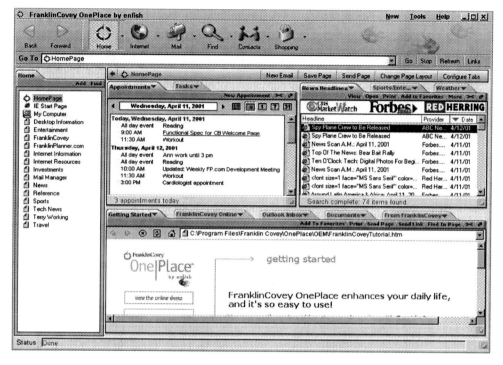

FranklinCovey OnePlace Opening Screen

- ➢ Microsoft Write
- ➢ Microsoft WordPad
- ➢ Rich Text Format (RTF)

- ➢ Microsoft PowerPoint
- ➢ Adobe Acrobat
- ➢ Bitmap, GIF, and JPEG files

Once the initial indexing is completed, the program can rapidly find what you need. Searches can be customized and saved, to save time and improve the accuracy of future searches (as shown on the following page).

If OnePlace lived up to its promise, we would recommend it with more enthusiasm, but we had mixed results installing it and getting it to work on a number of computers. In some cases we had trouble installing it, and in one case it crashed our computer repeatedly. This is a program worth having if you can get it to work properly on your system, but we suggest you test it thoroughly before committing to it. Fortunately, you can try it before you buy. A thirty-day free trial is available at www.franklincovey.com/ez/download/index.html.

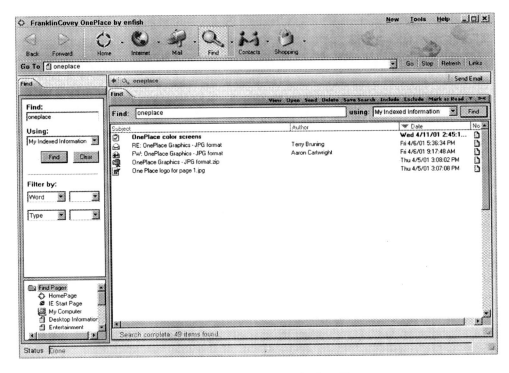

Searching for Information in OnePlace

Is Windows XP All You Need?

PERHAPS. IF YOU ARE STILL RUNNING WINDOWS 98 or Millennium operating systems, we recommend you upgrade to Windows XP, or similar operating systems that may have supplanted it by the time you read this, not just for its superior search capabilities, but for the significant improvements Microsoft has achieved in security and stability with XP.

The search capabilities of both Microsoft Windows XP and Office XP are, alone, a significant improvement over earlier versions. If most of your work is done from within Office applications, and document properties are religiously recorded when Office documents are saved for the first time, document retrieval will proceed smoothly. Even if some of your work product derives from other programs, the tools you already have may suffice. Windows XP's Indexing Service can read information from many other programs. The best way to determine if it works for you is to run some trial searches on your hard drive to see what gets cataloged and reported.

Windows XP Tips for Small Firms

WITH WINDOWS XP HOME selling for roughly half the price of Windows XP Professional, cost-conscious smaller firms may be tempted to opt for the cheaper Home version. Our advice is...don't. For many of you, Windows XP Professional is the only appropriate choice. According to Andy Rathbone, author of *Windows XP for Dummies* (John Wiley & Sons, 2001), "anyone in a business office environment should probably go for Windows XP Professional." At the very least, Rathbone suggests that your network file server run on XP Pro rather than XP Home: "If anything goes wrong with the network, the IT guy will prefer Pro, because he will have all the network tweaking options available to him."

Below we outline a few more reasons that XP Professional might be the appropriate choice for even the smallest financial planning office.

Security

XP Pro has security features not available in the Home version, including:

➤ **System policies.** According to a Microsoft technical support spokesperson, "Windows XP Professional can be joined to a Windows NT/2000 domain. This allows the system to be locked down centrally via a set of server-based security policies. For environments that are not utilizing a server, these policies can also be set locally on a Windows XP Professional machine, whereas they cannot be on a PC running Windows XP Home edition. Additionally, by joining a domain, a user can present a single set of credentials to other services in the office running on NT/2000 servers (such as secure websites or e-mail)."

➤ **Data encryption.** Windows XP Home does not allow for customers to locally encrypt the data on their hard drives. Windows XP Professional contains a strong encryption feature that allows data stored on the local machine to be secured in the case of theft. This is an additional level of security above and beyond the access control lists that regulate who can read or write to a specific file or folder.

➤ **User level access.** With Windows XP Professional, the user can set up unique user accounts and control the amount of access to a resource based on that user. This is useful when you have employees who need access to a shared printer or other network resources, but who don't need to be able to view sensitive information on your server.

➤ **Smart card security support.** This will allow you to secure access to your computer and your network with a physical smart card device. Without the card and the proper PIN, the user will not be able to log on to the system, which adds an extra layer of security.

Better Laptop Support for Mobile Users

These Pro features should appeal to laptop users:

➤ **Remote desktop.** One of the major features of Windows XP Professional not available in the Home edition is "Remote Desktop." Remote Desktop allows users of any version of Windows, starting with Windows 95, to remotely access all of their applications and data on an XP Professional host over a network connection. The Home edition contains the "client" version of Remote Desktop, which means it can connect to and control a "host" computer from a remote location; however, in order for the host to be controlled, Pro must be installed on the host, and only Pro contains the host software.

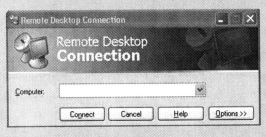

Remote Desktop

➤ **Roaming profiles/network location awareness.** If you use your notebook to log on to more than one network, you have probably been frustrated by the requirement that you change your network settings each time you move from one network to another. With Network Location Awareness, users can maintain multiple network profiles. Windows XP Professional is smart enough to know when the user has changed networks, and it will use the proper profile.

➤ **Offline files with encrypting file system.** More small businesses are investing in laptops for a mobile workforce. With offline folders, employees can copy documents from network servers onto their laptops so they can work on them away from the office. When they return they can synchronize their changes with the original files. They can work, read, and change documents without being physically connected to the network. However, laptops are more vulnerable to theft and require data protection. Encrypting File System encrypts files so that only authorized users can read or change them.

➤ **Power management/battery life.** Although Microsoft contends there is no difference between the two versions, others disagree. Rathbone states that he has communicated with numerous users who claim better results with the Pro version. He suggests readers consult the following Microsoft site, which appears to support his position: www.microsoft.com/windowsxp/pro/evaluation/experiences/mobility.asp.

Network Capability

The Professional edition has these other network-related advantages:

➤ **IIS (Internet Information Services).** Windows XP Professional includes IIS. A small business can host a website on its intranet or on the Internet. With a website, the small business can communicate information to sell products or services to customers, or with an internal website, make it easier to find and distribute business information to employees.

➤ **Scalability.** For the small business, there is a difference in using Windows XP Home versus Professional when the size of the network is increased. With Home Edition, the number of simultaneous computers that can connect to a single shared resource, such as File and Printer Sharing or ICS (Internet Connection Sharing), is five. For Windows XP Professional Edition, the number of users increases to ten.

➤ **Wireless network capabilities.** Although a Microsoft technical support spokesperson told us that both versions of XP should perform the same on a network, others disagree. Rathbone contends that Professional is the superior choice for wireless networks, which are often used by laptop users and sole proprietors who work at least part of the time in a home-office setting.

One Additional Reason You Might Want Pro

➤ **Disk backup and restoration.** Professional includes ASR (Automated System Recovery), a backup technology that restores your entire operating system and data. If your computer hard drive fails for some reason, you could conceivably replace the drive with an exact model and restore your computer to a working state without having to reload your applications and operating system from scratch. The retail version of XP Home includes a basic backup utility, but it is not part of the default installation. The file, Ntbackup.msi, can be found on the Windows XP Home edition CD-ROM in the following location: *CD-ROM Drive:*\VALUEADD\MSFT\NTBACKUP. Please note: if you received an OEM version of XP Home with your computer, the file may not be included on the disk.

Even if there are gaps, all may not be lost. Some programs that store files in their own native format may be able to output or export a version of their data in a format that the indexing program can read.

For example, NaviPlan Extended, a well-regarded financial planning program from EISI, can effortlessly create client reports in Microsoft Word format. Should you choose to save a copy of those reports on your hard drive, they will certainly be indexed. Other programs, such as WealthMaster, Integrate2000, StockOpter, and R$P, will work within, or can export to, Microsoft Excel, thereby allowing you to index them. If all else fails, a programmer may be able to customize the Indexing Service so that it can catalog the file types you use.

You may find that Windows XP and Office XP provide all that you need, or you may find them lacking, but either way we suggest that you experiment with them, if you haven't already, to provide a baseline for comparing other products and methodologies.

Before we leave the subject of eliminating paper in your practice, we will spend one more chapter on the subject, introducing you to several essential utilities to make your paperless experience as productive as possible.

Chapter Six

Software Utilities That Do Specialized Jobs

I N ADDITION TO THE MAIN TOOLS of the paperless office discussed thus far, there are various utilities—little known and underappreciated in most cases— that can help you eliminate paper and improve information handling. From print drivers to PDFs, OCR, PDAs, and even voice-recognition technology, the opportunities to better manage paper and lower costs are practically endless.

Virtual Scanning with the Printer Driver

A DRIVER IS SIMPLY a small program that controls a device, such as a disk drive or printer. You usually need to install a new driver every time you connect a new device to your computer. A driver acts as a translator between the device and programs that use it. The same driver that sends documents from your computer screen to your printer can be used in a paperless mode to send those documents to a *virtual* printer. The printer in that case is actually a piece of software—such as PaperPort Deluxe—and the printing medium is your desktop rather than paper. We might even call the process "virtual scanning."

Here's an example. Let's say we're surfing the Internet and see a page we want to print out. With an ordinary printer, we might elect to print it by clicking File, then Print from within our browser and selecting our favorite Hewlett-Packard printer as the device to which we want to direct the print job. A virtual printer, however, works like this: We still click on File and Print within our browser, but we select "PaperPort" as the printer. In doing so, the printed page appears as an image on the desktop of our

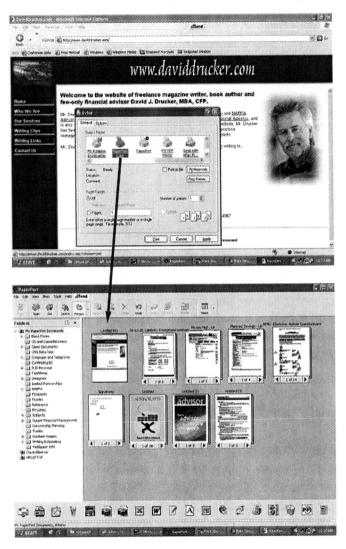

PaperPort scanning software rather than coming out of a printer as a physical item (at left).

Anything that can be produced on your computer monitor can be printed to the desktop of your scanning software—your archive for all things graphical. Is Charles Schwab & Co. one of your custodians for housing client assets over which you have trading authority? Do you use Schwab's Web-based trading system? Then, to make a copy of your trade order and file it away for SEC purposes, as well as for general reference needs, just obtain a listing of the trades you've placed at Schwab's website, click the Print icon, select PaperPort as your printer, and you've got a copy of your trade order on your scanner software desktop. Next, make a subdirectory within that software called "Trades." Finally, create a title for

Using the PaperPort Printer Driver to Archive
a Graphic Image on the PaperPort Desktop

your image (e.g., the date of the trade) and drag it to the Trades folder you've just created. That's all there is to it.

The process we've just described of getting images into your scanning software can be used to replace old, manual, paper-based processes, too. In the 1980s, Dave would pick up the latest copy of *Financial Planning* magazine, read an article that he'd want to refer back to later, cut or photocopy the article from the magazine, and file it in a "Subjects" folder in a file cabinet. Over the years, the number of folders in the Subjects drawer grew steadily. Eventually one file drawer became two. Dave seldom referred to the folders as often as their volume would suggest, and finding things grew increasingly difficult. Periodically, it would be necessary to weed out old articles and information that was simply taking up valuable space.

Dave is now more likely to read articles and other things of interest online, for example, at websites like Morningstar, Inc.'s adviser site (www.Morningstar Advisor.com) or Financial Planning Interactive (www.financial-planning.com). A Web page of any length sitting on his computer monitor can be printed to his PaperPort desktop. The driver will create as many pages as are necessary to capture the entire article and will batch them in the proper order as a single document. By virtually scanning the article, what would be the intermediate step, printing it out on paper and feeding the paper into a scanner, is avoided entirely.

Compressing and Exchanging Planning Documents as Graphic Files

TO EFFICIENTLY RETRIEVE these virtual documents and send them to someone else, there are some technical things you need to understand about graphic, or image, files. If you've worked with image files before, you know there are a small number of widely accepted image formats such as BMP (bitmap), JPEG, TIF, and GIF.

A bitmap, also called a raster image, is made up of individual dots called pixels (picture elements). The pixels are arranged and colored variously to form a pattern. The density of the dots, or resolution, determines the sharpness of the image. Resolution is expressed in dots per inch ("dpi") or simply by the number of rows and columns of pixels in the image, such as 640 by 480. The TIF, or "Tag Image File Format," is another example of a raster file format. Image formats other than the bitmap or TIF will generally be vector images. In vector graphics, objects are created as collections of lines and polygons rather than as a grid of pixels.

Of the two formats, raster images are better for photographs or other uses that require high resolution because they tend to offer greater subtleties for shading and texture, but they also require more memory and take longer to print. Vector images are better for drawings that need sharper lines, more detail, and easy modification. Vector images occupy a smaller file size and require far less memory and printing resources. GIFs (Graphics Interchange Format) and JPEGs (Joint Photographic

Experts) are both examples of vector graphics. These formats can compress images into a smaller file than a bitmap, the JPEG being the most compact of the three.

Scanning software will often compress files even further than GIFs and JPEGs can, a valuable feature as we capture many years' worth of data. To quantify the trade-offs between resolution and storage space, we took a client's one-page tax return extension form that had been scanned into PaperPort and measured its file size. PaperPort creates a proprietary file with a ".MAX" extension, and this tax return page measured 36 kilobytes (KB) in .MAX form. PaperPort will allow you to save a scanned image to a different format, if desired, so we saved our tax return as both a vector (JPEG) and a raster (bitmap) image. They measured, respectively, 355KB and 465KB, illustrating the greater compression possible with the JPEG format. The .MAX file, however, represents a 90 percent storage savings over the JPEG—and the legibility of the document, both on the screen and in printed form, is of a quality high enough to satisfy any financial adviser or SEC examiner.

When it comes to sharing our scanned information with others, a .MAXfile would tend to more readily fit on a removable disk and would move more quickly over networks and the Internet due to the extreme compression algorithm used by the .MAX technology. Even if our recipient doesn't own a copy of the PaperPort Deluxe software, he can be allowed to read this proprietary file. We're going to have him use a "miniviewer." Many software vendors now find it useful to create "self-executable" file formats that simplify dissemination of their programs' output. PaperPort does this by allowing the originator to save a scanned document as an .EXE file that contains a miniviewer. The recipient can access the file via Windows Explorer once he's downloaded it, click on the file name, and a tiny (free) version of the PaperPort desktop opens on his screen to reveal the contents of the file you e-mailed him. This can allow you, the tech-savvy planner, to share certain information with clients, regardless of their level of computer skill, as long as they know how to receive an e-mail and open an attachment.

An alternative method that is rapidly becoming the standard for document transmission is the Portable Document Format, or PDF. This results in a file size roughly equivalent to a .MAX file. You can read PDF files with the free reader available on the website of Adobe Systems Inc., and most PC users have a free copy of Adobe Acrobat Reader on their systems these days because some other software application they've already loaded has put it there. To write to (create or modify) a PDF file, you must buy the full Adobe Acrobat package that sold for $249.99 as of this writing.

The Portable Document Format allows you to replicate any report, spreadsheet, or other output in a fixed form that your recipient can read but not modify.

A file in PaperPort or any other scanning system can be exported in the form of a PDF using a printer driver that installs on your computer system with the Adobe Acrobat software.

In Chapter 4 we distinguished between graphic, or image, files and text files, and how best to archive each type. A PDF file is a hybrid in the sense that it is inherently a form of graphic file, but can be converted to text with the full version of Adobe Acrobat software. In other words, if you need a text version, you don't need to apply an OCR process to go from PDF to text, but simply select File, Save As from within Adobe Acrobat and then select the .RTF ("Rich Text Format") file option which will produce a file that can be read by any word processing software and which will retain the original formatting of the text as it appeared in the PDF file format.

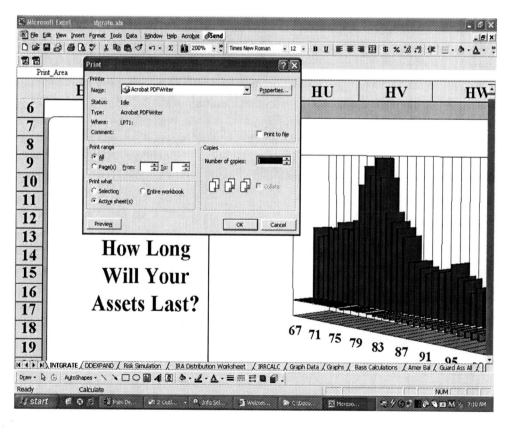

Creating a PDF Document from a Scanned Image

Six More Tricks for Simplifying Your Workday

YOU'VE PROBABLY BEEN USING certain paperless utilities for years, for example, when you download the previous day's investment transactions in your client's Schwab accounts from Schwab's website to your portfolio software (e.g., Advent, Centerpiece). Fifteen years ago you would have had to obtain the Schwab statements in paper form and manually type the information from those pages into your portfolio software. Don't remember doing that? You just haven't been around long enough. That was the *only* system available to the financial adviser in the early 1980s.

Now, here's a lesser-known paperless process. You may own a personal digital assistant, or PDA, but are you squeezing all the utility out of it that you possibly can? If you travel often enough, then you probably get most of your business reading done on airplanes, as Dave does. You likely scoop up a four-inch thick pile of magazines and newsletters and throw them in your briefcase before heading out the door to the airport. Did you know that you could download most of this information quite easily to your PDA? Most of the journals that planners typically read post some or all of their content on their websites monthly, including *Bloomberg Wealth Manager* (www.bloomberg.com/wealth/index.html), *Inside Information* (www.bob veres.com), *Investment Advisor* (www.investmentadvisor.com), *Financial Advisor* (www.financialadvisormagazine.com), *Journal of Financial Planning* (www.journal fp.net/), and even the fee-based *Wall Street Journal* (interactive.wsj.com).

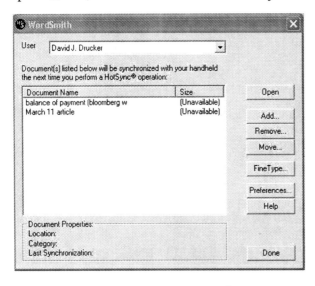

WordSmith's PDA Download Screen

A Palm PDA device like a Palm Pilot or Handspring Visor with 8 MB of memory will hold an almost limitless number of magazine articles, and even a book. It's a simple matter of saving the text of an article from a publication's website and HotSyncing that text to your PDA to be read by your PDA's installed word processor. Dave uses an after-market word processor on his Samsung I300 combination Sprint PCS phone and

Palm PDA called WordSmith by Blue Nomad software (www.bluenomad.com) to install and read his articles. With this technique, you'll be able to take all of your articles with you while relieving your shoulder of ten pounds of unnecessary paper. Repeatedly carrying excessive loads while en route can turn a swashbuckling, twenty-something adviser into an old man or woman really quickly, so consider this a health tip as well as an efficiency tip.

Here are some other tips for working more efficiently:

➤ You will vote proxies online at www.proxyvote.com instead of by U.S. mail, and then you'll print the proxy supporting information and a copy of your ballot to your scanning software.

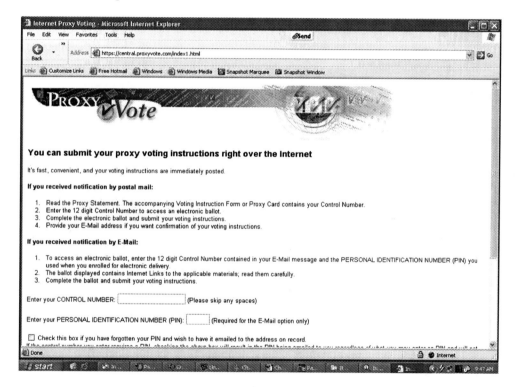

ProxyVote Home Page

➤ If you use audiotape courses from the College for Financial Planning to satisfy a portion of your continuing education requirements, you will take the tests online at www.cpeInternet.com/ and then print a copy of your test results to the "Continuing Education" folder you've created in your scanning software; when asked to report CE credits to the CFP Board every other year, all of the information you need will be right where you left it in one folder.

➢ You will read the *Wall Street Journal* online at http://online.wsj.com and save both paper and several times the subscription dollars you would pay to read the paper version.

➢ You will throw away your fax machine. Get an online fax service like Efax Plus from www.efax.com that will allow you to receive incoming faxes as e-mail attachments (which can then be virtually printed to your scanning software) and also to initiate faxes of any document you can replicate on your computer screen.

➢ You will trade in your postage meter and sign up with www.stamps.com so that you can start printing all of your postage directly from your computer; you'll never need to make another trip to the post office, pay meter rental fees, or worry about the correct rate for a particular postal item since rates are updated online in real time.

Stamps.com Home Page

When Voice Recognition Software Can Help You, and When It Can't

YOU PROBABLY CREATE A LOT OF DOCUMENTS and spend a considerable amount of time composing e-mails, client letters, reports, and articles. If you happen to be a master typist, you probably take this work in stride. If, on the other hand, you primarily type with your two index fingers, as Joel does, producing these documents can be trying and time-consuming.

Wouldn't it be great if you could bypass the keyboard altogether and dictate your thoughts directly into a word processor? We're sure it comes as no surprise to most of you that the technology to do just that has existed for quite some time now. Why, then, aren't more people making use of this timesaving technology?

One reason may be that when many early adopters first tried voice recognition software, they were working on 386 or 486 processors. Software vendors claimed that 486 machines were capable of running voice recognition software, and they were; but it was a slow, frustrating experience. Training the software took unacceptably long, and recognition was not up to expectations. Even those lucky enough to own a Pentium-based computer often ran into other hardware difficulties due to poor-quality sound cards and microphones.

A second problem was that Dragon Naturally Speaking, the most popular voice-recognition program on the market for many years, went through a series of upheavals due to financial difficulties at the parent company (the rights to the program have since been purchased by ScanSoft, Inc.). Concerns about corporate instability also may have kept people away from voice-recognition software.

A third problem is the investment of time required to get started. Even high-quality voice-recognition software needs time to learn the way you speak. The more you use it, the more accurate it becomes. Those who install the software and expect instant results are setting themselves up for disappointment. It takes a bit of patience to get the software working properly but, as the software is trained, the results progressively improve.

We hadn't thought about voice-recognition software as a potential efficiency booster until several events raised the issue. The first was a decision by Microsoft to include voice capabilities in Office XP applications. The second was totally coincidental. Joel happened to be giving a presentation at an industry conference in Orlando, Florida, and, during a break in his schedule, he ventured over to Epcot at Disney World where he participated in an IBM ViaVoice demonstration.

What he saw a convinced him that it was time to order a copy of the software and try it out at home.

Let's talk a little bit about XP first. There is a good chance that the voice-recognition capabilities of Office XP are not enabled on your computer, because default installation does not include them. If you are installing Microsoft Office XP for the first time, you can choose to do a custom installation and enable voice-recognition. If you already have Office XP installed on your computer, you can open an application such as Microsoft Word, click on Tools, then select Speech. You'll then be asked if you want to load the speech recognition files. A wizard will then walk you through the process of installing your microphone and the software.

Once the setup is complete, click on the microphone button to begin dictation. If your dictation is not being captured, try clicking on the Dictation button or say, "dictate." As you talk, a toolbar displays the current program status. For example, if you are not being understood, a "What was that?" message appears. Accuracy improves over time. If you perform only the minimum required training before trying to use the program, accuracy will be mediocre at best. Results will improve considerably if you spend an extra thirty minutes practicing before the first time you try to do any real work using your voice.

Overall, we found that we could dictate with about 85 to 90 percent accuracy after a short (less than fifteen minute) training session. The accuracy numbers apply to general vocabulary; dictation that includes technical terms will register lower accuracy rates until the software is trained to recognize the specific terms you use. Since Office XP is Microsoft's first crack at dictation software for the masses, it's not surprising that there are some problems. If you've never used dictation software, this speech recognition tool packaged with Office XP provides an inexpensive introduction. Give it a try when you have some spare time. If you feel comfortable dictating, but demand more accuracy and functionality, you're a prime candidate for a stand-alone package such as IBM ViaVoice Professional.

IBM ViaVoice for Windows is available in four versions: Personal at $29, Standard at $57, Advanced at $105, and Professional at $219. We think it is a solid choice if you are seriously considering the use of voice recognition software in your daily practice. We tested the top-of-the-line Professional version that includes a USB digital headset as part of the package. Our version included a detailed printed manual and a command reference card.

ViaVoice Pro contains a large set of features and functions that make dictation more effective. For example, ViaVoice Pro can scan and analyze existing documents on your hard drive to help you build a personal vocabulary list. The program includes specialized "Topics" (vocabulary lists) that you can activate with the click of a mouse. One of the available topics is "Business/Finance," and another is "Technology." Full, specialized vocabularies such as legal or medical dictionaries are available from IBM at an additional cost.

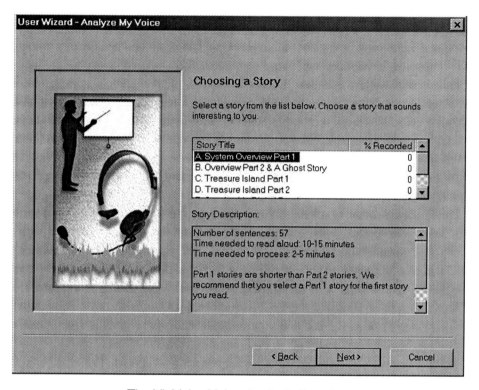

The ViaVoice Voice-Analysis Function

IBM's studies have determined that many recognition errors are actually caused by poor microphone acoustics. As a result, they developed the Recognition Wizard. This tool notifies you when audio quality is poor or when excessive background noise is present. The Recognition Wizard then guides you through the necessary steps to resolve the problem.

ViaVoice Pro provides a number of alternatives when you edit your documents. For those who prefer to edit manually with the keyboard, ViaVoice offers to add new words to your personal vocabulary when the document is saved. It is also possible to make edits and corrections using voice commands. Another option is to type corrections in the ViaVoice correction window.

The program offers three methods of dictating. The first method is dictation into SpeakPad, a word processor that has been optimized for dictation and is included with ViaVoice. With SpeakPad, you can dictate, say commands, make corrections, and edit with your voice. You can then print, save, or transfer the text into any other application. Dictated text can also be sent as an e-mail attachment. We found SpeakPad the most effective method for beginners since it is optimized for dictation. Once dictation is complete, documents can be cut and pasted into your normal word processor for advanced editing if required.

The second method is called "Direct Dictation." This feature allows you to dictate directly into any application that accepts text, such as text fields, dialog boxes, and table cells. The third method is "Dictate to Word." This allows you to dictate, correct, and edit with your voice in Microsoft Word. Direct Dictation and Dictate to Word work well for intermediate and advanced users, but we suggest that beginners stick with SpeakPad until both they and the software are properly trained.

There are a number of other ViaVoice features that improve usability. For example, dictation macros allow you to create voice shortcuts for text that you type or insert into documents frequently. You can also build dictation templates in SpeakPad that allow you to create forms with fields that can be filled in by voice. Navigation macros allow you to establish voice command shortcuts and automate tasks. A Navigation Macro Wizard is included to help you with the macro creation process. Voice Mouse enables mouse commands with your voice such as repositioning the mouse, clicking, or dragging and dropping.

A full-featured voice-recognition package such as ViaVoice Pro can be a real time-saver if used properly. It can speed the preparation of letters, memos, reports, and e-mails, decreasing the time you spend on office administration. And it may actually improve the quality of your records by enabling you to document more in less time. Just don't expect miracles overnight. After using the correction features of ViaVoice and allowing the software to analyze documents for several more hours, the accuracy improved from the initial 85–90 percent to more than 95 percent.

However, ViaVoice was not without its problems. For one thing, the program did not recognize many words and terms that we threw at it. Words can be added to the recognition dictionary by using the Add/Delete Words box, but this can become tedious if, for example, you're trying to write a financial or technology article with a lot of specialized terminology. We also found that the program froze from time to time when we performed certain tasks such as switching between modes or trying to use the voice command mode.

Your success with such a program will be heavily dependent upon your patience and preparation during the first two weeks of use. If you take the time to read the manual, train the software, correct errors, and scan your existing documents we suspect your experiences will be highly satisfactory. If not, you may be disappointed.

Is learning and training the software worth the effort? The answer depends on you and the way you work. If you are an excellent typist, or if you spend only a limited amount of time at the word processor, you may get some productivity gain by freeing your hands from the keyboard, but probably not enough to justify the effort. Even if you're an excellent typist, the software could help you avoid carpal tunnel syndrome. On the other hand, if you don't type well and you spend a fair amount of time at the word processor, ViaVoice will save you time and money. Just think about it: If your hourly rate is $150, one extra hour a week working with a client, as opposed to typing at the keyboard, could gross you an extra $7,800 per year!

Virtual Bookkeeping Tools

WE SUSPECT THAT almost every financial professional reading this book has some familiarity with Intuit. Over 23 million consumers use Quicken-brand products. QuickBooks, the popular accounting package for small to medium-sized businesses, has nearly 2.5 million users. TurboTax, Intuit's line of tax preparation software for consumers, is a perennial market leader. What does Intuit have to do with running a high margin, virtual financial practice? Quite a bit, we think. Intuit offers a tool to improve your business: QuickBooks and a website with user utilities.

A Tool to Improve Your Business: QuickBooks

It may seem that QuickBooks, a competent accounting program for the small business, has been around forever. What you probably don't know is that hidden inside the latest version are a variety of powerful tools for your virtual office. QuickBooks 2002 comes in two "flavors:" QuickBooks for the Web and QuickBooks for the Desktop, which is offered in a Basic, Pro, Premier, and Accountant's Edition. When the right version is paired with the right planner, the results can be impressive.

QuickBooks for the Web. A number of sole practitioners we know spend a lot of time on the road. If your accounting needs are basic, QuickBooks for the Web might be a great addition to your virtual tool kit. Wherever you are, if you can get onto the Internet, you can access your data twenty-four hours a day. Stranded in a hotel?

Stuck at the airport? Make use of that time by preparing invoices, receiving payments online, balancing your books, and analyzing your financial position. All transactions take place over a secure connection that uses 128-bit encryption and SSL technology.

Do any of your clients have small service businesses? Perhaps what they need is QuickBooks for the Web. Then not only can the client manage the books from anywhere, he can also grant you Internet access to the information as well.

QuickBooks for the desktop versions: Basic, Pro, Premier. The three mainstream desktop versions of QuickBooks—Basic, Pro, and Premier—all include the ability to print checks and track expenses, create customized invoices, generate reports, and perform other functions necessary to maintain a small company's books. But what makes QuickBooks for the desktop intriguing are the additional Intuit services that can be integrated into the system, sometimes at an additional fee.

➤ **Credit cards.** The QuickBooks credit card eliminates the need to manually enter purchase data. Authorized employees are issued no-fee credit cards for business expenses, and purchase data can then be downloaded directly into QuickBooks. Business owners can choose to receive a single consolidated statement, or each employee can receive his or her own statement.

➤ **Online billing service.** Online billing can save time, cut costs, and improve cash flow. This service allows users to e-mail payment-enabled invoices and statements from within QuickBooks. Clients will be directed to a private Web page where they can make payments, review their payment history, and print reports. Online bill payments can be made by direct fund transfers or by credit card. As payments are received, QuickBooks will download and enter the transaction, again saving time and minimizing potential data-entry errors.

➤ **Merchant account service.** This QuickBooks service allows business owners to accept credit card payments. It is specifically designed to work with the payment-enabled invoices described above, so no additional hardware or software is required (although many services require the purchase of a terminal and/or a dedicated telephone line).

➤ **QuickBooks credit check services.** Since the best way to deal with a "problem" client is to avoid the engagement in the first place, having timely, accurate information about new business prospects at your disposal is essential. The Credit Check Service offers access to online Dun & Bradstreet business reports from within QuickBooks.

➤ **Fax service.** QuickBooks Pro and Premier provide the option of using QuickBooks Fax Service, which is offered through eFax. Invoices and job estimates, each with a customizable cover page, are sent directly from QuickBooks in a fraction of the time it would take to do so manually.

➤ **Payroll service.** QuickBooks offers various levels of payroll services. Deluxe Payroll Service integrates with QuickBooks. It provides earnings and deduction calculations, tax tables, W-2s, electronic payroll tax filings, automatic payroll tax deposits, and the direct deposit of employee paychecks.

Many, if not all, of the Intuit services discussed above are available from other providers, often at a lower cost. Intuit, however, offers the convenience of "one-stop shopping" and integration with the QuickBooks system.

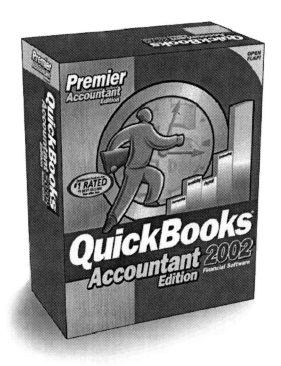

Tools to work more effectively with clients: Accountant Edition. We know quite a few accountants and financial planners working with small businesses who seem to spend more time in their clients' offices than in their own. Perhaps QuickBooks Premier Accountant Edition will help them get their lives back (at left).

The Accountant Edition has a number of enhancements, including better reconciliation reporting, improved accounting controls, sales tax coding, and easier data archiving; but the really important "virtual" improvement is the Remote Access Service. Remote access, powered by WebEx, is integrated into the Accountant Edition, activated through the software, and allows financial professionals to access their clients' computers over the Internet. QuickBooks makes Remote Access easy to sign up for. Simply click on Remote Access in the Company Navigator,

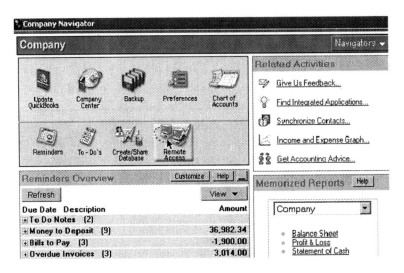

QuickBooks Company Navigator

follow the directions on the screen that appears (see below),

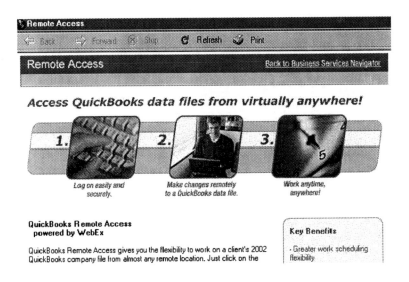

QuickBooks Remote Access Windows

QuickBooks Log In Window

and log in (as shown above).

The service can shorten response time, improve productivity, cut costs, and increase client satisfaction. One year's free service for an unlimited number of client accounts is included with the purchase of QuickBooks Premier Accountant Edition; following the twelve months, a subscription fee, undisclosed by Intuit at the time of this writing, will apply.

A Website with User Utilities

We think many financial professionals could learn a lesson or two about Web design by visiting the QuickBooks site. QuickBooks Retirement Solutions (www.qbrs.com) offers full-service 401(k) plans, online 401(k) plans, and other retirement plans through The Principal Financial Group. The site is easy to navigate, provides just enough information to be useful without overwhelming the lay person, and allows readers to compare plan features. Prospects can request further information and a price quote online.

Just eliminating paper can add a new degree of efficiency to your office. Doing so in conjunction with the utilities explored in this chapter will turbocharge it.

Part Three

3

The Tools
in Practice

C h a p t e 7 S e v e n

Communicating with Clients

W E RECOGNIZE THAT HANDLING CLIENTS is different from handling a piece of paper. Clients need to see your face periodically and determine that you and their money haven't fled to some far-off tax haven. But they can be "trained" to accept less face-to-face communication.

What Type of Adviser Are You?

WE ALSO RECOGNIZE that there are two types of financial advisers: introverts and extroverts. Severe introverts probably aren't dealing with clients in the first place. They're probably working behind the scenes with correspondence and spreadsheets and are in the employ of an extrovert. However, there are many borderline introverts in this business (Dave knows—he is one) who can spend limited amounts of time effectively with clients and then need to withdraw to their offices (or even to get away from the office) to do some planning in solitude. This type of adviser should take quite readily to the lessons in this chapter.

If you are an extrovert, sitting in front of clients as much as possible charges your batteries. The time you spend with them is essential to relationship-building, client longevity, and all the other things we value in growing our firms. But not *all* the face time is well spent. Some of it can be supplanted with forms of communication that are just as satisfying to the client but a lot less costly to you than scheduling time together in your conference room.

Clients don't necessarily value face-to-face meetings more highly than phone calls, or even e-mails. What they want is frequency of communication, however they can get it. As some wise person once said, clients can tolerate almost anything except neglect. It's the thought that counts—and the frequency of thought. Mix some face-to-face with some e-mails and an occasional phone call. You don't have to knock yourself out meeting with every client every quarter. That can become burdensome, even to an extrovert. (In fact, we are amazed at how many advisers tell their clients to invest for the long-term, but send a very different message by dissecting returns in excessive quarterly meetings.)

Being a Virtual Team Leader

AN IMPORTANT ASPECT of communicating with clients is dealing with each client's team: the lawyers, accountants, insurance salespersons, and other professionals. You, the adviser, may well be in the position of selecting the team members and quarterbacking the team. But, just as not every client interaction must take place face to face, not every team interaction has to be a committee meeting at the attorney's office, either. A lot of the collaboration we do with clients and their other advisers for wills, trusts, accounting systems, business plans, buy-sell agreements, and so on have, at their heart, a document. And we've already seen how to transform our process of document management.

Why not apply the same concepts to collaborative efforts with the client's team members? What have you got to lose? You may no longer get to take a red-eye flight to an out-of-state client's hometown. You might have to cut down on playing phone tag. Or your secretary may get fewer opportunities to track down mail or packages lost by the U.S. Postal Service. You might even have fewer forgotten or missed appointments. But we're betting you're willing to forego some of these experiences.

There are a variety of ways to replace the process of sitting around a table and passing pieces of paper back and forth to each other. In this chapter we will discuss substitutes, beginning with the workhorse of the arsenal—e-mail—and then going on to more exotic forms of communication and collaboration such as intranets, extranets, virtual private networks, and application service providers.

Clients and E-Mail

RIGHT ABOUT NOW you're probably thinking about Widow Thompson who will never embrace her VCR, much less a computer and the Internet. A segment of our client base isn't going to change *anything*, and that's just a bump in the road we'll have to live with.

In his practice, Dave has lobbied long and hard for less-frequent face-to-face meetings and more-frequent e-mail and other communication. He's weaned his clients away from time-consuming meetings and long phone conversations. But you can't get something for nothing. You must be able to show your clients what *they're* going to get out of the deal. And here's what you will give them:

First, you will give them greater *frequency* of communication. Dave learned the importance of this when he moved his practice 2,000 miles. He stayed in even closer touch with his clients to reinforce their certainty that he would be available to them anytime, anywhere.

The second incentive you will give your clients relates to that commodity we all value—money. You will explain that to remain competitive and (paradoxically) to continue giving them a high level of service, you've realized you must embrace many new technologies. But, you say, you expect to realize stable or falling costs as a result of some of the changes you want to make. And—here's the kicker—you're going to share some of these savings with them. As Dave began to institute many of the technologies we're going to discuss, he found his operating costs dropping—dramatically in some cases. What he promised his clients was that their fees would remain unchanged for some period of time. That is how he would share his cost savings in return for their "buying into" more digital (but also more frequent) communication. For the most part, this strategy of managing the clients' expectations was successful.

When Joel moved from New York to Florida, he took a similar approach: he told his clients that he would now be *more* accessible. He made good on his promise by providing clients with his cell phone number and by guaranteeing and following through on rapid responses to e-mails. Joel regularly checks his e-mail in the evening and over the weekend, too. What he has found is that younger clients with their busy work schedules almost always prefer communicating by e-mail from home as long as they receive a prompt response, and elderly clients often prefer this form of communication as well. During the day it is often difficult for working clients to focus on personal finance issues. It is in the evening, when they open the mail or review their accounts online, that a question is most likely to pop up. Overall, the system works very well. The client gets a rapid response, and Joel saves time by avoiding corporate voice mail systems and eliminating "phone tag."

The more you can get your clients to use e-mail and visit your website, the more efficient you can be. There is, in our experience, no fine line in terms of age between those who will adopt technology and those who will not. Younger clients will almost universally feel comfortable with it because they've been raised with it.

Middle-aged clients may or may not feel comfortable with it and, if they don't, they're probably too busy to make the time to learn it. Older clients have time on their hands if they're retired and, if they don't find computers inherently frightening, they'll often master e-mail and similar technology out of sheer curiosity and an opportunity to escape boredom.

For clients who are borderline—perhaps they don't like computers but are still willing to give it a go—you can help facilitate a smooth introduction. Dave has helped his own clients find computer training appropriate to their learning styles. Some attended classes while others worked from CD-ROM tutorials. In some cases, he's had computer consultants come into their homes, set them up with their first computer, install e-mail, and give them one-on-one training. On occasion, both authors have gone into a client's home and configured an e-mail system or installed for them a Quicken chart of accounts so that they could produce meaningful expense reports for planning purposes. This may seem like a lot of work, but it will pay off for you big-time in future cost savings.

Once you have a critical mass of clients using e-mail, the real economies can begin. You will realize the greatest savings from the use of e-mail in the form of your time and your virtual assistant's time, and in operational costs like paper and postage. Here are some examples:

➤ You will set up your clients in an e-mail group so that you can send notices to all clients with one e-mail. You put your client group address in the "bcc:" line of your e-mail so the clients can't see each other's identifying information on the copy of the e-mail they receive. Some advisers like to put themselves in the "to:" line of the e-mail so this line isn't left blank. Using this format, you can send all kinds of items:

  —**Monthly bulletins.** The text of your bulletin can simply be the body of the e-mail, or you can attach a full-blown graphically designed newsletter as a PDF file.

  —**Communications during market downturns.** Many advisers like to stay in closer contact with their clients during periods of market volatility in order to reassure them that they are experiencing temporary conditions and that the long-term strategy the adviser has designed for them will still prevail.

  —**Your office can send travel notifications and office closure dates.**

  —**Recommendations for actions to be taken in response to investment trans-actions affecting most or all of your clients.** For example, a particular holding might give the client a choice of receiving either a stock or cash dividend.

➤ Individual client e-mails can save you time and money as well, though perhaps not of the same magnitude as group e-mails:

—**Billing.** Some advisers print their clients' invoices from their accounting software directly to a PDF file and attach them to individual e-mails to the clients.

—**Reporting.** Some advisers also send individual client e-mails to transmit quarterly investment status or performance reports, though posting such reports to a secure website may do this more efficiently.

The saved time and cost of printing, folding, and stuffing newsletters into envelopes, not to mention affixing postage and getting them to the mailbox, will amount to significant money for advisers who produce fancy or frequent newsletters. Most of these costs can be avoided while still turning out a very professional-looking newsletter (via e-mail and PDF file) that doesn't spend two days or longer getting to your client.

During serious market downturns, most advisers pride themselves on having "prepared" their clients through previous extensive discussions about the inevitability of stock market volatility. When dramatic declines occur, these advisers don't hear from most of their clients at first and assume their teachings are having the desired effect. However, further into a downturn, even the most earnest believer will get frightened and pick up the phone for a bit of hand-holding. You can allay your clients' fears and reduce the number and duration of such calls by broadcasting your thoughts on the market downturn frequently while in its midst. There is not only an opportunity to save time and money here, but also a way to increase your value to your clients with a very modest expenditure of time.

Simply weaning all clients away from the telephone and turning them toward e-mail as their primary means of communicating will yield the dividends of more discretionary time and less stress for you. There are still occasions when you need to schmooze in conversations with clients ("How are the kids? What's your golf handicap these days? How does Mary like that new Beemer you bought her? What does your psychic think of tech stocks this week?"). But often you just need a quick response to a question. The client has paid for access to your time, and he may have a bit more trouble than you do distinguishing which situations warrant a call. But when you have a quick question, that is what e-mails were made for. In these instances, e-mail will save you loads of time by shortening your communications as much as possible and by eliminating the stress and accumulated hours wasted on everyone's favorite game—phone tag.

In Dave's practice, 75 percent of his clients use e-mail, and in Joel's practice it's about 95 percent. Dave would like it if his number were higher, and the level at which it has plateaued follows his best attempts to have each and every one of his clients use e-mail. Some advisers who practice near Microsoft headquarters in Redmond, Washington, or who have only younger clients claim their number is 100 percent. Although his numbers aren't that high, Dave finds that even with a simple majority of his clients using e-mail, his savings are tremendous. Those clients who don't have e-mail are generally not in a big hurry to get a piece of his time, anyway.

That raises a question: Will clients take more of your time once they know it's more convenient for you to respond? Some will. But some are probably the clients you needed to have more contact with anyway to keep them as clients. (However, your older widows who hate to call because "your time is so important" and their "questions are so silly" often balance these out.)

E-Mail Devices That Aren't Exactly Computers

CHERYL HOLLAND OF ABACUS PLANNING GROUP in Columbia, South Carolina, e-mails her clients all the time, including while she's on the road. But you don't need a laptop to get your e-mail while traveling. Says Holland, "I have a Blackberry, which I adore. It's my virtual office. I don't take my laptop on a trip because with Blackberry I can respond to e-mail, get Word and Excel attachments, and even browse the Web." For the uninitiated, Blackberry is a wireless e-mail and Internet device that looks a bit like a PDA but has a full, miniature keyboard on its lower half. It's made by a Canadian company called Research in Motion, or "RIM" for short, and costs about $400. Best yet, says Holland, when she comes back from a four-day conference, she's not behind in her work since she's kept up with all her electronic communications while away.

Similarly, Dave uses a new combination Sprint PCS phone and Palm handheld computer, the Samsung SPH-I300. Released in late 2001 and costing around $500, this device has a color screen, 8MB of RAM, does everything that either a Sprint phone or Palm PDA device will do, and integrates the best features of both in a stylish six-ounce package. For example, not only can you get your e-mail anyplace in the world that receives Sprint PCS digital phone service, but you can make a call to anyone in your Palm database by simply tapping the phone number on the Samsung screen.

When Palm devices communicated wirelessly only by forcing their users to sign up for a service over and above that of their existing cell phone carrier or by attaching a modem that sometimes worked and sometimes didn't, it was problematic to carry only a Palm while traveling. With the Blackberry or Samsung SPH-I300, a six-ounce handheld device is truly a replacement for a six-pound laptop.

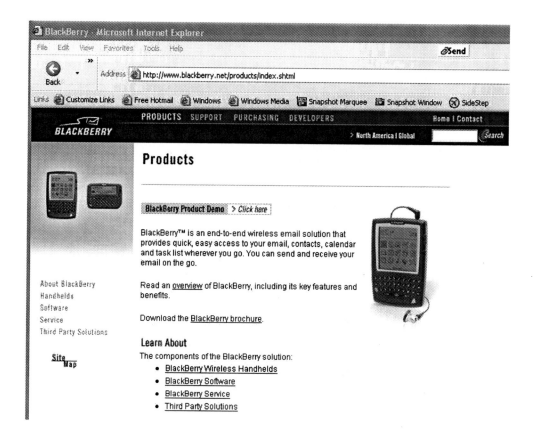

Blackberry

Other Nonverbal Client Communications

Intranets

The marvel of e-mail could probably be a chapter in itself, but let's move on to some of the slightly more exotic forms of technology you can use easily to your advantage. Intranets are a good example. *Intranet* is actually a misnomer in many of its uses. When the word achieved currency, circa 1995, it meant an internal company network that looked and functioned like a website and to which you could invite people outside of the company, like clients or suppliers, by granting them special permissions. Whereas this is still a great concept, true intranets have evolved into "virtual private networks" and similar tools that will be discussed in Chapter 9.

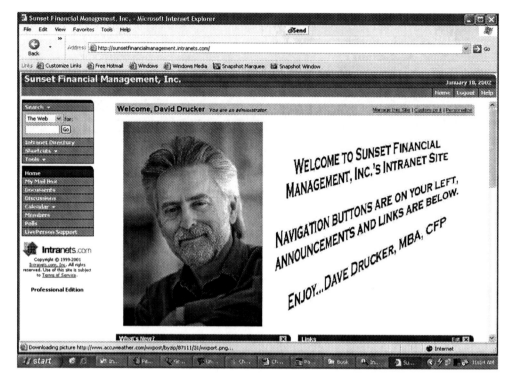

Home Page of Dave's Intranet

These days, the term intranet is often a reference to a website offering collaborative tools. Though such a setup exists for the use of only those who administer it and those who are invited to it, it is not an internal network and therefore should probably be called an "extranet." The semantics aren't important; the function is. Although you can attach all manner of information to client e-mails, it might be more efficient to upload that information to a website, into a secure folder accessible only to the client and to you. The information in question would be something that you produce for the client to read, like a quarterly portfolio report, or something requiring a collaborative effort, like a portfolio design project to which the client will provide input. Intranets, and a utility used in conjunction with them—Web Folders—are discussed more extensively in Chapter 9.

The Application Service Provider, or ASP

Another form of collaborative software that can not only involve the client in his own planning but also preclude the need for face-to-face meetings is the use of certain "application service providers," or ASPs. An ASP is a software program run from the Internet rather than from any individual's own computer or computer network. Let's use your favorite financial planning software as an example. You keep it on the hard drive of your company server or on your desktop computer. When you get a new client, you use the software to create a file for that client. When she's still a client three years later and she calls with a question that requires you to refer to her planning file, you load your program software and subsequently load her planning file.

An ASP does all of these things, too. However, its program code and the client's file all exist on the Internet and are run only from the Internet. You and your client may have a Windows Desktop link established by the program so that it can be run like any other program (i.e., users go to their desktop and double-click on the program icon), but very little actually resides on your computers.

The significance of some ASPs is that they provide another way to collaborate with your client from anywhere in the world, as long as you each have Internet access. Two examples of an ASP that can be used with your clients are Money-GuidePro and Financeware.com.

MoneyGuidePro

MoneyGuidePro, produced by PIE Technologies, is representative of the new type of ASP financial planning program that could change the future of financial planning. This tool, well suited for use by the virtual-planning firm, offers the ability to do financial planning collaboratively with your client and your client's other advisers over the Web.

Although its outward appearance is deceptively simple, it is a goal-based financial planning program that contains an innovative financial planning module, a well-designed asset allocation tool, and a retirement "spend-down" model that uses Monte Carlo simulations. Working on a financial plan in the traditional fashion places all sorts of limitations on the planner, the planner's staff, the client, and the client's other advisers. When the goal is virtual planning, however, MoneyGuidePro's virtual capabilities can overcome many of those limitations for you.

➤ *Planner.* With desktop financial planning software, the planner must be in her office to do financial planning. In small operations, there may be just one copy of a financial planning program on a single machine, limiting access and efficiency. Collaboration with coworkers is out of the question in that case. If, however, the planner uses an ASP like MoneyGuidePro on a network, two or more members of the staff can view the program and work on a plan at the same time. The cost of the service does not increase as more people access a particular client's MoneyGuidePro file.

➤ *Staff.* Sometimes a staff member can't make it to the office due to a last-minute problem at home or inclement weather. Under the ASP model, your staffers can access the needed program at home over the Internet. In fact, with a program like MoneyGuidePro, your staff does not have to be constrained by geography at all. Assuming your staff person has an Internet connection, plans can be shared with you or anyone else you authorize, in real time. MoneyGuidePro is an ideal program if you hire virtual planners to help with your plan preparation.

➤ *Client.* Sometimes your client needs answers but can't get to your office. Depending on the type of financial planning program you use, you may be able to post reports on the Internet or e-mail them. But with MoneyGuidePro, you don't have to worry about any of that because clients can directly access their financial planning software. Perhaps more importantly, the program empowers clients, significantly increasing their involvement in the planning process. Joel has been experimenting with this program, encouraging clients to enter data, view multiple scenarios, and interact virtually. Clients have reacted very favorably.

➤ *Other advisers.* Comprehensive financial planning in particular often requires the input, if not the active participation, of other professionals. With the client's permission, much of the interaction and information-sharing required of the professional team can take place online, creating efficient workflow and cutting costs.

➤ *Financial planning module.* MoneyGuidePro is divided into three distinct sections that share a common, centralized database—meaning you have to enter information only once, in any of the program's three sections. MoneyGuidePro's financial planner is goal-based rather than cash flow–based. The primary advantage of goal-based planning is that clients can relate to and understand it. Goal-based planning works the way clients typically think, focusing on life objectives rather than just cash-flow projections.

As you work through a financial plan with a client, MoneyGuidePro lets you prioritize the goals—something you won't currently find in other planning software. Cash flow models tend to spend assets as the need arises, rather than according to a client's priorities. If, for example, a client has three goals and the least important occurs first, most planning software will allocate assets to the first, though least important, goal on the timeline.

With MoneyGuidePro, however, assets will be automatically assigned to goals in the order the client specified, regardless of the year(s) in which the goal is scheduled (unless you override the defaults). If, for example, a young couple has two goals, their first priority being retirement and their second priority college savings for the kids, no money will be allocated to college until the first goal is met through a combination of current assets and future projected inflows. The results are presented in a clear illustration, allowing the client to grasp the current circumstances and to consider trade-offs when they become necessary.

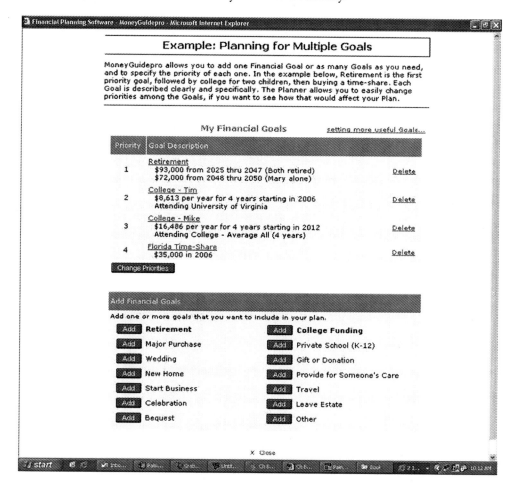

MoneyGuidePro's Planning for Multiple Goals Function

The module includes some features that will save you time and improve accuracy. For example, the education module includes detailed information about college costs. Social Security estimates and life expectancy information is also included.

MoneyGuidePro allows you to project the tax effect of a change in state residency upon retirement, something many high-end programs can't do. And, if you anticipate clients taking early withdrawals from an IRA or qualified plan before age

59½, you can instruct the program not to tax those withdrawals, as in the case of post-age-55 separation from service or a 72(t) withdrawal.

The risk management module can perform life, disability, and long-term care needs analysis. For long-term care analysis, the program offers a useful database of nursing care costs, covering both home care and nursing home care broken down by state. It also reminds the planner and the client to review property-casualty coverages.

An estate planning tool allows clients to set a target amount that they wish to leave for heirs and to treat the bequest as a goal with an assigned priority.

—**Asset Allocation.** This module begins by asking whether you have a lump sum of cash to invest or whether you want to reallocate an existing portfolio. If it's a lump sum, you just enter the dollar amount. If the client has an existing portfolio, you will be prompted to enter its contents. From there, you move to the risk tolerance questionnaire, which will help determine the asset allocation.

We particularly like the way this module is designed: It requires you to enter only the minimum amount of data necessary to perform a calculation, but allows

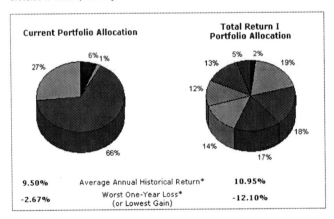

Example: Asset Allocation

MoneyGuidepro provides a comprehensive Asset Allocation system that includes a Risk Tolerance questionnaire, Model Portfolios, and suggested changes to move you from your Current Portfolio to Your Target Portfolio. The example below shows the Asset Allocation Results screen, which compares your Current Investment Allocation with the Target Allocation graphically, by dollar amount, and by percentage.

Results
Based upon the information you provided, **your Target Portfolio is Total Return I.**

This page compares your Current Portfolio Allocation with the way you should be allocated to match your Target Portfolio.

Current Portfolio Allocation / **Total Return I Portfolio Allocation**

9.50%	Average Annual Historical Return*	10.95%
-2.67%	Worst One-Year Loss* (or Lowest Gain)	-12.10%

MoneyGuidePro's Asset Allocation Function

you to add as much detail as you wish in the future.

From there, you could generate multiple "what if" scenarios in a matter of minutes. If necessary, you could later go back to the data and break out the individual assets in detail for a formal presentation.

Once this is done, you're presented with your current allocation in the form of a pie chart that presents the current dollar amounts invested in each asset class, along with their historic rates of return.

The next screen presents a range of portfolios along the efficient frontier, indicating the historic rate of return for each portfolio and, as a nice touch, the worst expected one-year rate of return. The program indicates which portfolio comes closest to your client's desired rate of return, and it also indicates which portfolio is compatible with your client's risk profile.

Once a new target portfolio is selected, the program generates a comparison of the new proposed portfolio versus the current allocations in both chart and table form. It also generates a list of transactions required to implement the new portfolio. The whole process is fast and efficient. Once the basic data is entered, it's easy to go back and run multiple scenarios.

—**Lifetime Income Plan.** The third section, Lifetime Income Plan, is a spend-down model designed to determine whether or not clients will outlive their resources. Once again, very little data is needed to do a "primary screen," particularly if you've already completed the other sections.

The program determines how long the portfolio will last, using Monte Carlo simulations based on historic rates of return. After the data are entered, the planner selects which assets to include in the simulation and selects a target portfolio. The program then runs 1,000 iterations to determine the probability of success. The results are displayed in a user-friendly format. If the results are not satisfactory, a "what if" box provides a convenient method to "tweak" the assumptions. One of the weaknesses of Monte Carlo analysis is that it can discourage clients or send them the wrong message. For example, if we treat all of a client's scheduled retirement spending as one amount, we will often have to instruct the client to implement a riskier portfolio to reach her target—even though not all projected retirement spending is equally important. One truly innovative use of the priorities function in MoneyGuidePro's financial planner is the ability to subdivide the retirement income need by goal and then to prioritize those goals. Under this approach, you might create one goal to cover essential fixed costs, and additional goals for vacations or a new car every so many years.

This methodology can lead to a discussion with the client of the trade-offs that different strategies or spending patterns will entail. ("You will not outlive your money; however, that trip around the world on a luxury yacht is not in the cards.")

Advantages

➢ It's a true, interactive, financial planning solution allowing for collaboration and "distance planning"

➢ It's easy to learn and navigate

➢ It's fast; you can put together the outline of a plan in one sitting

➢ The planner, not the program, dictates the level of detail

➢ A single database means you enter data only once

➢ The "priorities" feature is an extremely valuable tool

➢ Excellent output and ease of use means you can use it for client education as well as for more detailed planning

Disadvantages

➢ Although it works as well as can be expected with a dial-up connection, fast Internet access is required for optimal performance as it is for most ASPs

➢ Those who insist upon detailed cash-flow analysis won't find it here

➢ It may be conceptually different from the way you currently operate, and that will require some adjustments on your part

Financeware.com

Financeware, another ASP and virtual-planning tool permitting online collaboration, takes a more targeted approach than MoneyGuidePro. Financeware does not attempt to offer a full financial planning package online (although recent conversations with company spokesmen indicate the breadth of the product will expand over time). Instead, it concentrates on retirement, the area of primary importance to most clients. This concentration allows Financeware to offer more in-depth coverage of asset allocation, saving for retirement, and spending during retirement years, the topics these clients tend to care about the most.

For example, MoneyGuidePro offers a single methodology for modeling spending during the retirement years: actual historic returns in random order, which is a constrained form of Monte Carlo simulation. MoneyGuidePro's full-featured Monte Carlo capability applies only to modeling how long the client's money will last. Financeware offers actual historic returns in random order plus two additional methods: Historical Audit (rolling historical periods) and a full-featured Monte Carlo simulation (random returns in random order). Although we have some ques-

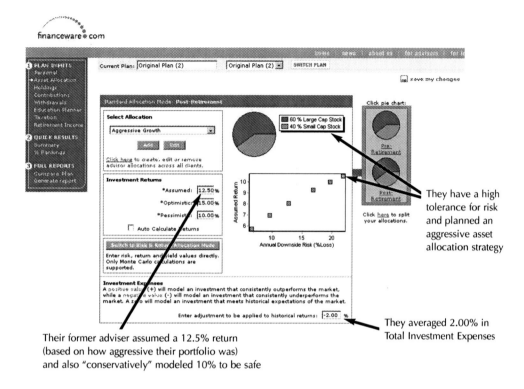

Their former adviser assumed a 12.5% return
(based on how aggressive their portfolio was)
and also "conservatively" modeled 10% to be safe

They have a high
tolerance for risk
and planned an
aggressive asset
allocation strategy

They averaged 2.00% in
Total Investment Expenses

Financeware's Retirement Planning Function

tions about the program's default asset class assumptions, users have the flexibility to substitute their own assumptions. Financeware also gives the user more control over assumed asset class standard deviations and cross-correlations than does MoneyGuidePro.

The company recently performed an overhaul of the reporting section of the program, further improving one of the software's strong points.

Probability analysis is not new, but its application in the field of personal finance is a fairly recent development. Clients may not be familiar with the concept. Employees may not be fully trained in conveying the benefits to clients. This is an area where Financeware really shines. The company has developed a series of tools (PowerPoint presentations and white papers such as company Chairman David B. Loeper's *The Use of Monte Carlo in Modern Portfolio Reality,* available at www.financeware.com) designed to educate advisers and to help them attract new business. They also offer live training classes in major metropolitan areas across the country.

A number of other services are available for purchase, including secure online storage and viewing of client documents, custom website design, and an online edu-cational program.

Advisers who focus primarily on investments, asset allocation, and retirement planning are likely to appreciate many of Financeware's charms. Further informa-tion is available at www.financeware.com.

Security Considerations

SOME CLIENTS (AND EVEN SOME ADVISERS) will resist using e-mail, intranets/extranets, or ASPs for communicating on sensitive subjects due to the perceived unsecure nature of the Internet. They will worry that confidential information that used to be exchanged orally or hand-to-hand will now be broadcast across the Internet for hackers to see and abuse. For this reason, you need to also know about security procedures, including encryption and the use of firewalls. These are dis-cussed in detail in Chapter 9 in connection with managing client work flow.

Web Conferencing: Conducting Meetings without Meeting

"FACE TIME" IS IMPORTANT, but it's also expensive. It entails travel time (for either you or your client) and often travel costs. We do not underestimate the importance of one-to-one meetings with clients, but we would argue that time devoted to such meetings is a precious commodity that should be spent with care.

Is there a way to better leverage your time? Can you save time and money by replacing some of your face-to-face meetings with another, more efficient format that will be beneficial to both you and your clients?

One way is through the use of Web-based conferencing services. The typical Web-based conferencing service is an ASP that allows two or more persons to meet at a designated time and place on the Web. What the participants see when they log on to the appointed site is anything from a "whiteboard" on which the advisor can write or draw while his client watches, to an application like a spreadsheet on which he can demonstrate to his client an analysis he's performed, accompanied by some real-time "what-ifs," or manipulations of the client's data. Both Dave and Joel have participated in Web conferences, as attendees and presenters, and have found that Web-conferencing lends itself very well to some tasks that financial advisers rou-tinely perform.

Probably the most frequently used Web-conferencing tool is the online slide show presentation. Typically, the audience calls in to a phone conference while simultaneously logging on to a website where the slide presentation takes place. Participants view the slides over the Web as the host provides commentary over the phone.

Here are some examples of how a Web-based slide presentation could be used:

➢ *Regular investment commentary.* Instead of calling or meeting with clients individually, present your regular economic and investment commentaries over the Web. Although some of what is said to clients is client-specific, your comments on the economy and the investment climate are probably repeated in just about every meeting you have. Furthermore, the questions you get from clients are often the same. Offering group presentations will save time and allow those clients who don't view such a setup as an invasion of their privacy to benefit from questions asked by others.

➢ *Seminars for existing clients.* Changes in the tax law often create new opportunities. Why not hold a seminar to alert clients to the possibilities? Regular seminars on financial planning topics, such as retirement distribution planning, college funding, etc. are good ways to provide general information.

➢ *Seminar marketing.* Organizing a live seminar can be time-consuming and costly. Web-based seminars save time, save money, and allow you to reach a broader audience. Polling, a feature available from most services, allows you to post a slide with a question for your audience and have the results displayed in real time. For example, if you are holding an investment seminar online, you can ask participants to rate their level of investment experience, or you can ask them to indicate on a screen the types of investments they currently hold. You get immediate feedback that you can use to tailor the presentation on the fly, and the participants experience a sense of community and interaction.

➢ *Advisory board meetings.* Many advisers have client advisory boards. No doubt, personal interaction is an integral part of advisory board dynamics. Nevertheless, there may be times when a fast reaction is needed or when members cannot get together in person. You can supplement the regularly scheduled live meetings with an occasional Web-based meeting.

Another thing you can do with Web-conferencing services is to share and annotate documents. This functionality might appeal to financial planners who often collaborate with a client's other advisers. For example, if you are working with an accountant and an estate planning attorney to update a client's estate plan, all three of you can meet online, view the documents, and mark them up as you work. This is clearly a great option if the team members are geographically dispersed, but it can also be a timesaver for those located crosstown.

With some Web-conferencing services you can share applications over the Web, allowing one participant to control an application on another participant's computer. Why would you want to do this? Perhaps to train clients in the use of a software product. Both authors have visited clients' homes occasionally to instruct them on the use of e-mail or Quicken. If you are trying to convert your less computer-savvy clients to use e-mail more, it might be more effective to do so with an online presentation. You could try sharing applications over the Web, or you could prepare a how-to presentation. Be forewarned, though, that application-sharing via Web-conferencing has limitations; so if you want to try it, test the application first on the platform you will be using.

In the course of our research, we examined four providers of Web-conferencing services: WebEx (www.webex.com), Placeware (www.placeware.com), Genesys (www.genesys.com), and Centra (www.centra.com). All offer the ability to make slide presentations, share applications, work on a whiteboard, and poll the audi-

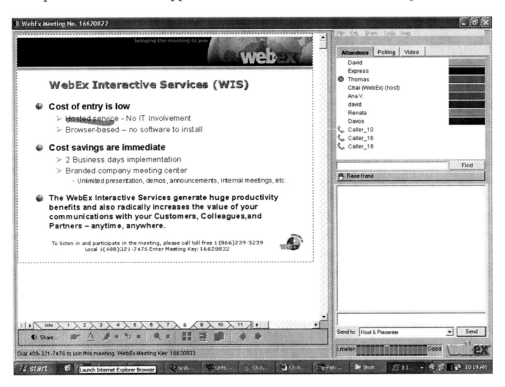

Sample WebEx Online Meeting Presentation Screen

ence—but each company employs its own software, some more intuitive than others. Some support only the Microsoft Windows operating system, whereas others can work with Apple and UNIX. Voice transmissions over the Web and Internet video-conferencing may be available, but we don't recommend these services as of this writing because most small-office computer systems will not produce satisfactory video and sound quality. A number of services also offer you the ability to set up conference calls through them, rather than through your regular telephone service provider, often at an attractive rate.

The prices charged by the providers vary significantly. Some charge a flat rate per month per license for unlimited use, some charge a lower fee per month and limit the number of participants you can have on one conference, and some charge a per-minute fee per user. License terms vary. One provider told us that a license is only necessary for each host (presenter). A host can invite numerous participants to a call. Another provider told us that a license was necessary for each participant on a call. Check terms carefully!

In some cases, the unlimited-user plans are not an option because they require a minimum number of licenses or a hefty setup fee. As of this writing, the best deal for small to mid-sized planning firms appears to be Genesys, which offers unlimited calls (up to fifteen participants per call) for $39.95 per month. Additional participants can be added to a call for forty cents per user per minute.

For smaller firms interested in unlimited monthly licenses but unable to meet the minimum, we'd suggest one of the following:
➤ Create a user's group, including enough users to meet the minimum
➤ Ask a vendor, such as a mutual fund company or custodian, to add you to their account
➤ Encourage an organization you belong to, such as the FPA or NAPFA, to establish an account so that members can purchase seats on an individual basis
➤ Purchase a subscription through an authorized reseller; for example, Hewlett-Packard Company resells WebEx services through its worldwide reseller network for its own products

Finally, don't underestimate the importance of customer support and technical support. Learning a new technology, and using it effectively, takes time. Good support can speed the process and provide help when you need it. Due to the rapid pace of change in this field, we urge you to do the following:
➤ Get recommendations from friends and colleagues
➤ Compare prices

➢ Try out a number of services, paying particular attention to feature sets and ease of use; many offer free trial conferences at their website

➢ Call customer support and technical support at different times; if you can't reach a human, or endure long hold times, be careful

Web conferencing will never, in our opinion, replace human contact. As a supplement to sitting down together, however, Web conferencing is a tool that can lower costs and increase client satisfaction.

A Look at Website Providers

WE DON'T NEED TO SELL YOU on the value of a website to client communications. Most advisers we speak with are well aware that a website has become an essential tool for doing business. Whereas many early attempts by advisers at establishing a Web presence amounted to little more than static billboards, financial professionals have come to realize that a well-designed website can perform a number of useful functions cheaply. Among the functions often cited are:

➢ Projecting a professional image
➢ Demonstrating that you are technologically adept
➢ Allowing potential prospects to reach you online
➢ Screening prospects
➢ Communicating with and enhancing service to existing clients
➢ Offering new services to existing clients
➢ Streamlining administrative tasks

One route that many early adopters pursued was to hire a local firm to design their websites. This idea has considerable appeal from the standpoint of access to designers and customization, but many advisers with whom we spoke indicated that generalist design firms did not grasp the nature of their business and could not come up with some of the services we know are essential.

What types of services are we talking about? Well, advisers seem to fall into two broad camps. One group is interested in providing market data and investment reporting to their clients over the Web. The second group, which comprised the majority of the advisers we talked to, was less interested in performance reporting and more interested in communicating with clients and prospects. To them, well-written content (or the ability to easily post their own) was very important. They were also interested in providing client services, such as online access to forms.

You can pay a lot or a little for a website. Costs are primarily determined by the services you desire and the level of customization you require, so it's helpful to know what you want before you compare prices. For example, you can probably purchase a basic package from any two website vendors for roughly the same price, but the look of one website will often be more customized than the other.

Considering client service and technical support are even more critical here than when evaluating financial planning software. In the area of website design, most advisers are clueless. This should not come as a surprise, since the skill set required for financial planning is not the same skill set required for constructing and maintaining a website. Most financial advisers are not experts in graphic design, and they don't know (and don't want to know) HTML. Under those circumstances, time spent working on one's website is time that could be more productively allocated elsewhere.

We looked at three of the best-known firms that market to our industry: LightPort Solutions (www.lightport.com), AdvisorSquare (www.advisorsquare.com), and AdvisorSites (www.advisorproducts.com).

LightPort had a lot of initial success in the adviser community because they were the first to offer online reporting capabilities for advisers. Joel was familiar with the firm because they had helped design a site for an FPA chapter with which he was affiliated. The person responsible for updating the chapter's site had complained to Joel that the interface was difficult to work with, and upon examining it himself, Joel had to agree. He played around with the site for some time and found formatting difficult, eventually discovering that he could accomplish much of what he wanted by creating documents in Microsoft Word and pasting or uploading them to the site. However, nobody suggested this technique until he specifically asked. In fairness to LightPort, they provided this site gratis as a marketing tool to reach FPA members, so paying clients might receive better tools and better service.

We went to the LightPort website to examine their client testimonials, looking for advisers we could talk to. One name immediately stood out: Deena Katz of Evensky, Brown & Katz in Coral Gables, Florida, one of the preeminent financial planners in the nation and author of *Deena Katz's Tools and Templates for Your Practice* (Bloomberg Press, 2001).

Ms. Katz told us that her firm was no longer a LightPort customer. (Her endorsement was subsequently removed.) She said that they used LightPort for a time but were not satisfied. According to Ms. Katz, "LightPort doesn't give you enough flexibility." She also complained that they "put links to places we would never send clients." She added that the "back office" was difficult to navigate and that she found tech support generally unresponsive. She told Joel that, adding insult to injury, LightPort continued to bill her firm months after it discontinued service. She says her firm is "temporarily" using AdvisorSquare, but she is very impressed with the work of AdvisorSites and expects to be working with them in the near future.

Another dissatisfied former LightPort client we talked with was Harry Kasanow, CFP, founder and President of Kasanow & Associates, a fee-only financial planning firm in Hawaii. According to Mr. Kasanow, "LightPort was a total disaster for us. We waited six months for our site, and it was never developed."

LightPort client Greg Friedman is no software novice. His firm was behind the development of Junxure, now a widely used contact management tool in our industry. According to Friedman, "They promise you a lot, but they hand you a blank template. The back office is kind of cool, but it's difficult to use. They have a new platform, but initially they didn't offer it to me."

Generally speaking, advisers who valued strong editorial content were not fond of LightPort. LightPort does, however, have its supporters. The advisers we talked with who like LightPort, such as veteran fee-only planner Al Coles of Financial Design Associates, Inc. in Stinson Beach, California, generally are looking for customized sites that they can fill with their proprietary content. Steven Cowen of Steven Cowen & Associates of La Jolla, California, values LightPort's portfolio reporting capabilities.

AdvisorSquare, the second website design company we checked out, forged numerous marketing arrangements with various "centers of influence" in our industry, such as broker/dealers, custodians, and providers of financial information. AdvisorSquare packages include client articles prepared by Liberty Publishing, as well as stock quotes and basic market news.

The first testimonial we found on their website was from Carter Financial Management, a well-known financial planning firm headquartered in Dallas, Texas. When we called Jennifer Lobaugh, marketing coordinator at Carter Financial, we were informed that they had dropped AdvisorSquare in favor of AdvisorSites. According to Lobaugh, her firm found the AdvisorSquare back office difficult to work with: "You have to know HTML to update your own text. When we updated our text, it sometimes didn't align properly. When that happened, the only way to correct it was to call in and have AdvisorSquare fix it." Lobaugh says her firm came to the conclusion that AdvisorSquare sites looked too similar to one another.

The firm of Armstrong, Macintyte & Severns, Inc. of Washington, D.C. is another former AdvisorSquare client who has been converted to AdvisorSites. Ryan Fleming found AdvisorSquare easy to use but disliked what he called the "cookie cutter approach." "There was no real design flexibility. There was nothing personal about it," he says. He often found that the stock quotes were stale, trailing the market by up to forty-five minutes. When he called customer support, his impression was that the employees had little understanding of his business. When he called tech support, "it sounded like a bunch of eighteen- or nineteen-year-old kids." Mr. Fleming is much happier since moving to AdvisorSites. "AdvisorSites is pretty responsive. They listened to what we wanted. It sounded like they took an interest in our business." He added that when talking to AdvisorSites, he felt he was talking to experienced businesspeople. "We told them what we wanted ... they gave us solutions," says Fleming.

If you are interested in doing business with AdvisorSquare, look closely at the various channels they sell through and select the least expensive one. When we shopped around, it appeared that their lower-cost package was attractively priced on MorningstarAdvisor.com, but that a better deal could be had on their premium package elsewhere.

When we turned our attention to AdvisorSites, we were deluged with enthusiastic endorsements. The message that we consistently heard was that the combination of superior content (much of it written by veteran financial journalist Andy Gluck), an understanding of the independent adviser, and superior service set AdvisorSites apart from the competition.

According to AdvisorSites founder Gluck, much of the firm's success is attributed to the fact that they started out as a supplier of custom-designed sites to high-end planners. These clients required customization, functionality, quality content, and good service. Their template packages are highly customizable, offering many of the benefits a custom-designed site provides at a fraction of the cost.

Lou Stanasolovich of Legend Financial Advisors, Inc. in Pittsburgh, Pennsylvania, an early AdvisorSites client, says, "not only do they offer website design, they offer excellent content." He adds, "They really understand our business. They are on the forefront of the profession."

Eric Rabbanian of Rabbanian Financial Planning, Inc. was impressed by the fact that he was able to work directly with the Web design staff to give his site the look and feel that he wanted. Content was another deciding factor: "Andy writes excellent articles," Rabbanian said.

Harry Kasanow is another satisfied client: "Ron Costa, our contact, is outstanding. We're in Hawaii, but we get twenty-four-hour turnaround. AdvisorSites understands the adviser market. They're looking for new and innovative things all the time."

Carter Financial is now working with AdvisorSites, and they are very satisfied

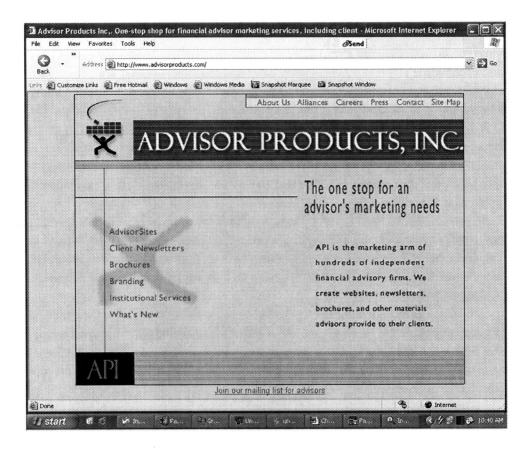

Advisor Products Home Page

with the service they are receiving. "We e-mail them the changes, and they post them promptly," says Lobaugh. "The content they provide is educational and informational in nature. The people at AdvisorSites understand our business," she says.

Dave recently moved his own website (www.daviddrucker.com) to AdvisorSites. He particularly likes the scripts that allow him to easily make design changes and post new content on his own without having to know any programming languages.

Our bottom line is that for independent advisers, particularly those who want to provide well-written editorial content without a lot of effort on their part, AdvisorSites is head and shoulders above the competition. The vast majority of advisers we spoke with want an attractive site, high-quality vendor-supplied content, and excellent support. If you fall into this camp, your first call should be to AdvisorSites. They do all the above, plus provide calculators, stock quotes, and

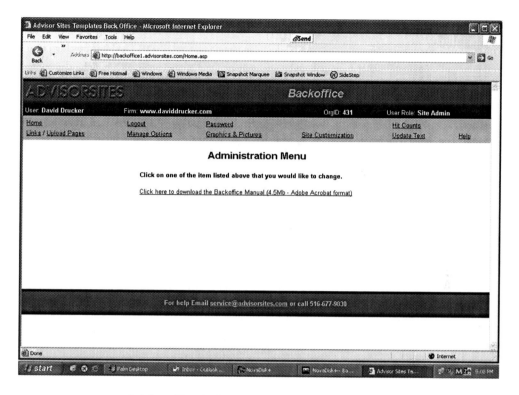

AdvisorSites's Site Management Home Page

other bells and whistles—all at an affordable price. They will even help you get all of your client service forms posted if you want them to. They are attuned to the needs of independent advisers, and their customer-service reputation is second to none.

We get a little nervous about a company in the business of producing websites that fails to keep its own site fresh. Both LightPort and AdvisorSquare had stale endorsement pages at the time we checked. We also worry when companies don't list their prices or list multiple prices through multiple channels. It's difficult to determine whether or not you are being treated fairly. The AdvisorSites's website makes it very clear what the costs are and what features are included at what price. (When we spoke with clients of AdvisorSites such as Chris Cooper, CFP in Toledo, Ohio, the words *honest, hard working,* and *ethical* peppered the conversation.) Pricing was much less clear to us when we visited rival sites.

Nonetheless, if you can live with the above criticisms, there are situations when the other companies might deserve a look. AdvisorSquare may be a viable option if

you want to get a basic site up fast. In view of the fact that AdvisorSquare has marketing agreements with many large B/D firms, reps are likely to find that their compliance department is comfortable with the work that AdvisorSquare does, speeding
the implementation process. Despite the negative feedback we got from a number
of planners, AdvisorSquare may also work for advisers who want content, quotes,
and market news that are at least adequate at a relatively low cost. Although we
didn't like the look and feel of AdvisorSquare's basic sites as much as we liked
AdvisorSites's, they do an acceptable job.

For large enterprise-sized jobs, or for advisers who have no need for vendor-
supplied content, LightPort is worth a look. Some of the advisers we spoke with felt
that they didn't get much attention from LightPort because the company was con-
centrating on servicing larger accounts, but if all you need are the tools and are willing to do much of the work yourself, the company might be a good fit for you.

Many of the communications techniques and tools that work for clients also work
for virtual work partners, or VWPs, as we'll show you in the next chapter.

C h a p t e r **8** *E i g h t*

Selecting and Working with Virtual Work Partners (VWPs)

S UPPOSE YOU WERE IN THE MARKET for an administrative assistant and were approached by someone who said, "I am an expert at what I do. The services I offer include not only secretarial work, but also bookkeeping, airline reservations, meeting scheduling, and other administrative functions. I don't need to be in your office to do my job as long as you're facile with e-mail and the Internet. I have all of my own equipment, software, office space, and access to as much of my own help as I may need. I charge a flat hourly fee for the work I do. And, if you're not satisfied, there are no strings ... since I have competitors, I have to do a good job at a fair price, and I intend to earn your trust. The prices I charge will be negotiated within the context of the free market in which we both compete. I have plenty of choices for employers, and you have plenty of choices of support workers. I am highly self-motivated and rarely seek or need guidance. I may sometimes bring you clients or business ideas that are so good you will want to implement them. In fact, you may sometimes voluntarily give me a generous raise because I've earned it and you are more than happy to compensate me."

What we have just described is the typical virtual firm owner/VWP relationship. A key element in the success of the virtual advisory firm is its reliance on outsourcing and virtual work partners ("VWPs") in lieu of traditional employees. Both the superior economics of the virtual firm and its ability to give more time back to its owner depend heavily upon hiring good VWPs and using them properly.

Two Flavors

VWPS COME IN TWO FLAVORS: independent business entities and independent contractors. An independent business entity is a small business formed specifically to provide a service essential to your advisory practice that you have chosen to outsource, as when Asset Management Solutions of Vista, California, does Centerpiece reporting for its advisor clients. An independent contractor is simply an individual who does the same thing. From a tax standpoint, the IRS may view the first as a corporation that will file a Form 1120 tax return each year, while Jane Doe, CPA, who provides accounting services to a few small business clients, will file a Schedule C with her 1040 at year-end.

The distinction may seem a little vague, but what's important is to understand the difference between independent business entities and independent contractors, on the one hand, and employees on the other. Businesses and independent contractors are both free agents and can deal with the virtual owner at arm's length. Dealings are not tinged with emotion or compromised by personal interaction, but are made with a certain detachment. Like the virtual owner, businesses and independent contractors are entrepreneurial in their thinking.

There's no "arm's length" when it comes to employees. After they've been around a few months, they begin to get absorbed into the family culture most small planning firms strive to create. At that point, they are telling you their personal problems, asking you for vacation time during your busiest season, and getting upset when you deny their request for a raise that would put their pay scale beyond the market rate for their job description. In short, they need a certain "care and feeding" that an independent business entity doesn't require.

Yet, most of us like to have real human contact, to be able to smile and joke with our coworkers, to commend them when they do a good job, and even to give them personal advice on occasion. Well, you don't have to give that up with a team of VWPs. Most of your communication will be by e-mail for greatest efficiency, but you don't have to lose the personal element entirely. It's just that you will stop at arm's length in your involvement with these employee substitutes.

A VWP, whether an independent business entity like Asset Management Solutions or an independent contractor, like Dave's virtual financial planner in Silver Spring, Maryland, generally understands the economics of what it's doing. A concept as fundamental as competition may be lost on an employee but is immediately apparent to a business. It knows it must provide a good service at a fair price, or Dave will find another reporting company or another virtual planner. It also knows that by doing a good job, it can turn its adviser client into a referral source. That's an advantage a business or independent contractor has over an employee. An employee's time generally belongs to one employer and he has no labor left over to give anyone else. A business, though, can have many bosses.

Another huge advantage that VWPs have over employees is that they come equipped with their own offices, equipment, and professional skills. We hope an employee will have high-level skills but, if he doesn't, we must either replace him or draw upon valuable time and money resources to train him. If a VWP agrees to take on a job for you that requires training, the VWP will foot the cost.

Does the typical VWP charge more than his employee counterpart? If he's smart, he will. He's got to take what you pay him and cover his entire overhead. If you pay your administrative assistant $17.50 an hour, you can't equate it to the $30 a virtual assistant might charge. The VWP must pay for his office space, his health plan, and his new computer. You pay these costs with an employee, too. They're just not apparent in looking at the employee's hourly rate.

Because a good business will run itself at least as efficiently as a good employee does, these costs are likely to be the same or lower for a business. And then, when you consider the other major advantage of the VWP—scalability—you can understand why the economics usually favor VWPs over employees. The VWP's time can easily be scaled to meet the demands of the job, with no excess, unproductive time left over. With an employee, you're either paying for time not worked, or underpaying for overtime, a condition that will eventually come back to haunt you in the form of a burned-out worker or seemingly excessive pay demands in the future.

Trying to establish a dependable team of employees can be like building a pyramid out of marbles: just when you think it's stable, one slips away and, in the smaller firm, that can be all it takes to unhinge the whole operation for a while. Turnover costs a lot because retraining new employees costs a lot.

Why do we have so much trouble retaining good employees? First, we're in an entrepreneurial business. We're all individualists, and the people we hire often are, too. Once they reach a certain level of competence and confidence, they judge themselves ready to do it their way. Many staff planners, for example, are destined to start their own planning firms, whether we like it or not. And this was true from the day we hired them.

Many principals bemoan the fact that their gross revenues are growing at 30 to 50 percent a year, yet their own compensation never changes. Perhaps they have forgotten an important lesson from Business Administration 101: Don't make something yourself if you can buy it better and cheaper from someone else. Put it in at the virtual owner can understand: Don't create a staff function in-house be accomplished better and less expensively by an independent busi- on.

In order to realize the economic benefits of VWPs over employees, you first need to be making the time for regular business planning. There are several software products that can assist you in this endeavor.

Business-Planning Software

AT THE HEART of every financial planning practice is a small business. Financial planners are often so busy working on solutions for their clients that they forget to tend to their own needs. In order to start a new business or improve an existing one, you need to have a plan. Many of us don't. Those who do often start from scratch, expending considerable energy building Microsoft Excel spreadsheets, formatting Microsoft Word documents, and then integrating the individual files into a finished product.

There is an easier, more cost-effective way. A number of software companies specialize in providing off-the-shelf business plan software and other business building tools. We examined a number of these products and found them to be effective and inexpensive.

Rated the top business plan software package by *Home Office Computing, Journal of Business Strategy,* and *Entrepreneur Magazine* is Business Plan Pro 2002 published by Palo Alto Software (www.paloalto.com). After putting the program through some tests, we can see why. This feature-rich program is well-suited to both novices and professionals. It includes an excellent manual called *Hurdle: The Book on Business Planning* (Palo Alto Software, Inc., 2000), by Tim Berry.

The Plan Manager, on the left of the screen, allows you to navigate the program. It is divided into six sections: Research It, Build It, Distribute and Deliver, Make It Happen, Help, and Tools. Research It allows you to view over 200 sample plans, conduct market research, and access expert advice. It also contains a list of useful Web resources. Build It helps you build your plan either by accessing an outline or using the EasyPlan Wizard.

The EasyPlan Wizard walks you through the process of establishing a business plan tailored to your unique circumstances. You are prompted with questions, instructions, and examples. Whether you are writing text or constructing spreadsheets, the Wizard does the formatting for you. The software is flexible enough to allow as little or as much detail as you wish to provide.

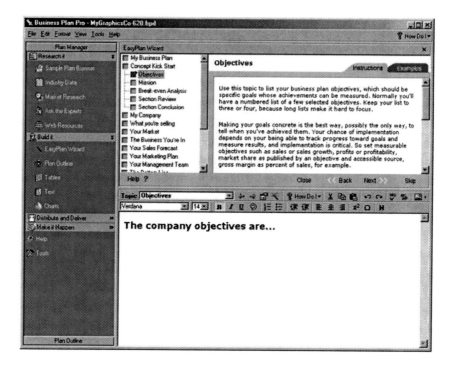

Business Plan Pro Sample Plan Company Objectives Page

Once your plan is finished, you can print it, export it, post it to a website, or turn it into a slide show. There is also an option to save the plan in a special format for use by Kinko's printing service. BusinessPlan Pro can export to Microsoft Office applications. It can also be made to work in conjunction with QuickBooks.

Plans can also be posted to a secure section of the Palo Alto website. As of this writing, posting for the 2002 version was in the read-only mode and was free. By the time you read this, you should be able to collaborate on your plan over the Web for a fee.

Make It Happen provides additional resources to implement your plan, including reminders, links to legal services, and help with funding.

Palo Alto Software provides some free resources that are accessible from its home page (www.paloalto.com). Bplans (www.bplans.com) contains a number of useful applets including a start-up cost estimator, a mini business-plan builder, and a mini Web-plan builder. The mini-plans allow you to export data into the full version of the product.

Two other Palo Alto Software products, Marketing Plan Pro and Web Strategy

Pro, use a similar interface to help you with other aspects of your business. You can import data from one program to another.

SmartOnline (www.smartonline.com) takes a different approach to building business plans. The product is a Web-based ASP that provides a wide range of software and services, including business-plan construction, for a monthly fee of $19.95. Business plans are built and stored online, but they can be downloaded for printing or e-mailing. Although its business-plan capabilities are somewhat more limited than Business Plan Pro's, it appears to be a good tool for collaboration.

The site also offers a wide range of other features that are included in the subscription price, including tools to conduct market research and to create job descriptions, employee manuals, and business letters. Numerous other services (credit card processing, professionally written press releases, and training courses) can be purchased for an additional charge.

Whether you are starting a new financial planning practice or improving an existing one, these products can help you get on track fast. Once you have mastered the software and created your own plan, you might want to think about creating plans for others. Producing business plans can be both a new source of revenue and a new source of financial planning clients.

Types of VWPs

THE FIVE BASIC TYPES of VWPs most virtual firms will need are (1) the virtual assistant, (2) the virtual planner, (3) a virtual reporting company, (4) a virtual trader, and (5) a virtual account administrator. Other personnel may be virtual as well, although you are probably using some or all in that mode already, such as accountants, attorneys, webmasters, compliance officers, and graphic designers. Let's explore the functions and abilities of the five basic types of virtual workers.

The Virtual Assistant

According to www.staffcentrix.com, a website that has been instrumental in developing the virtual assisting industry, a virtual assistant (or "VA") is "an independent contractor who can handle your noncore support needs from a distance via e-mail, fax, telephone, etc." Staffcentrix's definition goes on to say, "VAs, like many of their clients, are the CEOs of their own companies. Often they become the long-term 'growth partners' of their clients, handling such tasks as administrative support, bookkeeping, scheduling and client contact, or other more-specialized areas such as website maintenance and market research." A good employee brings to bear on

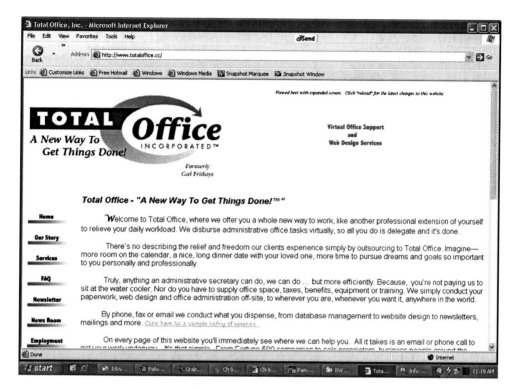

Total Office Home Page

your office systems the experience he or she has gained in working for a handful of previous employers. However, a good VA brings to bear the experience gained during possibly hundreds of other work engagements. The VA may be your best business consultant.

In other words, a VA is a virtual administrative assistant. However, some VAs can do even more than what's expected from the typical administrative assistant. Dave's VA, Sherry Carnahan, owner of Total Office, Inc. (www.totaloffice.cc.), is just as capable at doing Internet research, batch-mailing holiday cards, or maintaining customer lists as she is at printing and mailing client correspondence.

Of the various types of VWPs, the virtual assistant has probably been around the longest. Hence, there are more channels available for finding one. As our directory of VWPs on page 150 shows, there are various websites to help you locate a virtual assistant.

Staffcentrix.com allows you to submit a free, detailed Request for Proposal (RFP) to aid them in helping to find you the best VA for your business among its

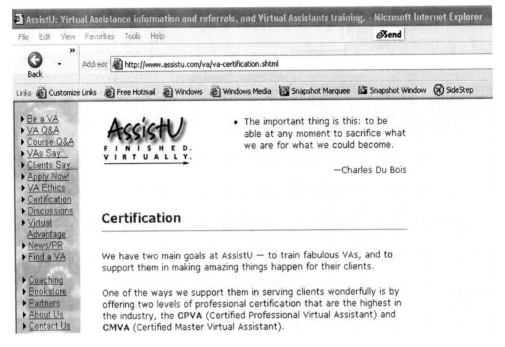

AssistU CPVA Certification Home Page

close to 2,000 international members. You can get as specific in your request as indicating what types of business equipment your VA must own or where they must be geographically located. Possible services range from the expected, like accounting and correspondence processing, to more specialized services such as database management, document OCR, and meeting planning. You may even have a need for a multilingual VA, and Staffcentrix will allow you to specify that in your RFP.

AssistU's primary mission is to train the best VAs in the world, but they also assist business owners in finding the ideal VA through their "Registry." AssistU first helps you figure out exactly what you're looking for. If you click on the first of three choices, "I am looking for a referral to a great Virtual Assistant who will support me administratively in a long-term, collaborative relationship," you will be taken to a detailed application, not unlike that of Staffcentrix' RFP. And if you answer, "I'm not sure what I need," you will be given the opportunity to join a teleconference about using VAs. If you don't want to commit to a long-term relationship with a VA but still want a VA's help, you are sent to Elance, where professionals bid on your project. (Another site like Elance, where you can locate professional freelancers for piecework, is FreeAgent.)

Of course, as is true with all valued business connections, word of mouth may produce the best results—*if* you can find an associate using a virtual assistant. Chances are, you may be the first among your group of closest colleagues to take this step, so you may need to be the pioneer. That means more risk but an earlier reward.

Through AssistU, VAs can earn professional designations: CPVA or CMVA certification. The first level of certification, the CPVA, or Certified Professional Virtual Assistant, is awarded to AssistU graduates who (1) do 150+ hours of industry-specific training, coaching, and independent study; (2) earn a high grade on a rigorous knowledge-based final exam; and (3) show high proficiency in more than fifty core skills during an eight-week long client simulated experience/certification exam.

The higher-level CMVA, or Certified Master Virtual Assistant, is awarded to CPVAs who achieve a place of Mastery in their profession. They have logged a minimum of 1,500 hours of work with virtual clients and have demonstrated that they can add premium value to these relationships.

What is probably more important than credentials in selecting a VA, though, is experience and entrepreneurial spirit. Years of experience as an administrative assistant with bookkeeping and computer skills are an excellent background to find in a VA. Also valuable is the VA's entrepreneurial know-how. This is true for any VWP you hire. Unlike the employee, they must be self-motivated and capable of running their own show. If you can't size this up adequately from the testimonials of others before you hire the VA of your choice, start out your working relationship on a trial basis with no strings attached for either party. This will give you a chance to see if your VA can truly meet your needs.

The Virtual Planner

The virtual planner is usually an individual Certified Financial Planner or small business offering the services of two or more planners to assist the virtual owner in various stages of the process of preparing financial plans. A virtual planner may do as little as entering a new client's raw data into the virtual owner's financial planning software. Or, he may have contact with the client and even make planning recommendations to the client.

Some good examples of virtual planners are Back Office Solutions (www.back officesolutions.net), a Georgetown, Texas, company headed and run by Naomi Scrivener, CFP, and Secure Financial Management, Inc. (www.sfmfinancial.com/home.htm), an Ashburn, Virginia, company run by Roron Wisniewski, CFP, and Barbara Clark, CFP.

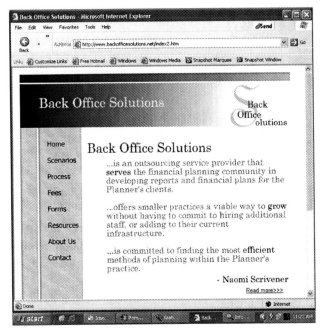

Back Office Solutions Home Page

Virtual planners can be found through commercial enterprises (see sidebar on page 150) or one might be on your staff right now. Confusing? Many virtual planners assume their role when it's time for a change. Dave's virtual planner had been Dave's employee for many years, and when he decided to start his own practice, he and Dave formed a symbiotic relationship that lasted about a year. Dave wanted as-needed planning assistance from a trained Certified Financial Planner, and his ex-employee needed a steady income while forming his own base of clients.

In another case, you may have a staff Certified Financial Planner who loves her job but must move out-of-state because her husband's company has just transferred him to their headquarters office. This is a great opportunity not only to convert an employee into a virtual planner, but also to experiment in setting up systems to work with VWPs long distance. Danelle Tainter was a receptionist for Hammel Financial Advisory Group, LLC in Brentwood, Tennessee, who was promoted to a client services role, and then to paraplanner position when she found out her husband would be taking a job in St. Louis. Melissa Hammel had recently heard of virtual planners and asked Tainter to stay on as a long-distance paraplanner. Tainter agreed and she and Hammel set up a system allowing Tainter to access a computer at Hammel Financial Advisory Group using pcAnywhere and a cable modem connection, which Hammel's firm pays for. "We primarily contact one another through e-mail and use attachments via Word, Excel, Centerpiece, and so forth," says Hammel. They also contact each other by telephone at least once a day and by fax as needed.

A similar situation developed at The Arkansas Financial Group, Inc. in Little Rock, Arkansas. Says principal Cynthia Conger, "The most 'virtual' thing we are doing is allowing one of our CPA/CFPs to live in Michigan and telecommute. We

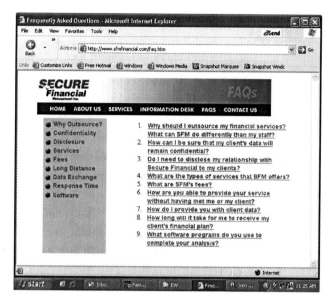

Secure Financial Management Home Page

hired her in September of 1999, and she moved from Lansing to Little Rock. In the spring of 2000, a family medical emergency developed and by summer she felt she had to move back to Michigan."

Conger and her firm experimented with VPNs, Laplink, and GoToMyPC (see Chapter 9 sidebars) but finally installed a terminal server and cable modem to keep their employee in the loop. Says Conger of her employee, "She is able to access our network and work at home. During tax season, she comes down about once a month, and we FedEx boxes back and forth. After May 1, her travel schedule is three days every three weeks. She arranges to meet with planning clients during those three days, and then takes more work home to do between trips."

This arrangement is not for just any employee, though. "The one caveat I would give," says Conger, "is that it takes a *very* structured and disciplined self-starter to do this. However, since she had come from a Big-Five accounting background, being able to make her own hours is heaven for her."

More and more Certified Financial Planners are leaving planning firms and considering working for planners rather than end consumers of financial planning services. When Naomi Scrivener's husband was transferred from an office in Tennessee to a job in Texas, rather than seek a successor employer to Resource Advisory Services, Inc. for which she'd worked for three years, Scrivener decided to go virtual. She set up Back Office Solutions in Georgetown, Texas, and now assists planners nationwide with everything from data entry to plan preparation.

Similarly, Barbara Clark and Roron Wisniewski had worked together two and a half years at The Advisors Group in Fairfax, Virginia, and hooked up in autumn 1998 to form Secure Financial Management, Inc. in nearby Ashburn. They now do financial plan preparation for a wide base of adviser clients. Says Clark, "We help our clients leverage their time to make each day more productive, profitable, and most important, enjoyable." Wisniewski characterizes the benefit they deliver their clients: "With a stroke of their pen, companies instantly create a fully staffed financial planning division utilizing the latest advances in tools and technology in order to efficiently deliver quantitative analysis designed specifically for their clients."

Sites like the aforementioned FreeAgent and Elance can also be used to find freelance or virtual planners, although more care must be taken to ensure that persons found through these channels have the necessary experience, since freelancers often offer their services in more than one profession.

In the end, your virtual planner will need to have strong computer skills, not only with transferring information electronically, but also with the financial planning software of your choice. If they must learn that software from scratch to take you on as a client, then you may find yourself paying for their training, their start-up inefficiency, and their mistakes.

The Virtual Reporting Company

Many financial advisers manage client money these days, and most prepare periodic reports showing portfolio positions and performance, both to inform their clients and to use in their own management process. Examples of popular software products used to track and report on client investments are Centerpiece by Performance Technologies, Inc. (www.centerpiece.com), Axys by Advent Software Inc. (www.advent.com/products/axys/index.asp), dbCAMS+ by Financial Computer Support, Inc. (www.dbcams.com), and Techfi by Techfi Corp. (www.techfi.com).

Rather than hiring a dedicated employee to operate one of these software products, virtual owners have the option of employing a reporting service. This type of VWP will get the virtual owner's "download," or daily price and transaction information, from the custodians she uses to house her clients' assets, run that information through her chosen portfolio tracking software, and publish reports.

The publication process can work many ways. Reports might be published to a website for password-protected access by the adviser and/or the client. They might be published the old-fashioned way and mailed to the client. Asset Management Solutions maintains a specialized, high-speed connection linking its server to each of its client adviser companies so that all updated Centerpiece information can be downloaded to the adviser's computer each night. That way, the adviser has completely current portfolio information each morning and can publish her own reports, as needed.

Examples of reporting services are Asset Management Solutions of Vista,

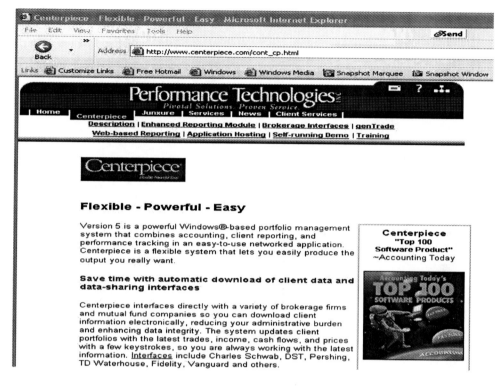

Centerpiece Home Page

California (www.assetsolutions.com/AMS.swf), or Krisan's BackOffice, Inc. in Charlottesville, Virginia (www.krisan.com). These names will pop up frequently if you're searching for a virtual reporting service via word of mouth.

A more structured approach to searching for this particular type of VWP, though, would be to start with the software producers. For example, a trip to Centerpiece's site yields the information that its owner, Performance Technologies, Inc., rolled out a service in 2001 called "Coworker" (www.centerpiece.com/cont_cp.html), which advertises to...

➤ Download data from your custodians

➤ Post transactions, prices, and any other information provided by your custodians to your Centerpiece database

➤ Provide price data for missing prices

➤ Adjust data for corporate actions

➤ Reconcile position data in Centerpiece with position data provided by your custodian

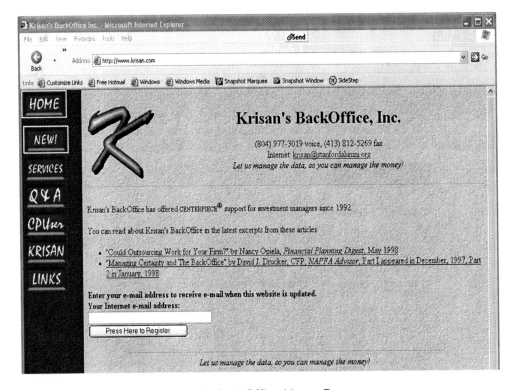

Krisan's BackOffice Home Page

> ➤ Input index data
> ➤ Run interval performance calculations at the end of each month
> ➤ Print client portfolio reports
> ➤ Calculate and print client bills

Techfi Corporation has a similar service called AdvisorMart (www.advisor mart.com) and FSCI, maker of dbCAMs+, has its own service bureau that you can check out at www.dbcams.com/services/svcbureau.htm. At Advent's site, you will find out about a service called Advent Browser Reporting (www.advent.com/prod ucts/browser_reporting/index.asp) that is another form of VWP.

Ultimately, what you want from a virtual reporting company is accuracy, a quick report turnaround after the end of a calendar quarter or year, and the ability to give you the most current share and price data for your clients on a daily basis in the reporting format of your chosen portfolio software. With that you can respond to your clients' questions as if you were still managing their data in-house.

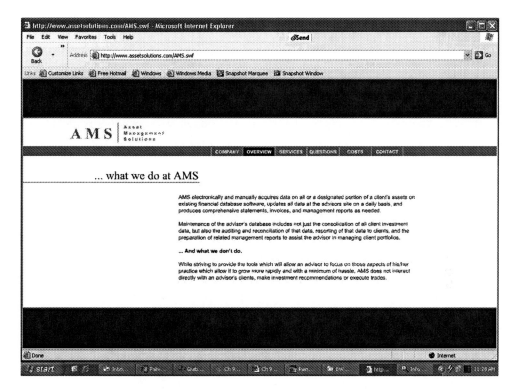

Asset Management Solutions Home Page

One other important point about virtual reporting companies: If you are completely new to outsourcing, this might be the best place to start. Compared to other VWP relationships, the output from the virtual reporting relationship is fairly standardized. In order to work effectively for you, a virtual assistant or virtual planner must understand much about the way you think and operate. Once you settle on the format of your reports, there is not much discretion required on the part of the virtual reporter, so startup difficulties and misunderstandings are less likely to occur.

The Virtual Trader

The term *virtual trader* covers a broad category that can include anything from a broker to a separate account manager. The concept of using a virtual trader is that the virtual owner is offloading the job of monitoring client accounts for liquidity sufficiency and conformity with asset allocation targets, along with the jobs of rebalancing the portfolio, selecting investment vehicles, and investing idle cash from maturing fixed income instruments.

Dave uses a broker, YieldQuest Investment Group of Atlanta, Georgia, that carries out the abovementioned duties via "trade-aways" for client accounts maintained at Charles Schwab & Co. (A *trade-away* is an arrangement for buying or selling a security through a broker other than the one with which the client's accounts are custodied, and journaling cash or securities out of the custodial account to pay for the trade.) The client is made aware of the additional costs he's incurring (trade-away fees of $25 per transaction), but he's also made aware of the trader's unique skills. YieldQuest has a team of highly skilled traders and analysts whom Dave could not afford to employ, but who add value to the management of his client accounts well beyond the reasonable commissions charged to Dave's clients.

In the case of a separate account manager, the end client usually understands that his adviser, the virtual owner, has made an arrangement with a third party to manage the client's investments. In most cases, the adviser is positioned as the professional who will monitor the performance of the chosen separate account managers and retain or replace them as necessary. In either case, though, the virtual owner has avoided the expense and hiring challenges of maintaining a staff of Chartered Financial Analysts to devise investment strategies and execute trades in client accounts.

As mentioned earlier, virtual trading can involve individual brokers, separate account managers, or any number of other arrangements you might find or construct to move your trading function "offline." Most large brokerage firms offer separate account management these days, from the "wrap" programs of full-service brokers to the more independent arrangements offered by discount giants like Charles Schwab & Co.

Large investment companies also offer virtual trading functions. A company long popular with financial advisers, SEI, offers what it calls its Investment Advisory Group that provides financial advisers with marketing materials, manager research and investment solutions, a process for monitoring managers that advisers have selected, and performance reporting (www.SEIBusinessBuilder.com).

Caution must be used in all of these arrangements. Investment management is one part of the financial planning process where many clients will seek the highest level of customization. Therefore, delegating their portfolio management to a cookie-cutter operation can be harmful to your relationship with your client if the details aren't taken care of with the same care you hope your office would provide.

For example, we have found that managing a client's funds consistently with their financial plan requires all of the following ingredients:

➤ Adherence to an overall asset-allocation strategy

➤ Maintenance of minimum cash balances to meet ongoing needs for income distributions, mandatory IRA distributions, and/or payment of the adviser's fee

➤ Recognition that the client can't or won't sell certain specific securities

➤ Recognition of the need for tax-wise sales of securities in which the client has inordinately large positions

➤ Knowledge of the client's state of residence in the selection of municipal bonds

➤ Knowledge of the client's tax bracket in selecting between taxable and tax-exempt bonds

➤ Awareness of the client's "target return" specified in the Investment Policy Statement tailored to that individual client

➤ Awareness of the risk tolerance and/or range of expected gains or losses the client can tolerate on an annual basis

The failure of a VWP to treat these variables with the same respect you would in delivering the management service in-house can cost you your client. Alternatively, you may decide to share these duties with your VWP; e.g., keeping the asset allocation functions and delegating the investment selection functions. However it is done, either your or your VWP must cover all of the bases.

The Virtual Account Administrator

"Account administrator" is a fancy name for the employee in your firm who deals with client investment accounts—not choosing investments, but handling the mechanics of opening and closing accounts, setting up automatic distributions from accounts, requesting one-time distributions from IRA accounts, and troubleshooting lost deposits to accounts.

This is a specialized position for which you won't find a lot of independent contractors offering their services. Generally, an ex-employee, or perhaps a virtual assistant who wants to learn a new skill, will be the ideal candidate for making this into a virtual position.

You might be able to locate a person with the particular skills you need through one of the abovementioned VA search functions, indicating back-office brokerage experience as a desired job skill. Or, as online brokerage utilities such as Charles Schwab & Co.'s Web Forms become more advanced, the adviser or a core staff person will more easily retain this job.

The most important traits to look for in the person or firm hired to fill this position are attention to detail, knowledge of qualified and nonqualified brokerage accounts and the various transactions affecting them, and the ability to clearly

A Short Directory of Good VWPs

Virtual Assistants

➤ Sherry Huff Carnahan, Total Office, totaloffice@neo.rr.com,
  www.totaloffice.cc
➤ Staffcentrix, www.staffcentrix.com
➤ AssistU, www.assistu.com
➤ Elance, www.elance.com
➤ FreeAgent, www.freeagent.com
➤ Association of Business Support Services International, Inc. (ABSSI),
  www.abssi.org

Virtual Office Consultants

➤ David J. Drucker, M.B.A., CFP, dd@daviddrucker.com,
  www.daviddrucker.com
➤ Joel Bruckenstein, CFP, joel.bruckenstein@prodigy.net
➤ Kevin and Jo Day, Trumpet Inc., jo@trumpetinc.com,
  www.trumpetinc.com

Virtual Planners

➤ Naomi Y. Scrivener, CFP, BackOffice Solutions,
  www.backofficesolutions.net, nscrivener@backofficesolutions.net
➤ Barbara Clark, CFP, and Roron Wisniewski, CFP, Secure Financial
  Management, www.sfmfinancial.com, bclark@sfmfinancial.com, or
  rwisniewski@sfmfinancial.com

Virtual Reporting Services

➤ Mike Kelly, Asset Management Solutions, www.assetsolutions.com,
  mkelly@assetsolutions.com
➤ Krisan Marotta, Krisan'sBack Office, Inc., www.krisan.com,
  krisan@stanfordalumni.org
➤ Sandy Derato, Planners Consulting Group, Inc.,
  www.plannersconsulting.com, sandy@plannersconsulting.com

instruct and guide your clients through the inevitable paperwork maze that is a part of every financial advisory practice.

Subadvisory Agreements

PERHAPS YOUR REACTION to outsourcing to VWPs has been "How could I entrust the confidentiality on which my client relationships are based to an outsider?" But think about it. A VWP is not much more an outsider than an employee. In both cases you must check their references carefully, assess their skills accurately, establish a clear agreement as to what will be expected of them and how they will be remunerated, and establish guidelines by which they will honor the trust your clients have placed in your firm by keeping confidential at all times private client information.

To do the latter, a subadvisory agreement should be made with all independent contractor VWPs. Independent business entities, such as virtual reporting services, will often have their own agreement forms in which confidentiality will be addressed. Although we are not attorneys and we advise you to consult one in the preparation of a subadvisory agreement, such agreements we have seen have included the following:

➢ Identification of the adviser and subadviser to the agreement
➢ The scope of the engagement (what each party will do)
➢ How and when the subadviser's productivity will be measured and how he will be paid
➢ Representation by the subadviser that he is an RIA, if that is a requirement, and that he is properly registered with all federal and state authorities with which he is required to be in compliance to serve the adviser's clients
➢ Attestation that the subadviser is not the subject of any regulatory proceedings that would disqualify him from performing the duties of the agreement
➢ Agreement that the subadviser and any employees of the subadviser will conduct themselves professionally at all times in serving the adviser's clients
➢ Agreement that the subadviser will hold adviser harmless for any damages suffered as a result of any violation of this agreement by subadviser or his employees
➢ Agreement that the adviser will hold subadviser harmless for any damages suffered as a result of any act or omission by adviser
➢ A termination clause
➢ A nonassignment clause
➢ An arbitration clause, if desired

➤ Agreement that appropriate disclosure, usually ADV Part II, will be provided to adviser's clients for both adviser and subadviser

➤ Statement as to which state's law governs the agreement

➤ Acknowledgment by the subadviser of the need to keep completely confidential the business practices and operations of the adviser, including information pertaining both to the operation of the adviser's company as well as to the adviser's clients

➤ Agreement by the subadviser not to solicit the adviser's clients for some period following the termination of the adviser's and subadviser's association

➤ Remedies for violation of the above items

➤ Signatures and dates

Now that we've got our paperless systems, and new, more efficient ways to communicate with our clients and work partners, let's talk about how to best manage client work flow.

C h a p t e r **9** *N i n e*

Managing Client Work Flow

O F WHAT DOES CLIENT WORK CONSIST? In its purest form, it consists of verbal advice, usually in conjunction with work products that would at one time have been created on paper alone. Aside from the obvious one—the financial plan—these documents include things like periodic investment reports the adviser sends the client, written correspondence, bulletins or newsletters sent to clients as part of their education process, and ad hoc analyses done at the request of a client.

These are the finished products, put together after work in progress has flowed between the adviser and her work partners. For example, two or more people may share the client's financial planning file in a collaborative effort to produce an analysis or the client's financial plan. The investment and reporting processes done on the client's behalf also generally require the attention of more than one person.

In a traditional financial advisory firm with, perhaps, two principals and six staff support positions, staffers will have occasion to deal directly with clients, if only to request and receive information needed by the principals. Two or more principals may deal with some of the same clients rather than segregating all the clients into "his" and "hers."

These collaborations all require some system enabling two or more people to access a common body of information about the client, modify that information, and then make it accessible to other workers within the firm. These days, most small to mid-size advisory firms have a LAN, or local area network, across which they share information. In some practices, the information on a client exists in an integrated system built on a platform like Lotus Notes. In other practices, information is more piecemeal, with the client's planning data existing as a proprietary file within the firm's commercial financial planning software, notes on client meetings existing within multiple Word files, and so on.

Now imagine how these systems might look if we transformed the entire in-house process to a system of VWPs. Let's assume there is one principal who sits alone in an office with six support persons spread across the country. Assume the same client base and the same information archives need to be shared with this workforce. The virtual owner, because his VWPs are offsite, now has a choice to make between a *centralized* or *decentralized* system of controlling the information everyone's sharing. As we will see, each has its advantages and disadvantages, and each requires different security measures.

Decentralized Control

DECENTRALIZED CONTROL OF client information looks much like the LAN we described above. Each coworker has autonomous access to all the information he or she needs, and the information resides on a computer network or website. We will call this "pull" technology because the virtual firm owner pulls the worker into her domain to access client data. The owner may give different security clearances, or permissions, to different people. A higher-level worker may have access to more information than a lower level worker, but they have in common their ability to dial or browse into a network or website and take what they need to complete the job you've assigned them.

In a system set up for decentralized control of client information, the files being accessed are the original files. Although there are presumably backups on tape or other media as a safety precaution, the data being acted upon by all workers is the main client database, the point of original data entry.

A distinguishing feature of decentralized control is the greater scope of the VWPs' role in the recording and tracking of work in progress. When all workers, including the owner or principal, have access to the same information, the VWPs can be treated more like employees in that they can be given higher-level responsibilities. For example, in a decentralized system, an owner may say to the virtual planner "you are responsible for collecting the client's information, recording it in his financial planning file, and producing the completed financial plan." In a centralized system, the owner would be more likely to break up these tasks into intermediate steps, retaining more of the responsibility for the ultimate product and its timely delivery to the client.

Centralized Control

IN A CENTRALIZED control system, the virtual owner says "I'm willing to sacrifice the convenience of enabling VWPs to access client information as needed in exchange for the security of knowing that I am better safeguarding this information by restricting others' access to it." In a centralized control system, the principal shares information with coworkers on an as-needed basis.

This generally requires a different set of technological tools. Whereas the decentralized system is based on a network concept, the centralized system is based on tools that "push" information out from the virtual firm owner to the VWPs, tools like e-mail and intranets/extranets to which individual files needed by a VWP for a specific task can be uploaded and from which the files can be later removed. VWPs do not enter the master files to work with original client information. They work with copies controlled by the virtual firm owner. Upon receiving a completed work product from the VWP, the owner will ensure that the information is accurate and then can choose to overwrite her original information database with the revised information.

As to recording and tracking work in progress, the virtual owner using a centralized control system is more likely to piece out work in small steps and do all of the tracking of the finished product herself. For example, if a completed financial plan requires collecting data, inputting data, and producing the plan, the owner may parcel out each of these three steps individually to a VWP while holding herself responsible for getting back each on time so that the finished product conforms to the deadline she has communicated to the client.

At Sunset Financial Management, Inc., Dave uses a centralized system of control over client data. This is not to imply that he believes this is better than a decentralized system or doesn't trust his virtual partners; it is simply his preferred method of operating. Some of the types of interactions that occur between Dave and his VWPs under a centralized system are described in Chapter 1.

Whether you choose a decentralized or centralized model for managing client work flow, many of the tools and methods you employ with VWPs will be the same as you use in communicating with clients, as discussed in Chapter 7. Under both setups, you may use ASPs, intranets and other third-party domains will become essential, and security measures will be necessary. With file attachments, much of the information that needs to be shared in a collaborative arrangement with VWPs can be transmitted using e-mail. However, when collaboration involves three or more people, it is often a better solution to use a third-party domain. Different types of third-party domains are discussed later in this chapter.

Security Considerations for Advisers

WHEREAS BOTH SYSTEMS require tight security, the types of security required are different for each. A pull system (decentralized control) requires security measures to protect the domain into which clients and work partners are invited. Password protection and firewall systems (both hardware and software) are paramount. The push system (centralized control) relies more on encryption methods to protect the confidentiality of the client data. Both systems require effective antivirus protection.

Hardware Security Measures

Many computer users are under the mistaken impression that if they have antivirus software installed on their computers, they are protected; unfortunately, this is not the case. Viruses are only one threat that Internet users face. For financial professionals, the risk that a computer hacker might access confidential records is particularly frightening. Firewalls are designed to protect your data by preventing unauthorized access to your computer system over the Internet. Those who access the Internet over a connection with a static IP address (most broadband connections are over a static IP) are particularly vulnerable.

There are two types of firewalls: hardware and software. For all but the smallest firms, we recommend both a hardware and a software firewall. Here's why: software firewalls work well, but if you are in a networked environment, software protection doesn't begin until the hacker enters your network and reaches one of your computers. Hardware solutions give you added protection because they stop hackers before they enter your network.

Hardware firewall solutions. As recently as a few years ago, hardware firewalls for small businesses were relatively expensive and difficult to configure—but no longer. Symantec (the company that produces Norton software products) makes an affordable line of firewall/VPN appliances that are easy to install and set up. These devices include a network hub for plug-and-play local area network (LAN) capabilities, broadband connections (both cable and DSL), VPN access (so satellite offices or virtual workers can access the network), and, of course, a firewall. Their function is to connect all of the computers on your local area network while also providing protection for the entire network against hackers. The Symantec Firewall VPN 100 entry-level version (four LAN ports) can be found on sale for under $300.

Those willing to spend a bit more should check out the Symantec Firewall VPN 200R. This system includes eight LAN ports, unlimited use of Symantec's Enterprise VPN software (including software firewall protection), two ports for broadband Internet access (users should consider subscribing to two services for redundancy), a serial port for an "emergency" analog connection, and automatic load balancing of outgoing Internet traffic. The VPN 200R lists for $1,200 but can usually be found online for considerably less.

Hardware strategies. Sometimes a simple strategy will do the job of lots of expensive hardware. If it's practical, try this: Keep your primary server off the Web. Download files and e-mail to a moveable medium—such as tape, CD, or removable hard drive—on a secondary computer that is not networked to your primary server. Then scan the data for viruses and transfer the files to your primary server. It's a little more work, but very effective. Besides, you were wondering what to do with that old Pentium 90 computer, right?

U.are.U Personal—the answer to password failure. One type of hardware security breach comes from the Internet, which is why there are routers like the two Symantec products we just mentioned. Another type comes from the office intruder or visitor who would walk right up to your computer and test your password system.

Password security fails more often than you might think. The most secure passwords contain a random combination of numbers, letters, and symbols, but these types of passwords are difficult to remember. Computer users often take the path of least resistance, using their address, phone number, or name of a family member or pet as a password, making it easier to crack, especially for someone who knows anything about your practice and anyone working in it.

In a small office environment, wandering eyes can be a problem, as when passwords are jotted down on a Post-it note affixed to somebody's computer monitor. It should come as no surprise then that the 2000 CSI/FBI Survey reported that over 70 percent of break-ins occur internally.

One compelling new high-tech solution is biometrics, the identification of individuals by biological traits, such as fingerprints and face recognition or retinal and iris scanning. Until recently, the cost of a biometric security system has been prohibitive for all but the largest corporations and the government. DigitalPersona, Inc. of Redwood City, California has removed the financial hurdle with the introduction of U.are.U Personal for Windows XP, an inexpensive and elegant biometric package designed to control who can operate a given computer workstation.

The system consists of a small fingerprint reader, measuring roughly 2" x 2" x 1", and some software, which requires an Microsoft Windows XP Home or Professional operating system. XP must be configured for "Fast User Switching," and documentation that accompanies the device will guide you through the reconfiguration.

If you value design as well as function, you'll be happy to know that the sensor

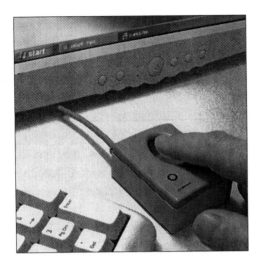

U.are.U's Fingerprint Reader

has been adapted as part of the permanent collection by the San Francisco Museum of Modern Art.

Installing the system is a snap. You log onto Windows XP, install the U.are.U Personal software, and plug the finger scanner into a USB port. Once the software and hardware are installed, a pop-up balloon and software "wizard" will prompt you to register your fingerprints.

Since Windows XP is designed to allow multiple users on a single PC, U.are.U Personal recognizes each additional user the first time they log in and prompts them to register their fingerprints and create a profile.

If U.are.U Personal did nothing more than provide a higher level of security in a small office environment, it would be worth buying, but it does much more. Since U.are.U Personal integrates with the Windows XP log-on and "Fast User Switching," users sharing a PC can instantly change from one account to another by applying a finger to the scanner, which elimi-

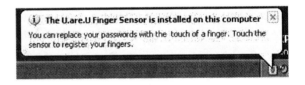

U.are.U's Fingerprint Registration Prompt

nates the need for password-driven log on and menu navigation. The advantage of separate profiles is that each user gets to maintain his or her customized desktop, icons, and other settings, facilitating maximum productivity.

More importantly, however, U.are.U Personal allows you to log onto password-protected websites with the touch of a finger. Active Web surfers typically end up with a large collection of hard-to-remember passwords, because different sites require different password conventions.

U.are.U's One Touch Internet eliminates password problems. You go to the site once, program your password and login name using the One Touch menu, and you're set up for future visits. Neither passwords nor special login procedures will again be required.

The next time you want to log on to the site, scan your finger and you're in. The program can add shortcuts to the One Touch menu for your favorite websites if you desire.

One Touch Internet is obviously a time saver for those of us who spend a lot of time on the Web, but it's also a great way to control employees' access to Web-based services. If you provide employees with a password, they can log on anytime from anywhere. With One Touch, you control the password, and you can limit their access to one computer in your office.

The program's One Touch Crypto feature enables the user to easily encrypt and decrypt sensitive files and folders using a fingerprint as the password. The program also includes a recovery utility to decrypt files should you need to access the file on another computer or uninstall the U.are.U software.

The only downside with the system relates to the One Touch Internet software. In order to

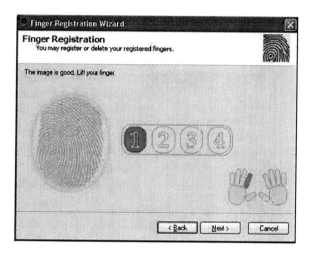

U.are.U's Fingerprint Registration Wizard
Screen #1

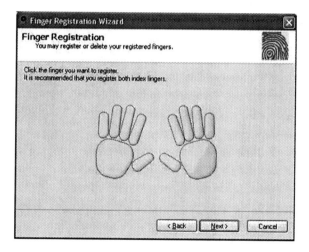

U.are.U's Fingerprint Registration Wizard
Screen #2

use it, every password-protected site must be programmed. One Touch is not capable of capturing your existing passwords already stored on your computer. Once we understood the process, it was not burdensome, but we had to read the instructions twice to get it right. We also think there is room for improvement with the Quicklinks feature. We'd like to have the ability to organize sites into folders and sub-folders.

U.are.U's One Touch Password
Replacement Function

Our overall impression of U.are.U Personal is highly favorable. We think it is a superb, easy-to-use security system and a great utility as well. We enthusiastically recommend it to all Windows XP users, and those organizations running workstations in a Windows NT or Windows 2000 environment should check out the U.are.U Pro Workstation package.

Software Security Systems

Software firewalls. All computers that access the Internet should have a software firewall installed, even those that are behind a hardware firewall on a company network. It is an unfortunate fact of life that many computer attacks come from within an organization. If you rely solely upon a hardware firewall, you leave yourself vulnerable to an attack from a disgruntled employee or anyone else who gains access to a computer on your network. Software firewalls can be configured to prevent those types of attacks by blocking others on the network from accessing individual machines that contain sensitive material.

For example, if you store nonsensitive data on one computer and client data on a different computer, you can create a rule that allows only the principals' computers to access by network the computer that contains sensitive data. Other computers in the office are blocked.

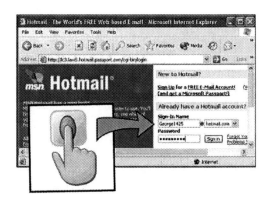

U.are.U Logging On
to an Internet Site

One standout in this product category that constantly garners praise from novice users and technology professionals alike is ZoneAlarm Pro (www.zonelabs.com). The software is easy to use, offers comprehensive protection, and is highly customizable.

Software products like Symantec Firewall (www.symantec.com) or McAfee Internet Security (www.mcafee.com) are also a fine choice for novices. From time to time, utility vendors offer package deals that are attractively priced. For example, when Joel upgraded to the latest version of Norton Utilities, a copy of Norton Personal Firewall was included at no additional charge.

Antivirus software. Every computer user should have an antivirus software program installed on every machine they own, but many don't. If you are one of the guilty parties, boot up your computer, access the Internet, navigate to www.panda software.com/activescan and bookmark the page. Through a service called Panda ActiveScan, this site provides free virus checks and repairs over the Internet without requiring the installation of additional software. We don't recommend using ActiveScan in lieu of antivirus software, but if you don't currently have any form of virus protection, it's a good stopgap measure. It is also a good backup to your primary antivirus defense system. Virus definitions are updated at least daily, so protection is always current.

For those of you who do have antivirus software installed, congratulations; but don't pat yourselves on the back just yet. Most programs from the major vendors, like Norton and McAfee, do a good job, but only if you update your virus definitions regularly.

ZoneAlarm Pro's Program
Configuration Screen

Most antivirus software programs allow you to schedule regular updates, but sometimes the time between updates becomes a window during which new viruses sneak into your computer. One solution is to schedule more frequent updates, another is to manually update whenever you hear about a new virus making the rounds, but perhaps the best solution is to purchase a program that automatically checks for updates every time you go online. One state-of-the-art program with this capability, as well as very good antivirus technology, is Panda

Antivirus Titanium, a more robust version of ActiveScan.

Antivirus programs as a category are highly effective, but nothing is foolproof; use a little common sense. If you receive an e-mail with a suspicious attachment from an unknown source, think twice. If you receive a file with an .EXE, .BAT, or .VBS extension, be suspicious—and check with the sender of the file before opening it.

Keep your software current. Hackers are adept at spotting vulnerabilities and exploiting them. They tend to target programs with the largest user base, such as Microsoft products. As vulnerabilities in programs are revealed, manufacturers release software patches. We recommend that you visit the Windows Update site (windowsupdate.microsoft.com) and the Microsoft Office Update site (www.office .microsoft.com/productupdates) often to make sure that you have the latest updates and fixes.

As for our software recommendations, Joel has used Norton Antivirus for many years, and he is very satisfied with it (bear in mind he updates definitions frequently). If you are constantly online and do not check for virus definition updates as often as you should, give Panda Antivirus Titanium a try. All of the antivirus products mentioned above sell for well under $100 in a single-user version, and enterprise pricing is available in most cases.

Antivirus strategies. Viruses often propagate through the use of e-mail. Some of the more malicious ones can take command of the host computer's address book and use it to spread the virus by sending a copy of the infected e-mail to every e-mail address in the book. The latest versions of antivirus software programs are starting to address this problem by enabling users to scan outgoing as well as incoming e-mails. Sometimes this capability is not part of the default installation and must be configured by the user. If your software is capable of scanning outgoing messages, be considerate of others and enable this feature. If not, we have another suggestion for you.

Create a bogus, invalid entry in your e-mail address book. It should start with a nonalphanumeric symbol, such as an exclamation point or a question mark. Replace the @ sign with a < (less than) sign.

A sample entry might look something like this: !catchthatvirus<now

As you are entering such an address in your e-mail program, you may get a warning telling you that you are about to enter an illegal or invalid address. You will be asked if you are sure you want to enter the address. Just reply that you do.

If a virus tries to send out e-mails using your address book, the first address it will attempt sending mail to will be the bogus entry because the nonalphanumeric character at the beginning of the address will keep it the first entry on the list. Depending on the e-mail server, one of two things will happen:

> All of the outgoing messages will be rejected, or
> The single bogus e-mail will be rejected.

In either case, you will be alerted to the fact that your computer is being used to attack others, and you can address the problem immediately.

Encryption Systems

Encryption can come in handy in the case of an office computer that many prying eyes have access to. If for some reason sensitive files must be stored on that machine, simple password protection may leave you feeling uneasy. Encryption can protect your data as it sits on your hard drive in exactly the same way it protects it during e-mail dissemination.

Encryption is also particularly useful in protecting the confidentiality of client data when the adviser disseminates those data by e-mail, Zip drive, or any other electronic format. E-mail messages more closely resemble postcards than letters. Anyone who can open them can read them. Encryption will scramble the characters in your e-mail into unrecognizable words and phrases. A password provided by the author of the e-mail will allow you to unscramble the letters and make sense of the message within the e-mail.

Readers who use McAfee Utilities already have a very good 256-bit encryption solution that goes by the name of Pretty Good Privacy (nicknamed "PGP"). This easy-to-use program can encrypt files, the contents of entire drives, and e-mails. PGP can also be used to e-mail self-decrypting files; just supply the recipient with a password. A stand-alone version of PGP Personal Security is available at the McAfee website (www.mcafee.com).

Our top recommendation for computer security, the U.are.U fingerprint recognition system discussed earlier in this chapter, includes 128-bit encryption as part of the package. In the case of U.are.U Personal, the encryption software, called One Touch Crypto, installs automatically during the default set-up process.

U.are.U Pro, designed for larger systems, includes encryption software called Private Space which does not install as part of the default set-up. Private Space works a little differently than One Touch Crypto, creating a private vault, or virtual drive, on a portion of your hard drive. To encrypt files, the user transfers them to the private vault.

If sending and receiving secure e-mail is your firm's primary concern, ZixMail, from ZixIt Corporation (www.zixit.com) may be the perfect solution. No special

ZixMail Home Page

software is required by the recipient to read an e-mail, and the service costs a reasonable $24 per year per e-mail address. A thirty-day free trial version is available at the ZixIt website.

Third-Party Domains

A THIRD-PARTY DOMAIN is a database of client information, needed to conduct one or more of the functions of the financial planning service, that exists on the website or server of an independent entity with which the virtual owner contracts for service. Third-party domains exist within both the centralized and decentralized frameworks. In any work system you adopt, you need to decide how much access to give employees and VWPs to client data maintained on third-party systems. There are three types of third-party domains: the custodian, the ASP, and the intranet/extranet.

Custodian Domains

Advisers who keep client assets with brokerage firms that cater to the adviser community, like Charles Schwab & Co., often have access to their clients' information on computers—or domains—maintained by the custodian. Schwab's institutional domain—www.schwabinstitutional.com—is an example. This domain incorporates those tools Schwab believes advisers should have to adequately protect their client information. If a third-party domain offers encryption, then encryption is available; if it doesn't, then it isn't. Schwab offers (a) password protection upon entering their domain, and (b) the ability to create "User Security Groups" to which you can assign different levels of permission to partners engaging in such tasks as accessing client account information, uploading trades, downloading file information, and uploading billing instructions.

The significance of third-party domains of this type is that they should be fully used in a virtual office environment for maximum efficiency. One of your VWPs

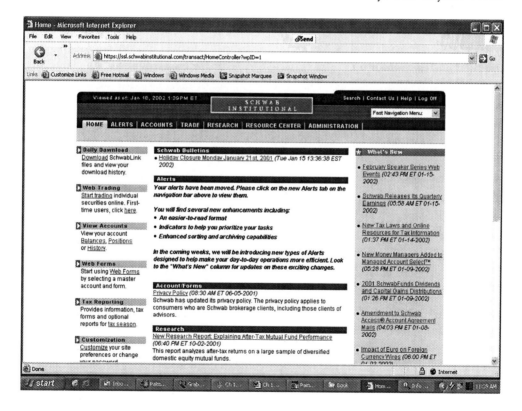

Charles Schwab & Co.'s Custodian Domain

may be a security trader or separate account manager. You will have a confidentiality agreement with this person or firm. At that point, it will be much more efficient to grant them direct access to your clients' Schwab database via www.schwab institutional.com than to act as a filter for this information.

Different VWPs may be granted different forms of access. For example, in Dave's firm, his virtual trader can view client accounts and upload trades, his account administrator cannot trade but can upload billing instructions, and his virtual planner can view client accounts but neither trade nor upload files. They don't need Dave's permission each time they perform one of these tasks for a client because he has already given it by the manner in which he assigned each of them access privileges on the "Administration" section of Schwab's website.

Application Service Provider (ASP) Domains

Application Service Providers provide a way for virtual firm owners, work partners, and clients to collaborate on a work product. Financeware.com, discussed in Chapter 7, is an example of this type of ASP. An ASP like a third-party domain is a software program that is run from the Internet rather than from any individual's computer or computer network. It is a website controlled by its owner and "leased" to the virtual planner, his VWPs and, sometimes, the firm's clients. By its use, it becomes a repository for certain client information that might otherwise be stored on the virtual owner's server in his headquarters office. By choosing to locate this information on an ASP, the owner is making a choice to use the collaboration technology offered by the ASP and sees the advantages of doing so as outweighing the disadvantages of not having more immediate control over the client data.

Intranet/Extranet Domains

Third-party domains also exist in the form of independent websites that can be leased and used as collaborative tools. These are more free-form than either custodian domains or ASP domains. Custodian and ASP domains exist for a specific purpose. Intranet/extranet domains exist for whatever purpose the virtual owner wants to use them. These services are offered in the form of websites to which you can invite members—VWPs, clients, or other professionals—to come and share information. The information may be shared by way of e-mail addresses sponsored by the intranet/extranet site, by file uploads to and downloads from the site, by instant messaging if the site offers that feature, or any of a number of other tools common to these sites.

Permissions can often be fine-tuned, allowing, for example, either groups or individuals to have no access to one or more areas of the site, read-only access, read-and-modify access, or full management (administrator) access. Some sites extend this type of hierarchical permission scheme down to individual elements of the site; for example, specific documents. With this level of control, a virtual owner can finely tune an intranet/extranet to meet many of the firm's collaboration needs.

Your authors practice what we preach. Dave lives in New Mexico, and Joel lives in Florida. Both travel often. We decided that the best way to collaborate on this book is through the use of an intranet. We selected Intranets.com as our ASP because Dave was already using it for other ventures he participates in. Intranets.com allows us to store and share documents in a central location. We set up a folder called "The Book" and populated the folder with sub-folders for each chapter as it was written. A sub-folder could contain, for example, a chapter outline, graphics associated with the chapter, and the chapter text itself. We could go back and forth working on different chapters using Microsoft Word, and could store multiple versions of a chapter, when desired, to better track changes.

Intranets.com allows us to use Web Folders, a capability built into the Windows 98, ME, and XP operating systems. By using Web Folders, the online files and folders appear integrated with our desktop. We click an icon on our desktop called My Network Places (or "Web Folders" in Windows 98), and our computers link to our folders online. From there, we can view a directory tree similar to the one used in Windows Explorer. Files can be uploaded to the site by dragging and dropping, just as if you were working on your own computer.

Intranets.com offers a host of other features. It allows users to maintain a group calendar for tracking appointments, meetings, and deadlines. Contact lists can be maintained, and they can be synchronized with handheld devices and with Microsoft Outlook. Larger groups may want to post announcements, enable private discussion boards, instant-message one another, poll members, or e-mail each other at the group's intranet site. Members can track tasks, submit expense reports, and share links to other websites with group members. As of this writing, Intranets.com charges a base fee for five members on a site of $29.95 a month plus $5.95 a month for each additional member. A significant break point occurs in its pricing for more than ten and fewer than twenty-six members. A user can have as many as twenty-five members on his site for a fixed rate of $99.95 a month. This limit will accommodate most independent planners, their staff, their VWPs, and other professionals they choose to invite to their site. Based on the suite of services offered, the functionality of the site, and the price they are currently charging, we consider it a bargain. *Forbes* magazine apparently agrees with us. In their Spring 2002 edition of *Forbes ASAP,* they designated Intranets.com a *"Forbes Favorite."*

Intranets.com is not the only service of its kind, and it's not the cheapest. There are some similar, advertiser-supported services that are actually free. One of the best known is Yahoo! Groups. Yahoo! can do much of what Intranets.com can do, but not everything. Yahoo!'s functionality and layout are OK, but we think Intranets.com is better. The utility of Web Folders, which we were only able to use with Intranets.com and not with Yahoo!, is a big plus. We also found Intranet.com's documentation, help, and support superior, so we think it is a good choice for business-related tasks.

That's not to say that you shouldn't use Yahoo!. We think Yahoo! works fine for discussion groups and other noncritical tasks. Both authors belong to a virtual study group that is hosted on Yahoo!, and it works well. The price is certainly right!

If the idea of online collaboration appeals to you, you may want to take the concept farther. Wouldn't it be great if an ASP offered an intranet with additional functionality, such as a financial planning program, presentation tools, a library of articles, account aggregation, and other tools all in one place? Actually, somebody already does. Collaborate! Financial (www.collaboratefinancial.com) offers an intranet with features similar to those offered by Yahoo! and Intranets.com, and it adds the option of subscribing to an online version of the high-quality financial planning program NaviPlan, a financial planning database and presentation tool called ForeMost Advice, and an account aggregation tool and bill-paying service called OnMoneyAdviser. Varying levels of access can be granted to planners, administrators, other advisers, and clients.

If you use all of Collaborate! Financial's functionality and pay annually to take advantage of volume discounts, its four service plans will run you from $550 to $1,800 a year.

Collaborate! Financial may be what you are looking for, but we don't mean to suggest that is the perfect solution, or even an appropriate solution, for everyone. Collaborate! Financial is, however, a good example of how one can construct a virtual work environment that meets the specific needs of financial professionals.

Virtual Private Networks (VPNs)

HOW YOU SHOULD COLLABORATE over the Web depends on what you are trying to accomplish. To simply share short documents that you have prepared with others, e-mail works fine, but perhaps you need more. Some e-mail services limit the size of e-mail files, and these days many are hesitant to open attachments.

If you are collaborating with others on a large document, right away e-mail has limitations. One person works on a document and sends it to another person. That person makes changes and sends it back. Who is responsible for storing the master document, and how do all members of the group access it in a timely fashion?

Our conversations with advisers around the country indicate that a portion of the financial planning community is very resistant to the ASP model. The reasons most often cited for this holding back are security concerns and skepticism about the financial viability of ASP providers.

One way to address these concerns is to set up your own virtual private network. That might sound difficult and expensive, but if your requirements are limited to

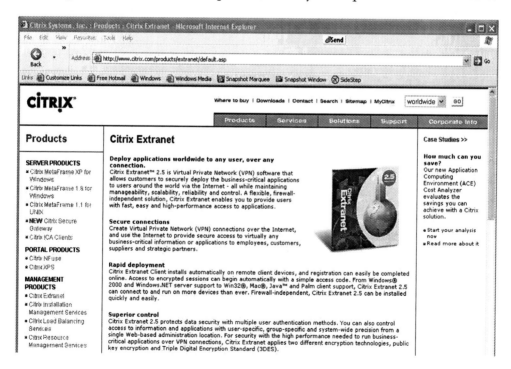

Citrix Extranet

document sharing and management, group calendars, secure bulletin boards, company directories, and the like, you might want to purchase an "intranet in a box" like IntraSmart by Mindbridge, Inc. (www.mindbridge.com) for a one-time fee of $65 per seat and maintenance and tech support at $13 per user per year. This type of program is designed to set up very quickly, with a minimum of installation or configuration headaches. Paired with an inexpensive server and a reasonably fast Internet connection, "intranet in a box" solutions represent an alternative to ASP solutions that allow you to control your data and security.

For more demanding jobs, like sharing multiple applications over a virtual private network, a more sophisticated software platform may be required. When Tom Batterman and his partners at Vigil Trust & Financial Advocacy in Wausau, Wisconsin established the National Independent Trust Company (www.nitco.org), they needed a platform that would allow affiliates throughout the country to access their back office software, which is physically located in Louisiana. Looking to the future, they wanted a system that was scalable, allowing them to add additional software applications and additional users to the network as needed. National Independent Trust Company selected a platform provided by Citrix Systems, Inc. (www.citrix.com) because it provided them with the functionality and the scalability they required.

Virtual Networks via Microsoft SharePoint

IF YOU ARE INTERESTED in online collaboration, and you haven't yet upgraded to Microsoft Office XP, perhaps you should. SharePoint Technologies from Microsoft extends the functionality of your intranet or virtual private network to a new level, but to take full advantage of its capabilities, you need Microsoft Office XP. SharePoint is a set of Web extensions that can be installed on a Web server to add additional collaboration tools and other features that were not readily available to nonprogrammers before. In addition to sharing folders and documents, SharePoint lets you create, edit, and exchange other kinds of information, such as contact lists and calendars, between a website and Office XP applications.

Microsoft offers two versions of SharePoint Technologies: SharePoint Team Services and SharePoint Portal Server. According to Microsoft, SharePoint Team Services are appropriate for workgroups of up to seventy-five people. A SharePoint Team Services site can be implemented in one of two ways: through the use of a type of ASP known as a WPP (Web Presence Provider) or by installing SharePoint on your own server. To find a WPP that offers SharePoint Team Services, visit

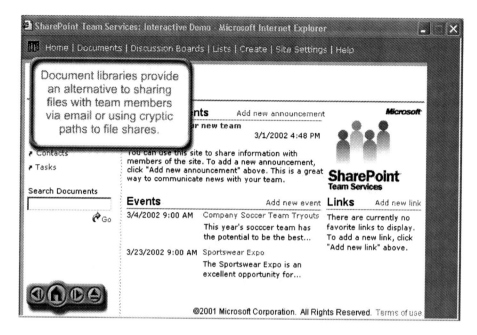

SharePoint Demo Screen

www.bcentral.com/services/sp/default.asp. If you choose to install SharePoint on your own server, you'll need a copy of Microsoft FrontPage 2002 or a version of Microsoft Office XP that includes FrontPage (Professional Special Edition or Developer).

To make use of SharePoint Team services through an ASP, the minimum required is a Web browser or Office XP, but to really benefit from what SharePoint has to offer Office XP is recommended (although many collaboration features will work with Office 97 or later). Microsoft recommends running Office XP on a Pentium III processor, or better. As for operating systems, Windows 98, Windows ME, Windows NT 4 with service pack 6.0 or later, Windows 2000, and Windows XP all work, but the more recent the operating system, the more satisfactory your experience is likely to be.

Here are some of the things you can do with a SharePoint Team site:

Create a document library. This feature is available using Web Folders, but SharePoint members using Microsoft Office XP can work on SharePoint documents from right within their Office application. Document libraries can be created for virtual workers, clients, etc., with you controlling who can access what.

Share templates. Team templates ease collaboration and add a professional, uniform look. Templates can easily be added to the document library. Once uploaded, team members can create new documents using them. Office XP users can launch the templates right from their Office application by going to the file menu and selecting the Templates on My Web Sites command. If you intend to employ multiple VWPs, you can ensure that all of them are using the latest copies of your forms and stationery by posting team templates and updating them regularly.

Create lists. Lists can be created for contacts, events, and tasks. For example, you can share client contact information with and assign tasks to VWPs, or list upcoming live Web events for clients.

Discuss an online document. Sometimes you will want to comment on a document without changing the document itself. Web discussions allow you to do so. Let's say a client wants you to review a trust document. You could upload the document, note areas of concern, and invite the client to review your notes. Perhaps you suggest that the client use a customized beneficiary designation for their IRA. You could invite the client's attorney to post the document for review by you and your client. Everyone has immediate access, and notes can be made without altering the attorney's draft.

Be alerted to changes. By subscribing to document libraries, discussions, or lists, you will be alerted by e-mail when the area you subscribe to changes. For example, you could subscribe to the contacts list to be notified whenever a contact is added, deleted, or changed. If you set up libraries for your VWPs, you can chose to be notified whenever they upload something to a client file. Users can control the frequency of notification.

Survey team members. Find out what members are thinking by creating surveys. Survey your clients to understand how they use your virtual services. What works? What doesn't? Is there anything you can do to improve the delivery of your services?

Customize the home page. Changing the layout of a home page is as simple as dragging and dropping components. This means you can start out slowly and add additional components, like live scheduling, as you progress through your virtual transition.

Refine your customization. The view feature allows you to further customize your pages. Columns can be adjusted and filters can be modified, for example.

Should you decide to go with an ASP model, much of the SharePoint functionality will be available whether you use Office XP or not. The advantage of using Office XP is that it provides a high level of integration with Office XP applications. When using an ASP provider, FrontPage is not required either, although, again, making use of FrontPage expands SharePoint's capabilities. FrontPage provides the ability to further customize a SharePoint site, such as adding graphics and applying "themes".

The server version of SharePoint Team Services is designed to establish a fully functional, formatted website right out of the box. Most current generation servers should be able to run the software without problems, but we suggest you check at www.microsoft.com/frontpage/sharepoint/sysreqs.htm to ensure compatibility. To

Remote Access

IT NEVER FAILS! You're out of the office (or home office) and suddenly you discover you forgot to load a critical file onto your laptop. Windows XP Professional now offers a remote utility that may help, but we suggest you spend a few dollars and try out one of the two programs described below.

Those needing to transfer multiple files on a regular basis should check out Symantec's pcAnywhere. pcAnywhere requires patience to install and configure, and the software must be installed on both the host and the remote machines, but it offers enhanced features such as AutoTransfer, which totally automate the file transfer process.

For elegant simplicity, GoToMyPC is tops. Register online, download the host software, and you're ready to go. When you are away from the host computer, log on to the GoToMyPC website, and a self-launching browser plug in allows you to see the host computer over a secure, 128-bit encrypted connection. Need to print something from your host computer? Not a problem, says Jeffrey N. Mehler, CFP, a fee-only planner practicing in Centerbrook, Connecticut. If the computer you are working from has a printer attached, GoToMyPC will load the print driver onto the host PC and print the files you need, he says.

GoToMyPC does not offer the level of automation and customization provided by pcAnywhere, but its ease of use, combined with its collaborative potential, make it a compelling choice for the small to medium-sized financial planning firm. Service for one host runs $119.40 per year. Sign up your home and office PCs for $179.40 annually. Corporate plans, which provide centralized management and administration, are also available.

GoToMyPC as a Collaboration Tool

MOST PEOPLE WHO KNOW GoToMyPC think of it as an alternative to pcAnywhere, a program designed to allow users to access their own computer from a remote location. Jeffrey Mehler tipped us off to a second, more potent use of the program. Jeff uses GoToMyPC as a collaborative tool.

Jeff e-mails clients an invitation to join him on his desktop. The invitation includes a hyperlink, where the client can download an applet that enables the session. Once the download is completed, which takes a matter of seconds, the client can view Jeff's computer screen as if he or she were in Jeff's office. For virtual client meetings, the visitor is placed in the view-only mode, although visitors can be granted full access (as might be appropriate in the case of a virtual assistant, for example).

Since all of Jeff's files are in digital format, primarily in PaperPort, Jeff can display financial plans, performance reports, and other documents to the client in real time. Jeff can use PaperPort's tools to highlight passages, add virtual sticky notes, or otherwise modify the document as a conversation takes place.

run the software on your own server, Microsoft Windows 2000 Server (or later) is required, as is Microsoft Office 2000 (or later) and Microsoft Data Engine (MSDE) or Microsoft SQL Server 7.0 (or later).

SharePoint Portal Server is an Enterprise solution designed for large workgroups of seventy-five or more. It is feature rich and powerful, but it is beyond the scope of our discussion. For further information about SharePoint Portal Server, visit www.microsoft.com/sharepoint/portalserver.asp.

We are well aware that the needs of our readers vary tremendously. It is impossible for us to suggest the best possible solution for each and every one of you. We can suggest that collaboration over the Web with clients, colleagues, and/or affiliated professionals may improve your efficiency and lower your cost of doing business. This is an area where a small time investment investigating an unfamiliar technology could pay substantial dividends.

In conjunction with an intranet, one might use a Microsoft utility called "Web Folders." A Web folder is a file transfer protocol that supports secure file transfers over the Internet. You can upload, download, and manage files on a remote com-

If, during the course of the conversation, the client has a question, Jeff can access a library of documents within PaperPort to illustrate a point. For example, if a client has a question about estate planning, Jeff can pull up a flow chart and walk a client through various options. If a client wants to open a new account for a child, Jeff can load an account application stored in PaperPort and fill out the application using PaperPort's form-filling tool as the client provides the information over the telephone. The client can view and proofread the information as it is typed in, eliminating data-entry errors.

Jeff has nothing but praise for GoToMyPC. "It passes the 'anybody-can-afford-it test,'" he says, adding, "I have never had it fail. It worked through every firewall, even those of the largest corporations."

Bottom line: GoToMyPC is an affordable tool that empowers advisers to conduct virtual meetings. It can also be used to allow virtual workers access to your system. And by the way, you can use it to access your files when you are on the road as well.

puter. Let's say you've created an intranet at www.intranets.com and, within the site, have created a folder of documents that you are sharing with a particular VWP. In order to modify a document, you or your VWP would ordinarily point your browser toward the website, sign in using your I.D. and password, go to the folder, download the document, open it on your computer, make modifications, save the document on your computer, go back to the intranet, delete the old document, and upload the new one with the modifications you made.

With Web Folders set up on your computer, you need only go to a separate directory on your hard drive or local server, click on the document name, make your modifications, and save the document. When you follow these steps, you are automatically downloading the document and later uploading it with the changes you made. There is no longer any need for the intermediate steps of going to the intranet via browser, etc.

Being Minus Paper Is a Plus

WHETHER YOU ARE MANAGING client work flow in a virtual firm or in a traditional firm, technology plays a key role. It's a worldwide phenomenon that internal office e-mail is replacing standing around the water cooler and shooting the breeze about the latest stock market trend. External e-mail is replacing phone calls and, in some cases, meetings. This shift is more pronounced, however, in the virtual firm than it is in the traditional one.

One reason is that VWPs are often geographically widespread. At the time of this writing, Sunset Financial Management, Inc.'s virtual assistant is located in Akron, Ohio, its virtual planner is in Silver Spring, Maryland, its webmaster (AdvisorSites) is in Syosset, New York, its Centerpiece reporting company is in Vista, California, and its account administrator is in Rockville, Maryland. (The functions of each of these types of VWP are discussed in Chapter 8.) We cannot easily convene a face-to-face meeting, either one-on-one or as a group. But we can communicate quite effectively using the tools discussed earlier in this chapter.

Here again you can see why a paperless office is so critical. If the virtual owner and his VWPs had to rely on U.S. mail, they would be at a disadvantage to the traditional firm where paper records can easily be passed from one office to another. But through the use of digitalized tax returns and attaching financial plans to e-mails, the balance of power shifts to favor the owner who can best master the technology and the techniques of virtual operations.

Case Study: Carolyn Sechler, CPA

A GOOD EXAMPLE of a professional using VWPs is Carolyn Sechler, CPA, with a very successful accounting practice in Phoenix, Arizona—Carolyn Sechler CPA PC (www.azcpa.com). Describing her virtual workforce, Sechler says "There are sixteen of us; I employ three, and the rest are independent contractors." Sechler's clients are internationally dispersed, and her VWPs are in six states and Canada.

Like Dave, Sechler uses a centralized system of controlling work flow. "I get about three hundred e-mails a day," says Sechler, adding, "I'm traffic control. I've had other setups in the past where phone calls didn't go to me, but clients have comfort reaching me, and I'm trying to avoid the large-firm issue where clients felt they were being passed off to a new guy."

Perhaps because she gets a lot of public exposure through her writing (she's an editorial adviser to the *Journal of Accountancy*), Sechler claims that, when it comes to finding VWPs, "I've never recruited anyone, they've just shown up. I don't have to sell either clients or virtuals on the concept." Sechler also gets clients from her website, from speeches, and from a few companies she runs that develop software and tools for clients.

Of her sixteen VWPs, eight are CPAs, six are bookkeepers, one is a full-time employee who serves as Sechler's business manager and supervises her bookkeepers, and one is a part-time employee doing bookkeeping and bookkeeper training. Sechler's CPAs each have a special expertise and his or her own practice because, says Sechler, "I believe that for this [system] to be successful, [my VWPs] must be entrepreneurial."

Because her system of working with her VWPs is centralized, Sechler needs a way to share work with them. Says Sechler, "We use a system of file cabinets on Yahoo! Groups. I have [VWPs] with different levels of ability in technology, and Yahoo! Groups allows me to create folders for each person on the team and upload standard forms for everyone's use."

One of Sechler's VWP bookkeepers is Annette Louise Peugh, also of Phoenix, Arizona. Peugh worked for seventeen years as an office manager at the United Association Plumbers, Steamfitters & Refrigeration Local Union #469, quitting when her first child came along and needed special attention. At that point, she and her husband joined in operating their own water treatment business from their home but gave it up after three years after her husband suffered a neck injury. They sold their business and spent their time caring for their children; then, after two more years, Peugh started going on job interviews.

"I received several job offers and turned every one of them down. There was no amount of money or benefits that could lure me back into a big office again. I was so stress-free that I suddenly realized just how physically and mentally sick office politics had made me before I quit," she says. "One of my strong points was always bookkeeping. My mother introduced me to Carolyn [Sechler], who operated her CPA firm from her home and was always looking for bookkeepers."

Describing her working relationship with Sechler, Peugh says, "I am an independent contractor, not an employee of Sechler CPA. Carolyn refers two types of work to me—her clients that need bookkeeping work done through her firm, and clients that are hers but whom I bill directly. Those that I bill directly are charged a higher rate than those that I bill through Carolyn. For instance: My rate through Carolyn is $15 to $20 per hour, when I bill the client directly, my rate is $20 to $35 per hour."

Sechler gets Peugh the information she needs on her clients in a variety of forms, sometimes paper—files, bank statements, etc.—and other times, client information that can be sent via e-mail. "I do my work on QuickBooks, then upload the data file to Yahoo! where Carolyn can pick it up and review it," says Peugh. If the work was given to Peugh in paper form, she delivers it back to Sechler; otherwise, it's e-mailed back. For day-to-day communications, Peugh says she and Sechler will use a live chat program, e-mail, or "last resort, we'll use the phone."

The point of Carolyn Sechler's story is that she has a top-notch reputation in the accounting community and a thriving practice, and she's doing it all with a fully virtual firm.

Case Study: Brian Wruk, M.B.A., CFP

UNLIKE CAROLYN SECHLER, Brian Wruk is fairly new in business. That gives him an advantage in using virtual office processes: he doesn't have to undo any mistakes. Wruk owns Transition Financial Advisors, Inc. in Gilbert, Arizona. His niche is working with Canadians moving to the United States.

"I look at the virtual office two ways," says Wruk: "One, a 'resource gatherer,' a way to combine the services of immigration attorneys, CPAs, estate planning attorneys and investment folks on both sides of the border, without having to bring them in-house." In fact, Kathleen Day's firm serves as Wruk's back office and investment manager. "I develop the Investment Policy Statement with my client and then hand him off to Kathleen's firm," says Wruk.

Secondarily, Wruk views the virtual office as the ability to leave home and go anywhere, to design a lifestyle and build a practice around it. "I'm a dual Canadian-U.S. citizen and have family in Canada, so I'd like to spend three to four months a year there," says Wruk. "I need to be able to relocate my office to Canada periodically."

Wruk used the services of Trumpet Inc. (discussed in Chapter 4) to set him up with a Visioneer One-Touch scanner and Paperport software, and he has been scanning all his documents from day one. He finds high-speed Internet access a must, and he has a server in his home, along with a laptop and his main workstation. As for his other office configurations, Wruk says, "I fax from the desktop, have no copier or fax machine, and have both a Hewlett Packard laser printer and Canon inkjet printer." Eventually he'll consolidate to one color laser printer.

Both Sechler and Wruk offer a glimpse into companies that are largely based upon nontraditional, virtual systems.

Chapter Ten

Managing Information about Your Clients

P APERLESS TECHNOLOGY and outsourcing opportunities will increase your efficiency tremendously. However, you still need a way to deal with all the minutiae that are left over—the many details about your clients and your business that originate in daily phone calls, meetings, and other interactions that are essential to your building a successful relationship with them. In this chapter we discuss the systems available to you to put these thousands of details right at your fingertips.

Software for Managing the Client Relationship

THE SOFTWARE AVAILABLE to help you manage your interactions with clients ranges from very simple to very sophisticated, but all products in this category are designed to do three things for you:

1 Store information
2 Organize information
3 Retrieve the information when you need it

Why is this type of software so important? Because our business is a people business, first and foremost. Many successful planners we come in contact with attribute their success primarily to the relationship they have with their clients, not to the quality of their financial plans or the precision of their optimizers.

Strong client relationships are built on a foundation of mutual trust and respect. One characteristic that will weigh heavily in the way clients evaluate you is your organizational skill. If you seem always to have good information at the ready and can field client questions in a timely manner, you earn trust. If you remember client birthdays, the names of grandchildren, and the upcoming and ongoing events in their lives, you solidify the relationship. So there is a lot more than efficiency at stake in having your information organized in such a way that you can find the information you need when you need it.

The type of information you store and manage will depend on the nature of your business but will likely include most of the following:

➢ Client contact information
➢ Client documents (contracts, account applications, wills)
➢ Letters
➢ Reports (investment policy statements, financial plans, and research bulletins)
➢ Important dates and account numbers
➢ Agendas
➢ Client-related tasks assigned to in-house employees or virtual assistants
➢ Notes

If offered a choice, most planners would like to be able to run their whole office from one application or one suite of applications that work seamlessly together. Unfortunately, for many of us no one-stop solution exists yet, even though the industry is moving in that direction. Until more integrated solutions become available, independent software applications that specialize in solutions for distinct practice needs will be your answer.

As a practical matter, when it comes to the trivia we all must deal with, most planners think, and therefore organize their records, in a client-centric fashion. That's why the software you pick to manage client relationships is one of the most critical software decisions you make.

A good contact manager can help you

➢ Organize and maintain client records
➢ Schedule appointments
➢ Enter, track, prioritize, and assign tasks
➢ Communicate effectively
➢ Prospect (and track results)
➢ Save money
➢ Find what you need when you don't have time to hunt for it

Let's take a look at each of these in turn.

Organizing and Maintaining Client Records

YEARS AGO THERE WAS A CLEAR DISTINCTION between personal information managers (PIMs) and contact management software (CMS). PIMs were basically electronic Rolodexes that stored names, addresses, and phone numbers, and offered a calendar as well. Contact management software did all of the above and was capable of tracking phone calls, letters, schedules, and tasks, too. Business people tended to use CMS, but there were constant complaints:

➤ Software often wasn't able to communicate with other programs (word processors, e-mail programs, and database software, for example)
➤ The structure was rigid (limited customization)
➤ Search capabilities were limited
➤ It was often difficult to move information into or out of a program because of proprietary formats

The picture is brighter today. Programs generally communicate well, and many offer a useful degree of customization. Search capabilities are much improved, as are import/export functions.

With full-featured programs affordable by even the smallest firms, it's difficult to argue that you should make do with less. However, some readers may not understand what these programs can and cannot do. It's also worth pointing out that a program poorly suited to act as your primary client management system might serve very nicely in a supporting role.

Let's take a look at some programs practitioners might encounter in their search for a tool to improve client interactions:

➤ *Microsoft Outlook Express.* An e-mail program that includes an address book
➤ *Franklin Planner.* A hybrid product that combines a PIM with additional functionality
➤ *Microsoft Outlook and ACT!* Full-featured, off-the-shelf contact management programs
➤ *ProTracker and Junxure*. Industry-specific programs

Microsoft Outlook Express

You are probably familiar with Microsoft Outlook Express, which comes bundled with Microsoft Internet Explorer. It is primarily designed to be an e-mail and newsgroup reader, but it does contain an address book that allows you to track contact information and limited personal information, such as names of spouses and children and birthdays. Outlook Express's search capabilities are fairly basic. The address book provides a space to enter contact notes, primarily a storage space for small amounts of uncategorized, miscellaneous information. Customization is limited, and you can't link information to contacts.

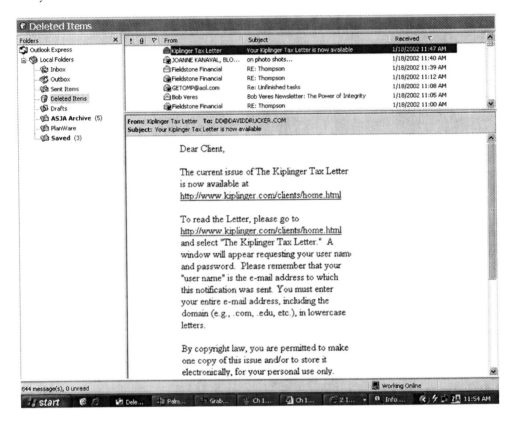

The Deleted Files Screen from Outlook Express

We are not knocking Microsoft Outlook Express. It was designed for a simple task and does it quite well. It can store, organize, and retrieve both basic contact information and e-mails. It is widely installed, and it's available for free.

Advantages
➢ Very good e-mail capabilities
➢ Very good newsgroup reader
➢ Good basic electronic address book

Disadvantages
➤ Outlook Express doesn't do much more than what's listed above.

Outlook Express is well-suited for
➤ Storing basic client contact information at home or when you are on the road
➤ Sending and receiving e-mail from office, home, or on the road
➤ Reading newsgroup messages

It may be all you need on your home computer or a light notebook that you take on business trips. It can help you keep up with your electronic correspondence, and it can store contact information, but that's about it. We don't suggest that you use Outlook Express as your primary program for client management.

Franklin Planner

The Franklin Planner is a niche product. Viewed strictly as a PIM, it does a good job, but there are more compelling choices for advisers whose needs exceed the capabilities of any Personal Information Manager. However, Franklin Planner may be just the ticket if you have trouble rationalizing your life, defining your mission, or prioritizing your tasks, and if you are familiar with FranklinCovey methodology and like it.

Many of us don't take the time to stop and think about missions and priorities and balancing work with family life, let alone get things done. Those of us who fall into this trap derive less satisfaction from our professional and personal lives than we should. Perhaps that's why Steven Covey's books, such as *The 7 Habits of Highly Effective People* (Simon & Schuster, 1990), and Franklin Covey's "What *Matters Most*" seminars are so popular. They provide disorganized souls with a framework to get on track. The software is really a PIM combined with organizational tools. It is not a true CMS, but it does possess a few key advantages that may appeal to you.

What really sets Franklin Planner apart is its ability to help you determine your values, examine the various roles you play in other people's lives, construct a personal mission statement, and plan your days accordingly. In its simplest form, Franklin divides planning into three phases: Discover (what's important to you), Plan (set long-term and intermediate goals), and Act (plan your day and complete the tasks). The program contains a number of wizards that walk you through these processes. Once the wizard-generated exercises are completed, tasks have been prioritized based on the framework you have created.

We often hear that financial planners are so involved with ordering their clients' lives that they do not devote sufficient time to addressing their own personal and business goals. If you find yourself falling into this all-too-common trap, using Franklin Planner may help you, although it may be more appropriate to use this product as a supplement to, as opposed to a replacement for, a CMS.

Another advantage of this program is that it is designed to work with other Franklin products. If you are using a paper-based Franklin planning system, this PIM is a strong companion. Franklin software can even be synchronized with hand-held devices using the Palm operating system, which makes it a handy way to take client information on the road with you.

An add-on program, Franklin Planner Handheld Suite, provides additional functionality for both Palm and Pocket PC systems. It includes the utilities Key Information, FileLocator, and EZ-Convert. Key Information lets you systematically enter and retrieve personal medical and financial information about you and others. FileLocator allows you to create a catalog of where you have stored articles, documents, and notes. EZ-Convert is a weight and measurement conversion calculator. You also get electronic editions of some FranklinCovey publications formatted for downloading to a handheld device.

One interesting feature of this program is the Information Manager. It contains something called Turbo Files, which allows you to quickly track various bits of information such as the title and date of a newspaper article, the location of documents, etc. Turbo File allows the user to enter a description, keywords, location, category, type, and date entered. You could use this feature to track where clients store their original documents so that, if a tragedy struck one of your clients, you could help the spouse locate all necessary documents in a hurry.

A Quotes module lets you track any interesting quotes. The quotes can be categorized, and they can be indexed by keyword. For those of you who speak publicly or write on a regular basis, the utility of this module is readily apparent.

Information Manager provides Journal and Notes for entering various types of text. For some inexplicable reason, Journal entries can only be assigned a date, whereas Notes only can be assigned a description and a category. Both would be more useful if they offered all of the index fields that Turbo File offers.

Advantages
➢ Good basic PIM functions
➢ Particularly helpful for prioritizing
➢ Some nice organizational tools

Disadvantages
➤ Not a full-fledged CMS
➤ Limited customization

Franklin Planner is well-suited for
➤ Organizing your personal life
➤ Prioritizing personal and professional goals and tasks
➤ Storing client contact information at home or on the road

Microsoft Outlook 2002

Many Microsoft Office users are familiar with Outlook, and it's probably fair to say that users of previous versions had plenty to complain about. Outlook's e-mail capabilities were inferior in many ways to Microsoft's free e-mail program, Microsoft Outlook Express; security was poor; and the overall feature set trailed popular third-party programs by a wide margin.

With the release of Outlook 2002, part of Microsoft's Office XP, Microsoft has narrowed the gap in a number of areas. Microsoft Outlook is now a full-featured CMS suitable for individuals or workgroups. For those of you unfamiliar with the program, Microsoft Outlook is designed to help you

➤ Store contact information
➤ Create and maintain a personal calendar
➤ Schedule and track appointments
➤ Manage tasks and track projects
➤ Send receive and file e-mail
➤ Keep a journal
➤ Access the Internet from within Outlook

Microsoft Outlook 2002 has one thing going for it that other programs don't: more compatibility with other Microsoft products. In the past, Microsoft didn't exploit this advantage much, but things are starting to change. Outlook 2002 users will benefit from new Microsoft Office suite-wide enhancements, such as a better clipboard that can store and display up to twenty-four items, the "ask a question box" that provides help in a hurry, and speech recognition, allowing you to dictate and issue commands to Office programs.

Microsoft Office 2002 contains a long list of program-specific improvements to make your life easier:

Tracking appointments with Calendar. Microsoft has made numerous improvements to the Calendar, many of them targeted at workgroups. For example, previously, when a group member proposed a time for a meeting, the only available replies were to accept or decline. It is now possible to suggest an alternate meeting time. Another new feature is the Internet Free/Busy Service. This lets users publish a list of their free time to other workgroup members on the Web, so that coordinating group activities becomes easier. The improved calendar makes it much easier to coordinate tasks with VWPs and assistants. It also means you can schedule meetings with clients and coworkers virtually, even when you are out of the office.

Keeping better records with Journal. The Journal can be a powerful tool for financial planners. Once the Journal is activated, Outlook will record any document you create, edit, or print in an Office XP application. It will keep a record of e-mails, meeting requests, and task requests. You can also manually save items that are created, modified, or printed in any Office application by dragging them onto the Journal icon. Journal entries can contain additional file information, including category and client. The more data you provide, the easier the retrieval process will be.

Other types of files can be entered in the Journal, but the process is more complicated. First, you navigate to the My Computer icon by clicking on the Other Shortcuts bar, then locate the file you need in the directory tree. Click on the My Shortcuts bar and the Journal icon will appear. Drag the file onto the Journal icon and the Journal entry form appears. Enter any information you wish, then click Save and Close. If you need to find something at a future date, you can view Journal entries by contact, category, date, or type. Assuming the journal entry contains the necessary information, Journal's capabilities allow the planner to keep good records for both client service and compliance purposes; but the process is not intuitive, and the program is not optimized specifically for use by planners.

Using e-mail effectively. Some long-overdue improvements have been made to Microsoft Outlook's e-mail capabilities. Configuring e-mail accounts is simpler and more intuitive. AutoComplete, a feature available in Microsoft Word and Microsoft Internet Explorer for some time, has finally made its way into Outlook 2002, cutting down on keystrokes. Type the first few letters of an addressee's name into an outgoing message, and AutoComplete will fill in the remainder for you.

Word is now the default e-mail editor. This means that you can create your e-mails using Word's full bag of tricks, such as templates and enhanced formatting capabilities to project a uniform "look," whether you are corresponding by e-mail or snail mail. If you prefer using the plain text editor, you can deselect Word as the e-mail editor.

Users of Hotmail, another Microsoft product, have long complained about the lack of integration with Outlook. Planners typically use Hotmail to access their e-mail messages when they are out of the office. Thankfully, Microsoft has finally addressed this issue. Hotmail accounts can now be accessed from Outlook, and you can drag and drop e-mails from Hotmail right into your Outlook inbox.

Improved file management. Outlook 2002 has improved file-management capabilities. Users with heavy e-mail volume will want to make use of the new archive feature, available on the File dropdown menu. Archive will move old e-mails to a permanent storage place on your hard drive based on user-defined preferences. By archiving, you will keep Outlook running rapidly while maintaining a permanent record of all your communications.

Can instant messaging improve productivity? Joel's never been a big fan of instant messaging. At one time he had an AOL account, but it seemed that whenever he was trying to do some research, friends and family used to pop up on the messaging service, keeping him from his appointed task. He took the coward's way out and dumped AOL.

It may be time to take another look at instant messaging, though, since Microsoft has decided to integrate IM into the XP environment. IM support is enabled in Outlook 2002 by default, so whenever you start Outlook, you will be immediately logged on to the Instant Messaging service. You enter a contact's IM address on the general tab for the contact. If the person you want to reach is online, it is now possible to send files, collaborate on documents, and conduct meetings over the Web. Theoretically, instant messaging can now be used as a productivity tool to collaborate with clients and VWPs, but the jury is still out. One potential stumbling block to universal IM use is the incompatibility of competing IM services. If this barrier is removed, we suspect that organizations will make a serious attempt to exploit IM's potential.

Keeping your data secure. Outlook automatically blocks attachments that it determines could be unsafe. It is supposed to prevent viruses from taking over your address book and using it to attack other computers. Password security is also improved. It would be naïve to say that these measures will eliminate all vulnerabilities, but they should make hacking more difficult, and that's a good thing.

Outlook is now a much more complete generic solution.

Advantages
➢ Full-featured contact management
➢ Improved calendar
➢ Journal to track activities, documents, and other information

➤ Task management
➤ Scheduling
➤ E-mail
➤ Integration with Microsoft Office Suite
➤ No additional cost if you already use Microsoft Office

Disadvantages

There are some disadvantages to working with Outlook, however. Anthony DeVito, PhD, CFP, of ADV Financial Planning and Investment Management in Pelham, New York, cites one complaint that we often hear: "Outlook is very powerful, but it is not easy to learn. I often have trouble finding answers to my questions in the Help section." Another criticism is that because Outlook tries to offer so much, it requires a lot of system resources. This is not much of a problem for users with brand-new computers, but it is a problem for machines that are a few years old.

Outlook is well-suited for

➤ Practices on a tight budget that already have Microsoft Office installed
➤ Practices that do most of their work in Microsoft Office
➤ Those that need strong scheduling features combined with good contact management

ACT! 2000

ACT! can do all of the other things you expect from a program of this type. The scheduling and task-tracking functions have long been a strong point, offering extensive flexibility and customization. Calendars can be displayed in numerous formats. Icons make it easy to distinguish among types of tasks on the task list, and the user can assign priorities, color-coding, and notes to each. When an activity is scheduled with a client or VWP, an e-mail confirmation of the event can be sent from within the program.

Why would so many planners go out and spend additional money on contact management software if they already have a CMS bundled with their office suite? There are a number of reasons, but a more user-friendly interface, a client-centric approach, the ability to customize, and the availability of third-party add-ons are among the main ones.

User interface. From a financial professional's point of view, we like ACT!'s user interface more than Outlook's. ACT! is a client-centric program. The default view is the contact view, divided into two sections. The top section contains "primary" information, such as name, address, company, phone, fax, e-mail address, and status (or category). The bottom section accommodates additional screens for notes/history (similar to the Journal in Outlook), activities, sales opportunities, groups, profiles, user-defined fields, phone/home (home contact info), alt contact (alternate contact at a company), and status. Any of the secondary screens can be reached by clicking on the related tab at the bottom of the screen. If you don't like the default contact view, ACT! allows you to select from a number of predefined alternate layouts, and additional layouts are available from third-party vendors.

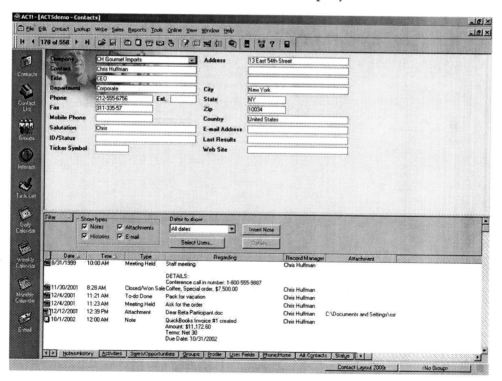

ACT's User Interface

The thing we like most about ACT! is that it "thinks" the way we do: in terms of the client. If you schedule a client task, for example, it gets associated with the client file, not with the person responsible for the task. Anyone on your team can look at the client's ACT! record and see outstanding tasks. Take the time to set up ACT! properly, and you can manage and track all of your client interactions from this one program.

This feature-laden program offers a lot of things planners want. Here are some highlights:

Track what you do. ACT! allows you to enter unlimited notes for any client contact; each note is accurately identified with the date and time of entry. If you send letters, faxes, or e-mails from within your client's ACT! file, ACT! automatically logs these items as they are completed. It also tracks a contact's status. Changes in field values are logged to a contact's history, so you know things such as when a prospect becomes a customer.

Keep better records with Notes/History. The Notes/History function is powerful. When used properly, all documents, letters, faxes, e-mails, notes, completed tasks,

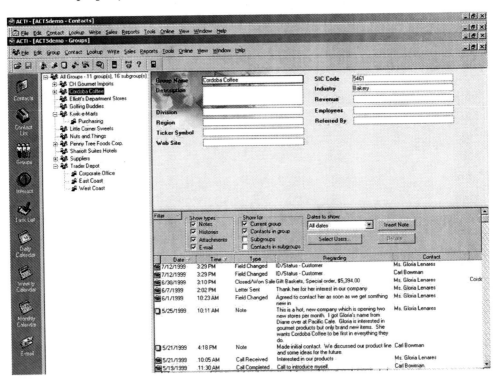

ACT's Notes/History Function

and everything else associated with a client will be documented in one place. If you print a spreadsheet for a client, you can attach a file to the client's record. If you scan a document into your computer, you can create a shortcut in the ACT! client file linking the file to the appropriate client. If you assign a client-related task to a virtual assistant, document it here. Notes and histories can be maintained for groups as well as for individual contacts. An example of a group, with notes and history, is pictured below, at left.

Much of the above functionality is available from Outlook, but ACT! is more intuitive and user friendly.

Find what you need. One of the biggest challenges facing all of us is finding the information we need when we need it. ACT! 2000 greatly improves the search capabilities of earlier versions. ACT! now includes keyword searches.

Keyword search looks through the entire database to find the information you need. Traditional screen and formula-based queries with Boolean operations are supported. For example, users want to find every contact for which "Roth IRA" is an entry in Notes/History. With ACT! 2000's keyword search, you can filter your

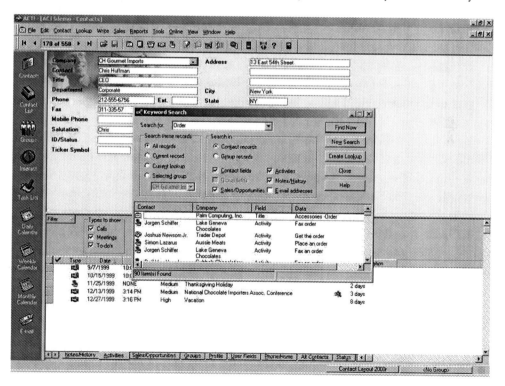

ACT's Search Function

search to look in the Notes/History tab or Activities tab. Keyword search can also be used to find a word or phrase in a single contact record or in a group. Instant lookups examine information in a field. For example, if you wanted to screen for overseas contacts, you could look up all contacts that have any notation in the country field. If you wanted to find domestic clients, you could screen for contacts that have blank country fields.

Group contacts. Organize groups of contacts in a way that is meaningful for you. Create and access groups of contacts, such as Hot Prospects, A-Clients, and Mutual Fund Wholesalers. Users can set up a system to automatically put a contact name into a group or subgroup, based on a defined set of rules. Users may define the rules based on one or two fields or a saved query. You can then easily create customized communications for members of a group. For example, if you create a group of clients that are small business owners, you can send them e-mails addressing their particular needs.

Phone calls—outgoing calls. It is possible to make all of your phone calls from within ACT!, and you may want to do so to track billable hours and tasks or to have a history of client conversations. When you make a call from within ACT!, the program prompts you to enter the topic of the call and any detailed notes. Using this feature helps you track tasks and supplies a history for compliance purposes.

To dial out using ACT!, you need either a modem that shares the same phone line as your telephone or a telephone equipped with a Telephone Application Programming Interface (TAPI). Your operating system must also support TAPI; if you use Windows 98 (or later) or NT with service pack 4 (or later), you have it.

To enable the dialer, go to the Edit menu, select Preferences/Dialer. Then check the Use/Dialer box. You can then select your connection method from a drop-down list of lines and modems. If you select Modem, ACT! will configure your modem automatically. You then configure the dialing properties (area code you are dialing from, code from outgoing line, and code to dial long distance).

To make a call to a contact whose record is displayed, simply click the Dial Phone icon on the toolbar. Calls can also be initiated in the Task List by highlighting a task, clicking on the Contact menu, and selecting Phone Contact on the drop-down menu.

Phone calls—incoming calls. If your system is properly equipped, ACT! will determine who is calling before you enter the phone number and display their contact record. Can't remember what you last discussed? Don't remember the daughter-in-law's name? You'll never be caught off guard again. All of the information will be in front of you before you pick up the phone.

Map work flows with Activity Series. This is a great timesaver that allows you to predefine a series of activities and automatically schedule the steps of the series with the contacts in your calendar. If you have a standard procedure with new clients, for example, you can schedule all of the steps with one entry. These steps might include sending out a data questionnaire, following up with the client to make sure he received it, following up again to see if he has questions or needs help with the form, scheduling the next meeting to review the data form with the client, and so on through the end of the initial planning engagement. ACT! includes an Activities Series Wizard, greatly simplifying the process of series construction.

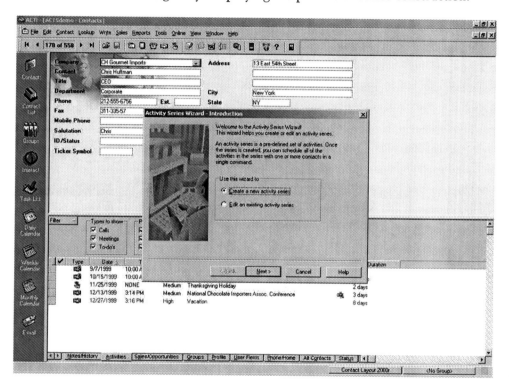

ACT! Activity Series Wizard

Gain a competitive edge with the Instant Profile tab. If you have clients who work at major corporations, or are targeting prospects there, this feature may appeal to you. ACT! will download contact-specific information from the Internet directly into itself with a single click. Contact-specific information includes: News, Company Snapshot, Individual Stock Quotes, Stock Comparisons, Weather, Maps, and Driving Directions.

Prospecting, with help from Dale Carnegie. ACT! 2000 added support for sales development, based on a proprietary system developed by Dale Carnegie Training that the user access via ACT!'s Sales pull-down menu. With minor modifications, this functionality can be used as a "prospect development system." Essentially, the program provides a marketing blueprint with a system for tracking results.

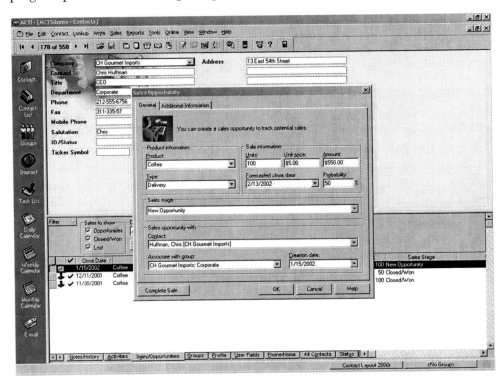

ACT!'s Prospecting Function

You can use ACT! to create and mail-merge letters, faxes, and e-mails, keeping a history of each one. A number of predefined reports come with the program to get you up and running right away; you can custom design your own additions if you wish.

Add-ons. One advantage of deploying a well-established program like ACT! is that it has a large-enough installed customer base to attract third-party software providers who have developed add-ons to extend the functionality of ACT!

Oakhurst Software Products, for example, offers a number of enhancements that expand ACT!'s capabilities and can improve your efficiency. Oak!Zip! not only validates zip codes a new contact may have given you as part of his address, it auto-completes the city and state fields when you enter a contact's zip code, saving you the effort of manually recording these two items. eConvert automatically converts contact information from e-mails and Web submissions, or registration forms submitted online, into ACT! Entries.

Allied Financial Software, Inc., produces ACT4Advisors, a custom ACT! database and layout template designed specifically for financial services professionals. ACT4Advisors allows financial professionals to input information such as asset allocation, insurance, goals, and security holdings without having to customize ACT! on their own.

The list of add-ons is extensive. The ACT! website (www.act.com) lists add-on products grouped by function, as well as information about books and consultants.

Advantages

- Client-centric
- Full-featured contact management
- Robust calendar
- Task management
- Work-flow management
- Links to e-mail from within the program
- Some integration with Microsoft Office Suite
- Can maintain a record of all client-related contacts and activities
- Ability to search by all fields and by keywords
- Provides a good record for compliance purposes
- Excellent at scheduling and task tracking
- Customizable
- Can work with older systems
- Easy to learn; program includes detailed, well-written users' guide
- A library of third-party add-ons can extend ACT!'s capabilities
- Relatively low cost

Disadvantages

Although anyone can use ACT! out of the box and improve their productivity in short order, some personalization will be needed to optimize it for the specific work you are doing. Customization within ACT! may be as simple as defining a number of fields and tweaking a few templates, or it may require extensive work, like producing custom layouts or creating controls for drop-down menus.

Note that the ability to customize ACT! is listed as both an advantage and a disadvantage, depending on your willingness to invest some time in the program. If you are so inclined, you can customize the program's utility for both you and your clients with slight tweaks or major changes, such as

➤ Adding, deleting, or modifying fields in contact and group records

➤ Changing contact or group layouts

➤ Changing field attributes

➤ Limiting the number of characters that can appear in a field (for example, limiting the "state" field to two letters, or the "zip code" field to either five or nine numbers)

➤ Setting rules for a data entry field (for example, only numbers, only letters, or specifying it as a URL field)

➤ Adding drop-down lists to data fields

➤ Changing colors and fonts

➤ Creating or modifying a report or envelope label format

➤ Creating macros to automate certain functions

➤ Specifying the view a user sees when the program launches

➤ Customizing menu bars and menus

➤ Modifying keyboard shortcuts

Based on what we have seen, ACT! deserves serious consideration if you are looking for an "off-the-shelf" solution. Customization is helpful but, nevertheless, optional. ACT! is client-centric, robust, well documented, and one of the easiest programs to master in its class.

ACT! is well-suited for

➤ Those who need strong contact management and scheduling features

➤ Tracking each client interaction

➤ Tracking work flows

➤ Prospecting

➤ Customization (in-house or through the purchase of add-ins)

Industry-Specific Solutions

ProTracker

ProTracker is a powerful program that was originally developed by fee-only planner Warren Mackensen of Mackensen & Company, Inc. in Hampton, New Hampshire, for use in his own financial planning practice. As is the case with all programs of this type, ProTracker is a name-centric, or client-centric, program. Within ProTracker, we make a distinction between name centric and client centric because ProTracker offers you two options for initially entering information: the name screen and the client screen. The difference between the two is the type of information and the level of detail that can be entered. The names screen is ideal for entering prospects, related professionals, centers of influence, and media contacts.

The prospect name data screen contains input fields for just about everything a financial professional would want to know about a nonclient, including name, addresses, phone numbers, birth date, profession, photo, relatives, referral source, military service, education, comments, and preferred refreshments when visiting the office.

The name input screen can also be used to assign a priority to the contact, add the contact to the firm's newsletter subscription list, and track ADV forms sent to the contact.

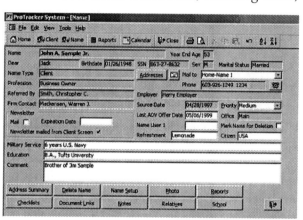

ProTracker Prospect Name Data Screen

The client screen is the place to enter and control client-related data such as assets and liabilities, beneficiaries, cash flow, checklists, estate planning information, goals and objectives, insurance coverages, notes, and tax information.

As an example, clicking the Insurance button leads to the insurance screen, where the user selects the type of policy. Each of the

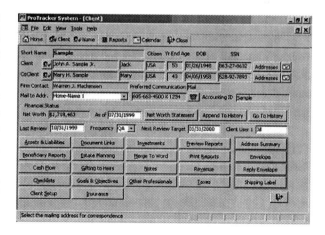

ProTracker Client Data Screen

insurance input screens is customized to accept detailed data for that particular policy type. In the case of the Disability Insurance screen, fields are available for crucial information such as definition of disability, monthly benefit, maximum benefit, elimination period, and other policy features and limitations.

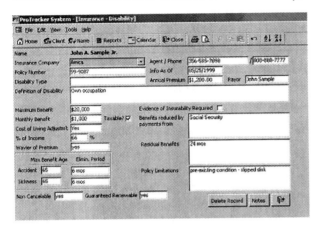

ProTracker Client Disability Insurance Screen

Retirement planning features include the ability to track retirement contributions and retirement contribution status, print letters reminding clients to make their retirement plan contributions, record Roth rollover data, and track required minimum distributions from retirement accounts.

ProTracker does a nice job of tracking essential income tax data, including filing status, adjusted gross income (AGI), current tax liabilities, alternative minimum tax exposure (AMT), tax loss carryforwards, state income tax information, and marginal tax rates. For planning firms that prepare taxes, it is possible to designate which clients are tax-preparation clients and which IRS district the client files in. The program can also prepare envelopes or mailing labels to mail the returns from within the Taxes screen—a nice usability touch.

The estate planning section tracks all of a client's essential documents. Wills, trusts, powers of attorney, health care proxies, and final arrangement preferences can all be easily recorded and stored. To illustrate, in the Wills section a planner can indicate whether a copy of the will is on file and note the executor, date of will, state law governing the will, organ donor preferences, and a summary of key will provisions.

As our profession evolves, more and more planners are questioning the advisability of evaluating the client/planner relationship solely in terms of investment performance. Clearly, financial planners do more for clients than manage investments, but measuring the value of some financial planning services is problematic. ProTracker's Goals & Objectives page, loosely modeled on Ross Levin's (Accredited Investors Inc. in Edina, Minnesota) *Wealth Management Index,* presents planners with an area to input client goals, assign a dollar amount to the goal, weight the importance of the goal, and track progress toward the goal. The planner and client then have a basis to evaluate client progress and the effectiveness of the financial plan. As is the case with many sections, the client can generate a report for review.

ProTracker is well suited to serve as your client communications center. Client lists can be sorted in numerous ways, including keyword and preferred communication method. Monthly reports can be generated to remind the planner of dates such as upcoming birthdays, anniversaries, retirement plan distribution deadlines, and the like. Letters (or e-mails) can be generated and mailing labels can be printed. Of course, all communications can be linked to the client record.

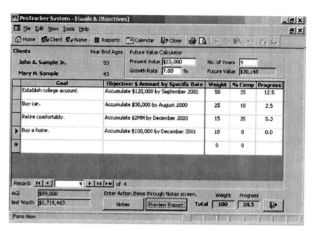

ProTracker Client Goals Screen

If ProTracker is installed on a system using the full version of Microsoft Access (as opposed to the runtime version), a ProTracker System button is installed on the toolbar of Microsoft Word, Microsoft Excel, and Microsoft PowerPoint. This button can create links to ProTracker from within the Microsoft Office application.

Notes are another powerful ProTracker tool. Notes resemble index cards that can be categorized and time stamped. The program comes loaded with an assortment of fifty-one common notes to get you going, including: overspending (to advise a client that he is spending beyond what was budgeted or to keep track of that fact internally), review meetings, missing or outdated documents, mailing date (to inform a client that a letter mailed to her two weeks ago needs her attention or to track mailings for internal follow-up), and a request for a tax return, to name a few. Notes can be e-mailed, and they can be marked for action. They can later be retrieved and sorted by category, name, keyword, or date.

Managing your business. ProTracker can do much more than manage client data and communication; it can actually help run your business. Let's look at a few examples:

➤ **Compliance.** Compliance is an important aspect of all financial service firms, and keeping good client records is an important component of compliance. Taking notes of telephone conversations, etc. is extremely helpful, but more is required. Should you be audited, you will want to have information such as the date a client engaged you, the date an agreement was terminated, the last ADV offer date, the discretionary status of each account, account values, and billing methods readily available. ProTracker can store all of the above information and produce reports for compliance use.

➤ **Client revenues.** If a client management system (CMS) is going to help you manage your business, it must be able to report client revenues and allow you to view them in the context of assets under management, client net worth, or client income. ProTracker meets this requirement by allowing planners to import data from two of the most widely used small business accounting packages: QuickBooks and Peachtree.

➤ **Scheduling and task management.** Schedules are entered in either the ProTracker calendar or the Outlook calendar. Action items can be posted to either calendar as well. Individual client action items are assigned to an employee and tracked to completion. Tasks or processes can be grouped into checklists, linked to a client, executed, and then archived.

➤ **Finding the information you need.** Compiling and storing information is only half the battle. Without the ability to rapidly retrieve information in a useful format, data gathering and storage is an exercise in futility. Fortunately, ProTracker provides over eighty reports, enough to meet the needs of most planning firms.

➤ **Exchanging information between programs.** We've already mentioned ProTracker's ability to import information from small business accounting packages. Perhaps of more importance to the many financial advisers who manage client investments is ProTracker's ability to import investment account data from popular portfolio management programs such as Centerpiece and TechFi Portfolio. Advent Axys users can import information into ProTracker, but an additional step is required.

What about moving data into ProTracker from your current system? Will you have to manually re-enter everything? Highly doubtful. For an additional fee, the ProTracker staff can almost certainly convert the data for you.

In summary, this is a capable, powerful program, but it is more difficult to use proficiently than most of the programs discussed earlier.

Advantages
- Comprehensive
- Organizes and stores extensive client information
- Manages client and staff tasks
- Tracks important dates
- Excellent compliance tool
- Excellent sorting and reporting capabilities
- Interfaces with popular portfolio reporting software
- Friendly, competent support staff
- Online Knowledgebase
- Training available at a modest cost

Disadvantages

The complaints we hear about ProTracker are generally usability issues. ProTracker is not the most intuitive program on the market, and some find it difficult to master. We believe that the Knowledgebase and training will allow most potential users to become proficient with the program, but the ProTracker user's manual could be better. If you don't have any database experience, or are the type of user who demands instant gratification right off the bat, you may be frustrated or disappointed initially.

ProTracker is well-suited for
- Detail-oriented practices that want to store and track extensive client data
- Tracking work flows
- Prospecting
- Maintaining superior compliance files
- Integration with portfolio management software
- Those who require personalized service

Junxure Version 1.3

We view Junxure, marketed by Performance Technologies, Inc., as the only strong competitor to ProTracker. The company, owned by Charles Schwab & Co., publishes Centerpiece, a portfolio management program used by many independent financial advisers.

Due to a recent change in the marketing agreement between Performance Technologies, Inc. and the program's developers, two versions of Junxure will be available by the time you read this: the Schwab/Performance Technologies version for Schwab advisers, and Junxure-I (as in independent) version, from CRM Software, Inc. (www.crmsoftwareinc.com) for everyone else.

Managing client relationships. Like ProTracker, Junxure is a client-centric program. It interfaces well with Microsoft Office as well. We were able to install the program easily after quickly browsing through the *Getting Started Guide.* Those installing the program on a network will want to read the guide more thoroughly.

Navigating Junxure was, for the most part, intuitive. Upon boot up, you are brought to the control center of the program, which allows you to access all of the program's features. Across the top are six buttons labeled People, Letters, Reports, Database Tools, System Setup, and Maintain System. Clicking on the People button reveals nine activities.

When you highlight one of the nine items, further information appears to the right of the screen. For example, if you highlight the second subitem (My Pending Actions), a summary of pending actions appears.

Let's double-click on item #1 in the left column of the screen, labeled People, which transports us to the main client information page, pictured at right.

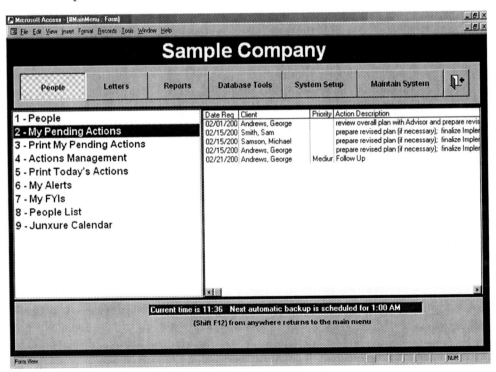

Junxure Pending Actions Screen

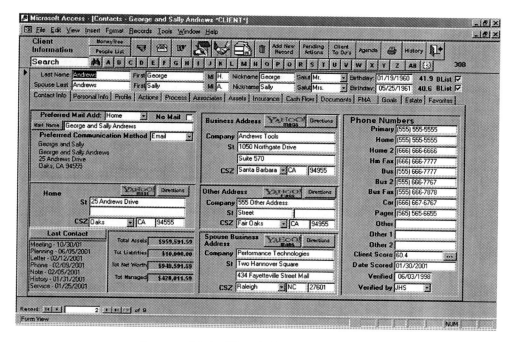

Junxure Main Client Information Screen

The client information form contains additional subsections, providing space for just about any type of information a planner needs to track. It is here that you enter and access data such as contact information, client profiles, actions related to the client, assets, cash flows, tax and suitability-related info (filing status, IRA Distribution method, investment objectives, investment experience, etc.), insurance policies, financial planning goals, and much more.

Many of the subsections contain nice usability features. For example, on the main contact info page, each address can be linked to a Yahoo! Map and/or driving instructions. Many fields, where appropriate, contain drop-down menus, speeding the data entry process.

The main profile page is particularly well designed. It allows the user to enter quickly a great deal of important information, like client type, classifications, keywords, interests, account types, and custodians, thanks to the intelligent use of check boxes and drop-down lists. If you wish to include a field that Junxure doesn't provide, the program allows you to add approximately fifty additional user-defined fields.

Once all of the data is entered, users can begin to experience Junxure's many features. The program tracks letters, e-mails, phone calls, and documents related to

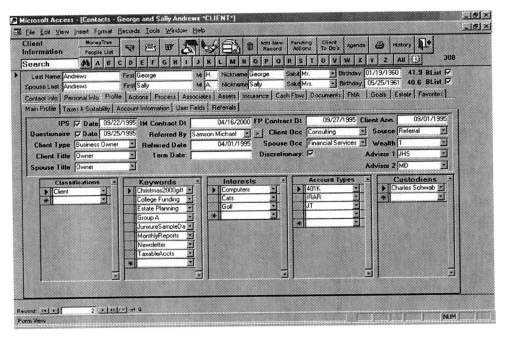

Adding User-Defined Data Fields to Junxure

each client or prospect. It allows you to set up recurring actions, assign actions to a specific client, assign actions to staff members, and set reminders. "Processes" such as opening a new investment account, transferring client assets, and processing a new financial plan can be scripted and entered into the system in one step.

As is the case with ProTracker, Junxure provides a library of reports that will meet the needs of many, but it takes usability a step further by including a Report Wizard that greatly simplifies the creation of custom reports.

Alerts remind users of actions that have been assigned to them. Various operations can be performed on assignments that arrive. They can be confirmed, edited, postponed, or used as a link to the appropriate client page for further information. Junxure can send a copy of an action to someone in the office other than the person the action is assigned to. To distinguish between the two, Junxure terms the copies FYIs.

Wizards are available to guide users through other common tasks such as creating letters, envelopes, and global e-mails. There's also a Referral Wizard that automatically creates a thank-you letter for the referrer as it prepares a welcome letter to the referral. Another useful tool is the Rules Builder. Rules are used to select groups of clients for reports or actions. For example, you can create a rule to list all clients with 457 plans to inform them of a change in the law regulating those plans.

Junxure's Wealth Management Assessment Worksheet

A Wealth Management Assessment worksheet is available for tracking client objectives and goals. Similar to Goals and Objectives in ProTracker, this is another takeoff on Ross Levin's *Wealth Management Index.*

Managing your business. Junxure can perform many of the same functions and create many of the same types of reports that ProTracker can; differences are minor. It is worth noting that Junxure now offers users the option of either the Outlook calendar or Junxure's own calendar; early versions of Junxure did not have a calendar built into the program.

Finding the information you need. Junxure has solid search capabilities. For example, contacts can be found by name, spouse, address, phone number, referral source, or adviser. If none of those work, you can always try running a custom report. Searches can be run on actions as well. Let's say an adviser needs to find something related to an IRA that he did for a client. The program can do an IRA keyword search. Should that search yield too many results, it can be narrowed using additional keywords, like "IRA" and "Roth."

Exchanging information between programs. Junxure can bring in most asset data from Advent and dbCams. Since Performance Technologies would like you to use Centerpiece, they don't really promote these capabilities, but they are available. For Centerpiece users, this product is particularly attractive, since they will soon share a common database. Contact information can usually be brought in from other applications, for an additional fee.

Overall, we think Junxure is another good choice for financial planners. We list some advantages and disadvantages below:

Advantages
➢ Comprehensive
➢ Fairly easy to learn
➢ Organizes and stores extensive client information
➢ Manages client and staff tasks
➢ Tracks important dates
➢ Excellent compliance tool
➢ Excellent sorting and reporting capabilities
➢ Interfaces with popular portfolio reporting software
➢ Training available at a modest cost
➢ Owned by an established firm with strong finances

Disadvantages
➢ Users more than occasionally complain about the interface with Centerpiece. We expect this complaint to disappear once the two programs are united under a single database structure.
➢ Whereas it's fairly easy to learn the basics, mastering the program is more challenging than it is with ProTracker.
➢ Reports from users regarding customer service and technical support are mixed.
➢ Documentation is acceptable, but could be much better.
➢ The lack of templates to get you started is a big disadvantage.

We continue to be annoyed by the lack of templates. We understand that no two practices are the same, meaning that designing templates and sample processes is a challenge, but our experience is that it is easier to modify existing works than to create them from scratch. If products like Microsoft Office and ACT!, with much more diverse customer bases, can design helpful models to help their users save time,

Junxure can, too. CRM Software has indicated to us that templates will soon be offered in the Junxure-I edition.

Junxure is well-suited for

➤ Detail-oriented practices that want to store and track extensive client data
➤ Tracking work flows
➤ Prospecting
➤ Maintaining superior compliance files
➤ Integration with portfolio management software
➤ Firms transitioning from ACT! or Goldmine

Finding the Right Solution for You

THE THREE MOST USEFUL FACTORS to consider when you are trying to decide upon client management software are (1) the size and nature of your practice right now, (2) where you want your practice to be in a few years, and (3) your budget.

All things being equal, we have a strong preference for programs like Junxure and ProTracker that were designed by financial planners for financial planners, particularly for established, multi-person practices. There are minor differences between the two programs, but both offer a solid client management platform that is scalable enough to meet the needs of a sole practitioner or a much larger firm. Both have the ability to link to Microsoft Office applications so that you can launch Microsoft Word or send an e-mail using Microsoft Outlook right from within the program (doing so will link the action to a client record).

Could you hire someone to design a custom database for your firm? You certainly could, but we have talked to a number of very bright and successful planners who have tried, and in most cases it was an expensive and frustrating endeavor at best, with total failures common.

Programs like Junxure and ProTracker incorporate not only the experience of their developers but also the wisdom of countless financial professionals (and their staffers) who use the programs and offer feedback. These programs may not be 100 percent to your liking, but they probably contain most of the features you've wished for. They may also contain some features you could use but never thought of, like mapping and linking digital pictures of your clients to their database records.

If your firm concentrates primarily on financial planning, compare programs to one another on the basis of the features that are most important to you. For example, if you are accustomed to using ACT! or Goldmine, you may find the Junxure interface more to your liking. Is ease of use very important? Again, we'd give Junxure the nod. Perhaps personalized service is very important, or you like the ability to track ADV offerings for compliance purposes. You may find yourself gravitating to ProTracker. We think both programs are capable of doing a fine job; the ultimate decision may come down to just personal preferences.

If your office is primarily investment oriented, performance reporting may be a more important consideration than CMS. If you fall into this camp, the best solution may be to select your performance-reporting package first and compatible CMS second. Many Centerpiece users will find Junxure a natural fit, although ProTracker also works well. Portfolio 2001 users might check out Contact (TechFi produces both products), but we think ProTracker is a much richer program than Contact right now.

If you are a sole practitioner, a new practice on a tight budget, or a firm that just does not need to track as much client detail, ACT! or Microsoft Outlook might suit your needs perfectly. Personally, we have had good results with ACT!, and we like the fact that you can buy add-ons to relieve yourself of some customization chores, but Outlook may be all you need, and odds are you already have it. Should you decide to go with ACT! or Microsoft Outlook, it's a good bet that you will be able to move much of your data to Junxure or ProTracker at a later date if you need to.

Chapter Eleven

Making the Virtual Transition

WHENEVER YOU ARE CONTEMPLATING a major change in how you work, the first step is to clear your mind. Meditate, go on vacation, do whatever you have to do to be able to step back from your office and really see it for the first time—problems and all. Take an inventory of all your operating systems. See and thoroughly document the status quo, being careful not to take anything for granted as unchangeable. Resist the temptation to bypass inefficiency because "we've always done it this way," or "I can't imagine how we could do this differently." And above all, keep an open mind to new technologies. Focus on the benefits, not on the obstacles, as you rise to the challenge of creating a more efficient and profitable working environment.

The Four Phases of Conversion

THERE ARE FOUR PHASES to any virtual conversion. The first is to convert physical records to digital records. The second is to convert employees to virtual workers. Next, you need to establish systems to accommodate your off-site workers. And last, you must install systems that facilitate the retrieval of your digital information. Underlying all of this is the requirement that you not only identify your present systems but cost them out as well. The business planning software we discussed earlier can help you here.

Consult the expense portion of your company's accounting records. If yours is a traditional financial planning firm, you will find that your employees are one of your major cost categories. Think of your employees as one of your internal systems, because you have other options for staff support, and it is now time for you to compare the cost of these options with the system you now employ.

Converting Physical to Digital Records

Now, the task at hand is for you to comb through all of your firm-wide systems looking for opportunities like the outsourcing opportunity just mentioned. Some will be associated with employees, but others will be associated with paperwork inefficiencies. Thus begins the important first phase of remodeling your practice—converting physical records to digital records.

There are three steps in the conversion of physical records, all of which have been touched on in other chapters, but we'll outline them here again. First, historical records will need to be scanned and filed. Scanning is a menial task and is something you can hire a low-paid temporary worker to do since it just involves feeding paper into a machine. Filing, however, is something you will want either to do yourself or to have an experienced employee do under your supervision. By filing we mean determining into which subdirectory within your scanning software you want to move the documents you've scanned from their initial desktop repository, as well as how you want to label each scanned item. However, before either scanning or filing, you must "unfile" what you've accumulated in paper form, i.e., go through all of your client files and decide what to keep and what to throw out before beginning the scanning process. As we all know, papers (and digital files, too) have a way of growing to fill the space available.

Deciding what to throw out immediately versus what to keep, scan, and then discard is a matter of personal preference, regulatory requirements, and risk management. Personal preference will dictate whether you keep and scan records you could duplicate from other sources, if necessary. For example, your client file may contain some old monthly statements from his investment custodian that could be duplicated. You might choose to shred those without scanning them. Regulatory requirements (for now, at least) require that you keep certain signed documents in original form, such as client contracts. And your own risk management preferences will guide you in deciding whether to scan more "peripheral" documents. For example, in helping your client select a 20-year level premium term policy five years ago, you might have collected illustrations and marketing materials from four different insurance carriers. Do you scan all of those materials? If you don't, the risk is that you might have to defend this decision in the future. On the other hand, if you figure the probability of that happening represents a negligible risk you are willing to accept, then you may pass on scanning these usually bulky materials.

Converting from Employees to Virtual Workers: The Process and the Economics

We are financial planners who wouldn't hesitate to do a thorough analysis of a client's options were he to contemplate changing jobs or relocating across country. Yet, when it comes to our own strategic planning, we often fail to dedicate enough time and make snap judgments. Let's go a bit further this time and find *all* of the costs of your employees.

The framework for this analysis is constructed with the knowledge of what the virtual competition looks like. So, for example, if we are comparing the cost of dedicating an employee to client reporting (i.e., downloading and reconciling custodial trade data within a program such as Centerpiece or Axys, establishing accurate price files, and producing periodic status and performance reports for your client and your own professional staff) against using a virtual counterpart to carry out this function, our framework for our employee cost analysis must include all of those items that we will *avoid* with the virtual option.

Let's say you are considering using a Centerpiece reporting service for the first time. You manage $90 million, an average of $1,200,000 per client, and each client has, on average, four different accounts. The reporting duties for 300 accounts require a full-time effort from a staff person. That person is responsible for doing all of the day-to-day tasks associated with maintaining your Centerpiece (or other portfolio reporting) database. Reporting duties consist of sending quarterly status reports to clients, or uploading them to a website, and annually producing performance reports and realized gain/loss reports for tax purposes. This employee also must compute month-end account balances, prepare invoices based on those numbers, and distribute those invoices by fax, e-mail, or U.S. mail to either the client or the custodian for payment.

For this particular set of services, the Centerpiece reporting company you've narrowed down, should you decide to use their service in lieu of your employee, would charge $10.50 per account per month. That results in an annual cost to you of $37,800. You pay your employee $35,000, so your first inclination is to pass on this reporting service since you can produce this service in-house for less money. But, as the sidebar on the following page makes very clear, there are a host of costs associated with your employee that can be totally avoided by using a reporting service. First, there are direct costs you've forgotten, such as employer payroll taxes, sick days and vacation leave, and various employee benefits. Then there are additional costs that are also quite direct though less obvious, such as office space rental, equipment costs, etc. Finally, there are indirect and *much* less obvious costs such as the cost of turnover when you must hire a replacement worker, incurring

The Annual Cost of Employee Care and Feeding

Salary		$35,000
Payroll taxes		3,500
Vacation and sick leave		2,000
Benefits		5,850
Health plan	$4,200	
Pension plan	1,050	
Parking	600	
Office space		2,400
Square footage of employer's office	120 feet	
Annual rent per square foot	$20	
Training/continuing education paid by employer		1,500
Turnover costs (training of employee's replacement)		1,000
Dedicated equipment (annual depreciation)		1,200
Computer	$700	
Phone system	200	
Other	300	
Total cost of care and feeding		**$52,450**

the search costs associated with that hiring as well as the training costs. A review of the sidebar above shows how one might structure a comparative analysis.

The true cost of your employee is no less than $52,450 (and this is probably conservative), whereas the reporting service still costs just $37,800. That's a savings of 28 percent. And guess what—all of the headaches you experience in the care and feeding of your employee, such as integrating requested leave with work schedules, meeting the employee's need for additional training, or dealing with unexpected resignations, are absorbed and endured by your reporting company, not you, when you outsource this activity.

Converting Systems to Accommodate Off-Site Workers

Our third conversion phase is the conversion of systems to accommodate off-site workers. These could be virtual workers living thousands of miles from your office, or your own employees living just three miles away but desiring to work from home. One example of accommodation is the use of online research capabilities. Let's trace the evolution of one of today's research services for financial advisers and how it is representative of the path many have taken.

In the 1980s, Morningstar Inc. marketed to financial planners *Mutual Fund Values,* which contained the familiar one-page mutual fund analyses Morningstar became famous for. This paper version eventually gave way to one-page analyses on CD-ROM that, in turn, gave way to Morningstar's website. Each step up the evolutionary ladder has brought not only greater efficiencies, but also improved products.

Only one employee could use paper-based research volumes at a time, and keeping the services updated after replacement pages were received was annoying and often given a low priority. CD-ROMs improved this process in that a disk could hold an entire set of volumes, eliminating the need to replace pages. But the one-person-at-a-time limitation remained, unless multiple disks were ordered or the CD-ROM was installed in a network version. Migration of these services to the Web not only eliminated this remaining roadblock, but permitted Morningstar to update information daily, or even hourly, rather than monthly or quarterly as it once did. A research company should be able to save enough money using the Web as a cheap distribution system that it can provide far timelier information than it offered before, for the same or even a lower rate. Even more important, for the purpose of our discussion, these Web-based services make it possible for your workforce to do their research anywhere, anytime.

Systems to accommodate off-site workers are those we've discussed in some depth, such as intranets and VPNs. The reasons to set these up are not just for virtual workers' use, but to have backup systems for your clients' protection as well. Suppose you have a traditional office with ten on-site workers plus yourself. Everyone communicates across a LAN that is not accessible from outside your physical office because no one ever works off-site. You aren't interested in working from home, and that is not something you permit your employees to do. When you vacation, you pride yourself on being able to leave the firm in someone else's hands. You leave your cell phone and laptop at home. Is it conceivable that some situation in your life will someday necessitate your needing to work from afar? What would happen if one of your parents needed your extended attention, as for a health-related problem, requiring you to be off-site for an indefinite period—and not for vacation purposes?

What we all need to move toward in our increasingly computerized world is the portable office. In other words, we need to be able to go virtually anywhere and do anything while still retaining the full capability to reach out electronically to our clients and coworkers.

Installing Systems for Digital Retrieval of Information

All of the digital systems we've discussed in this book facilitate rapid retrieval of information. One of your objectives should be to eliminate multiple and duplicative software programs, lost client files, client phone tag, and other sources of inefficiency in how you receive, store, retrieve, and use all of the various types of information on which your service depends.

A contact manager, for example, can be brilliantly constructed to provide office-wide network access or flawless mail merges. But if it doesn't facilitate the rapid retrieval of information, pass it by and look at the next entry on your shopping list. In spite of our universal societal trend toward multitasking, there is something to be said for completing tasks without interruption. The faster you can get from A to Z, the more efficient the trip will be. If you can't locate information quickly and must call back your client to answer his question, then the interven-

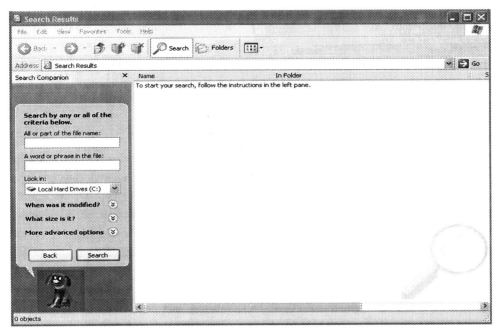

Windows XP Search Window

ing trips to the file cabinet or sessions of phone tag will allow for interruptions, possibly causing you to forget to complete the task or, at best, resulting in a poor response time.

Computers retrieve information by searching for text. However you store your text-based records, you want to minimize the number of searches and/or the time it takes you to perform a search. If you keep copies of letters to clients in Word files scattered throughout various subdirectories, and e-mails to and from clients in Outlook Express, then reread Chapter 5. Working out of several applications' default directories may be the way Bill Gates wants you to do it, but it's not the *best* way. That becomes obvious if you need to search for a document containing, for example, the text "generation-skipping trust." You know you've recommended these estate planning vehicles to five of your clients, but you don't remember which ones or when. You click on your Windows Start button, select Find (or Search, depending upon the version of Windows you're using), and search for all files containing your selected text passage. This can take up to five minutes depending on your processor. A program like Info Select, in which you might centralize all of your text-based records, will find your documents in less than five seconds. And because those documents are all filed within one archival system, you only need to open one software program to view the documents rather than searching your entire hard drive.

For graphic files, discussed in Chapter 4, we recommended you use software that will OCR the documents you scan, convert them to fairly accurate text automatically, and create an index allowing you to search on any word that appeared in your scanned image.

A Conversion Cheat Sheet

HERE ARE SOME QUESTIONS to stimulate your thinking about work habits or conditions in your firm that might lead you to consider converting them:

Daily Routine

➤ If you've been away from your office, do you return to be overwhelmed by urgent phone messages?

➤ Are you spending hours in traffic each day to reach your office or that of a client?

➤ Are you unable to take time out from your daily routine for physical exercise?

➤ Are you or an employee stuck repeating inefficient processes each day when you could outsource the activity to someone with the right tools for the job (e.g., payroll services)?

➤ Are you making one-day plane trips to meet with regional clients who would be just as happy hearing from you by phone, or having a "whiteboarding" session with you online?

Outsourcing Employee Functions
➤ What does each employee do? Does an outsource opportunity exist for duplicating his or her function?
➤ Have you performed a cost-benefit comparison between outsourcing versus keeping certain employee functions in-house? Does the cost-benefit analysis suggest the outsourcing option should be considered?
➤ Do you offer services to your clients requiring skills that are difficult or expensive to hire?
➤ Do you have full-time employees whose time you cannot profitably fill during seasonal periods or temporary periods of reduced demand for your firm's services?

Client Communications
➤ What percentage of the firm's clients have e-mail addresses?
➤ Can clients who are not using e-mail be persuaded to begin using it?
➤ Is the total number of actual plus prospective client e-mail users sufficient to warrant a higher degree of online communications?
➤ If so, consider which of the following can be moved from paper to online:
  Client correspondence
  Invoices
  Portfolio reports
  Bulletins and newsletters
  Other communications
➤ How many phone calls do you and your staff take from clients daily? What percentage of these calls is to transact business that could be just as effectively conducted using e-mail?

Digital Information
➤ What kinds of records do you keep in paper form?
➤ Does a government body by which your firm is regulated require this paper?
➤ Can you retrieve information needed during a client phone call, or for a rapid e-mail response, in one minute or less?
➤ What would be the results of a cost-benefit analysis comparing the costs of scan-

ning/digitizing of historical client records with the future productivity gains of having this information at your fingertips?

➤ When you receive digital information, do you store it in a digital form or convert it to paper (e.g., incoming faxes)?

If you answer these questions honestly, they will help you zero in on the operational areas where you can benefit from a virtual conversion.

C h a p t e r   T w e l v e

Looking Ahead

EVERY DAY FOLLOWING THE PUBLICATION of this book there will be
advances in the art and science of the virtual office. The tools we've
reviewed will continuously change and improve. We would like to think
therefore that the underlying lessons of this book will only increase in applicability
as these office technologies become more essential to the work you and we do as
planners. To reap the greatest possible rewards, you must ideally be a daydreamer
and believe that whatever you can imagine doing virtually instead of physically can,
in fact, be done.

And as you work to envision new possibilities for your own business and life,
don't get hemmed in by the constructs of others, even when they're delivered with
apparent authority and strength of conviction. In the preface to this book, we made
reference to the 1999 and 2000 studies on the future of the financial advisory industry by Undiscovered Managers LLC (UM), which challenged all advisers to rethink
their business models in light of rising costs of competition and the narrowing of
profit margins. The solutions UM recommended were, in essence, twofold: growing
much larger to meet the competition head on, or developing an impenetrable niche
while retaining one's present size.

In this book, we have suggested that small and mid-sized firms can prosper
without massive growth by applying virtual-office concepts and harnessing associated technologies. UM's spokesman, Mark Hurley, argued that investments in
infrastructure will be expensive. Perhaps, but they don't have to be. Hurley's definition of infrastructure depends to a great extent on people and physical capaci-

ty, both expensive commodities, whereas ours is much more technology-oriented and virtual.

For example, hiring more administrative support could help you handle more business and spend less time on that portion of your paperwork, but converting to a paperless office could greatly reduce the cost of administering client accounts. If you're going to add people, add them because they will enhance client service to the net benefit of the firm, not because inefficient systems require more people. The reason for using technology, such as paperless systems, is to raise the productivity of the minimum number of staff needed to maximize the virtual owner's bottom line in the context of the lifestyle and work style he or she wants to have.

And if we can hold down the cost of staff, so can we also minimize the cost of technology. In the process of acquiring a paperless solution, for example, you could spend upwards of $20,000 on some of the products we have deliberately avoided reviewing due to their poor benefit-to-cost characteristics, or you could copy the mid-sized firms we've showcased in this book that are doing it for a grand or two with WORLDOX, or other comparable products. If yours is a small operation, you could even do it for a few hundred dollars with PaperPort. Technology marches on, and prices never seem to stop their free fall. You, the reader, can reap the benefits.

In the preface we looked at typical profit margins of advisory firms, i.e., net income before taxes plus total owner compensation divided by gross revenues. *The 2000 FPA Financial Performance & Compensation Study of Financial Planning Practitioners* showed this percentage, regardless of company size, to be in the range of 55–61 percent. Yet, Dave and Joel know through experience that virtual firms can retain for their owners as much as 80 percent or more of their gross revenues. This jump of 20–25 percent can mean the difference between a workaholic lifestyle and the freedom to allow time for family, friends, and hobbies—in short, a well-rounded, low-stress life.

This promise of greater profitability will direct us not only to learn our technological lessons but, in a very beneficial way, to be introspective and holistic in figuring out the best business model for our own well-being. Many of us may never examine our true feelings about the life we are living because, as inefficient small business owners, we never expect to have enough time to really live it. Ask yourself this question: If you could earn enough money to provide you and your family a comfortable lifestyle with adequate long-term savings to meet all your essential goals, and you still had a spare ten hours a week left over after spending all the time you wanted to with your family, what would you do with that ten hours?

If you've been as overworked as most small business owners, your first inclination may be to say "sleep" or "watch nonstop golf on T.V.," but when that passes, one of three things will happen. You may be unable to think of anything else you'd rather do with your time and, as is sometimes the case with younger entrepreneurs, you may just want to work on making your business better. Or, you will spend your extra time doing something you already know you have a passion for, like tennis or reading or music or photography. Finally, you may even discover a new interest, something that brings you a level of fulfillment you haven't experienced before. (Faced with his own spare ten hours a week, Dave discovered a yearning to volunteer at his local Animal Humane Association to help stray and abandoned dogs avoid euthanasia and find new homes.)

It is our duty to aspire to an identity that isn't just our businesses. It's our duty not just to ourselves, but to our families and to our clients, because all of these constituents will suffer if you don't get your life in order, get beyond the same money anxiety that brings many of your clients to you, and get to a place where you can truly enjoy what you're doing.

It's also the duty of our institutions to help us realize these promises. The same professional associations, certifying bodies, and peer groups we depend upon for professional education and guidance must begin to include a more holistic viewpoint in the business advice they offer the financial planning professional. If they can teach the planner how to construct an appropriate estate plan for a client, or how to analyze a tax return, they should be able to teach him how to organize his own business affairs.

It is our sincere hope that you have found gems in this book that will make a difference in your life. In fact, please let us know if you do. Dave can be reached at dd@daviddrucker.com, and Joel picks up his e-mail at joel.bruckenstein@prodigy.net. We look forward to hearing from you.

Acknowledgments

THE AUTHORS WOULD LIKE TO THANK the following people for their help on *Virtual-Office Tools for a High-Margin Practice.*

For their support and encouragement, we want to acknowledge the editors and writers with whom we regularly work in the financial planning press: Robert Casey, editor, *Bloomberg Wealth Manager;* Mary Ann McGuigan, executive editor, *Bloomberg Wealth Manager;* Robert Veres, editor and publisher of *Inside Information* newsletter; Olivia Barbee, T. Rowe Price (formerly of Morningstar Advisor.com); Jerry Kerns, MorningstarAdvisor.com; Mitchell Rose, senior editor, horsesmouth.com; Kevin Adler, editor, *NAPFA Advisor;* Ed McCarthy, financial journalist; Geoffrey Michaelson, writing coach; and, of course, at Bloomberg Press, editorial director Jared Kieling and Tracy Tait, associate editor.

For their willingness to share their experience and wisdom, we want to thank the financial and accounting professionals who made a contribution to this book: Kathleen Day, Kathleen Day & Associates; Norman Boone, Boone Financial Advisors; Cheryl R. Holland, Abacus Planning Group, Inc.; Deena Katz, Evensky, Brown & Katz; Harry Kasanow, Kasanow & Associates; Greg Friedman, Friedman & Associates; Albert Coles, Jr., Financial Design Associates, Inc.; J. Steven Cowen, Cowen & Associates; Jennifer Lobaugh, Carter Financial Management; Ryan Fleming, Armstrong, Macintyte & Severns, Inc.; Louis P. Stanasolovich, Legend Financial Advisors, Inc.; Eric Rabbanian, Rabbanian Financial Planning, Inc.; Chris Cooper, Chris Cooper & Company, Inc.; Danelle Tainter, Hammel Financial Advisory Group, LLC; Melissa K. Hammel, Hammel Financial Advisory Group, LLC; Cynthia Conger, Arkansas Financial Group; Thomas W. Batterman, Vigil Trust & Financial Advocacy; Carolyn Sechler, CPA, P.C.; Annette Louise Peugh; Jeffrey N. Mehler, CFP; Brian D. Wruk, Transition Financial Advisors, Inc.; Anthony J. DeVito, ADV Financial Planning and Investment Management; and Warren J. Mackensen, Mackensen & Company, Inc.

For their help on the book and their general contributions to the virtual office movement we want to thank Kevin and Joanne Day, Trumpet, Inc.; Andrew Gluck, Advisor Products, Inc.; Mike Kelly, Asset Management Solutions; Sherry Huff Carnahan, Total Office, Inc.; Roron Wisniewski and Barbara Clark, Secure Financial Management, Inc.; Naomi Scrivener, Back Office Solutions; Jay Chitnis and David Summers, YieldQuest Investment Group; Bob Curtis, PIE Technologies; Steve Thalheimer, Thalheimer Financial Planning; Maria Camacho, account administrator; and Krisan Marotta, Krisan's BackOffice, Inc.

Dave wants to acknowledge his wife, Susan Drucker, and daughter, Gracey Sofia Torres Drucker, for their usual but nonetheless extraordinary love and support. Joel likewise wishes to acknowledge his wife, Viviana Bruckenstein, and sons Kevin Adam Bruckenstein, Alan Jake Bruckenstein, and Eric Jordan Bruckenstein.

Recommended Resources

Antivirus Systems

Antivirus software is a must on each computer you operate to prevent the corruption of sensitive files or entire networks.

McAfee, www.mcafee.com
535 Oakmead Parkway
Sunnyvale, CA 94085
408-992-8100

Panda Software, www.pandasoftware.com/activescan
230 N. Maryland
Suite 303
Glendale, CA 91209
818-553-0599

Symantec, www.symantec.com
20330 Stevens Creek Boulevard
Cupertino, CA 95014
408-517-8000

Application Service Providers

Application Service Providers (ASPs) host software applications on their servers, eliminating the need for you to install and maintain the software on your own hardware. Some, like Proxyvote.com, cost you nothing to use, while the majority are subscription-based services.

FAXES BY E-MAIL

The absolute best way to receive faxes: Have them delivered to your e-mail inbox. You probably need to print only a small percentage of the faxes you receive; archive or delete the rest. Basic service is free; add additional bells and whistles for a modest monthly fee.

E-Fax, www.efax.com
J2 Global Communications
6922 Hollywood Boulevard
8th Floor
Hollywood, CA 90028
800-958-2983

FINANCIAL PLANNING SOFTWARE

Old-style, non-ASP planning software products did not permit access by the client. Let the providers below keep you updated on the latest financial and tax-planning algorithms and provide a cyberspace location where both you and your clients can have input to the planning you do for them.

Financeware, www.financeware.com
100 West Franklin Street
Richmond, VA 23220
804-644-4711

MoneyGuidePro, www.moneyguidepro.com
PIE Technologies, Inc.
2820 Waterford Lake Drive
Suite 103
Midlothian, VA 23112
804-744-5900

NaviPlan Software, www.naviplan.com
900-125 Garry Street
Winnipeg, MB
R3C 3P2
Canada
888-692-3474

PORTFOLIO DEVELOPMENT AND OPTIMIZATION

An online version of Principia, and more. For example, data is always current, and there are no CD-ROMs to deal with.

Morningstar Workstation, http://advisor.morningstar.com
Morningstar, Inc.
225 West Wacker Drive
Chicago, IL 60606
800-735-0700

PORTFOLIO MANAGEMENT SYSTEMS

These providers offer both traditional and ASP portfolio management systems.

Advent, www.advent.com
301 Brannan Street
San Francisco, CA 94107
800-727-0605

Techfi, www.advisormart.com
Techfi Corporation
620 16th Street
Suite 300
Denver, CO 80202
720-891-2000

POSTAGE

No more trips to the post office, and no more postage meter rentals. Order your postage online and print your own stamps.

Simply Postage, www.simplypostage.com
Neopost Online
30955 Huntwood Avenue
Hayward, CA 94544
887-397-8267

Stamps.com, www.stamps.com
3420 Ocean Park Boulevard
Suite 1040
Santa Monica, CA 90405-3324
310-581-7200

United States Postal Service, www.usps.com
If you prefer conventional postage stamps, you can order them online through
the U.S. Postal Service.

PROXY VOTING

Save time and money! Vote your client's proxies online and receive a digital record
for compliance purposes. Best of all, it's free.

Proxyvote, www.proxyvote.com
ADP Brokerage Services
2 Journal Square
Jersey City, NJ 07306
201-714-3000

Backups

LARGE-CAPACITY BACKUPS

Tape is a cost-effective solution for large backup needs.

Exabyte, www.exabyte.com
1685 38th Street
Boulder, CO 80301
303-442-4333

OnStream, www.onstream.com
OnStream Data, Inc.
9600 Great Hills Trail
Suite 150W
Austin, TX 78759
512-637-1381

Seagate, www.seagate.com
Seagate Technology
920 Disk Drive
Scotts Valley, CA 95066
800-SEAGATE

Small- to Medium-Capacity Backups

External hard drives are the recommended solution for small to medium-sized backups. They are inexpensive and portable. USB 2.0 and FireWire drives speed up the process.

LaCie, www.lacie.com
LaCie, Ltd.
22985 NW Evergreen Parkway
Hillsboro, OR 97124
503-844-4500

Maxtor, www.maxtor.com
500 McCarthy Boulevard
Milpitas, CA 95035
408-894-5000

QPS, www.qps-inc.com
8015 East Crystal Drive
Anaheim, CA 92807
800-559-4777

Western Digital, www.wdc.com
20511 Lake Forest Drive
Lake Forest, CA 92630-7741
949-672-7000

Mini-Capacity Backups

Mini USB backup systems are the best new storage products in years. Carry an impressive amount of data around in your pocket.

DiskOnKey, www.diskonkey.com
M-Systems Inc.
8371 Central Avenue
Suite A
Newark, CA 94560
510-494-2090

Sony Micro Vault, www.sonystyle.com/electronics
877-865-SONY

Trek ThumbDrive, www.thumbdrive.com
TrekStor USA Inc.
2411 Old Crow Canyon Road
San Ramon, CA 94583
925-837-4506

USBDrive, www.usbdrive.com
JMTek, LLC
18034 72nd Avenue South
Kent, WA 98032
425-251-9400

Client Contact Database Software
Create, store, and retrieve essential text-based client and administrative records with one of these products.

ACT!, www.act.com
Interact Commerce Corporation
8800 N. Gainey Center Drive
Suite 200
Scottsdale, AZ 85258
480-368-3700

Info Select, www.miclog.com
Micro Logic
666 Godwin Avenue
Midland Park, NJ 07432
201-447-6991

Junxure, www.crmsoftwareinc.com
CRM Software, Inc.
P.O. Box 30607
Palm Beach Gardens, FL 33420-0607
866-CRM-TOOL

Microsoft Outlook, www.microsoft.com/office/programs/default.asp
Microsoft Corporation
One Microsoft Way
Redmond, WA 98052-6399
425-882-8080

ProTracker, www.protracker.com
ProTracker Software, Inc.
6 Merrill Drive
Hampton, NH 03842
603-926-8085

Document Publishing

An essential part of the virtual financial planner's toolkit. Allows you to easily e-mail properly formatted digital documents. Documents can be locked to prevent tampering.

Adobe Acrobat, www.adobe.com
Adobe Systems, Inc.
345 Park Avenue
San Jose, CA 95110-2704
408-536-6000

Document Scanning and Management Software

You can't have a paperless office without one of these:

CEO Image, www.ceoimage.com
CEO Image Systems
340 N. Main
Suite 203
Plymouth, MI 48170
800-523-1066

DocuXplorer, www.DocuXplorer.com
Archive Power Systems, Inc.
DocuXplorer Software

15 West 72nd Street
New York, NY 10023
212-496-9871

Image Edition, www.imageedition.com
Ovation Data Services, Inc.
10650 Haddington Drive
Houston, TX 77043-3229
713-464-1300

PaperPort Deluxe, www.scansoft.com
ScanSoft, Inc.
9 Continental Drive
Peabody, MA 01960
978-977-2000

WORLDOX, www.worldox.com
World Software Corporation
124 Prospect Street
Ridgewood, NJ 07450
201-444-3228

Online CE Credit Sources
The periodicals listed below regularly offer free continuing education tests to readers:

Bloomberg Wealth Manager, http://wealth.bloomberg.com
Financial Planning Interactive, www.financial-planning.com/Education
Investment Advisor, www.investmentadvisor.com/ed_center.asp

Additional sources of continuing education credit (that will set you back a few bucks):

College for Financial Planning, www.fp.edu/students/ce_info.asp
6161 South Syracuse Way
Greenwood Village, CO 80111-4707
800-237-9990

Journal of Financial Planning, www.journalfp.net/ce_online.cfm
3801 E. Florida Avenue
Suite 708
Denver, CO 80210-2571
303-759-4900

Online Financial News

Bloomberg, www.bloomberg.com
Financial Times, http://news.ft.com/home/us
The New York Times, www.nytimes.com
The Wall Street Journal Online, http://online.wsj.com

Online Financial Planning Publications

Bloomberg Wealth Manager, http://wealth.bloomberg.com
Financial Planning Interactive, www.financial-planning.com
Inside Information, www.bobveres.com
Investment Advisor, www.investmentadvisor.com
Journal of Financial Planning, www.journalfp.net
Morningstar Advisor, www.MorningstarAdvisor.com

Optical Character Reading Software

For those OCR tasks requiring extra muscle.

Abbyy FineReader Pro, www.abbyy.com
Abbyy USA
46560 Fremont Boulevard
Suite 105
Fremont, CA 94538
510-226-6717

OmniPage Pro, www.scansoft.com
ScanSoft, Inc.
9 Continental Drive
Peabody, MA 01960
978-977-2000

PDA Software

Visit these sites to squeeze more productivity out of your handheld device with PDA reviews, message boards, software downloads, Web clippings, and the capability of downloading important documents to your PDA for anytime-anywhere reading.

WordSmith, www.bluenomad.com

PDA Street, www.pdastreet.com

PalmGear, www.palmgear.com

AvantGo, www.avantgo.com

LandWare, www.landware.com

Stand Alone Inc., www.standalone.com

Scanners

Fujitsu ScanPartner 3091DC or ScanPartner 4110CU, http://fcpa.fujitsu.com

Fujitsu Computer Products of America, Inc.

2904 Orchard Parkway

San Jose, CA 95134-2009

408-432-6333

Hewlett-Packard 6350, www.hp.com

Hewlett-Packard USA

3000 Hanover Street

Palo Alto, CA 94304-1185

650-857-1501

Kodak i50 and i60 scanners, www.kodak.com

Eastman Kodak Company

Document Imaging

343 State Street

Rochester, NY 14650

716-724-4000

Search Engines and Directories

Google, www.google.com

Teoma, www.teoma.com

Wisenut, www.wisenut.com

Vivisimo, www.vivisimo.com

Yahoo!, www.yahoo.com
Alta Vista, www.altavista.com
Northern Light, www.northernlight.com
All the Web, www.alltheweb.com

Security

FINGERPRINT RECOGNITION

For added security, we highly recommend biometric authentication. These two products are effective and affordable:

DigitalPersona U.areU., www.digitalpersona.com
DigitalPersona, Inc.
805 Veterans Boulevard
Suite 301
Redwood City, CA 94063
650-261-6070

Targus DEFCON Authenticator, www.targus.com/accessories_security.asp
Targus, Inc.
1211 North Miller Street
Anaheim, CA 92806
714-765-5555

FIREWALLS

Antivirus software alone will not protect your computer from uninvited intruders. Firewalls are a must to block Internet-based intrusions and attacks. Some of the leading providers in the field are:

McAfee, www.mcafee.com
535 Oakmead Parkway
Sunnyvale, CA 94085
408-992-8100

Symantec, www.symantec.com
20330 Stevens Creek Boulevard
Cupertino, CA 95014
408-517-8000

ZoneAlarm, www.zonelabs.com
Zone Labs, Inc.
1060 Howard Street
San Francisco, CA 94103
415-341-8200

Virtual Assistants

Total Office (formerly Gal Fridays), www.totaloffice.cc
1170 Sutherland Avenue
Akron, OH 44314
330-753-8881

Virtual Assistants, Sources of

AssistU, www.assistu.com
76 Cranbrook Road
Suite 192
Cockeysville, MD 21030
866-829-6757

Association of Business Support Services International, Inc. (ABSSI),
    www.abssi.org
5852 Oak Meadow Drive
Yorba Linda, CA 92886-5930
714-695-9398

Elance, www.elance.com
820A Kifer Road
Sunnyvale, CA 94086
408-524-7600

FreeAgent, www.freeagent.com
800-445-5775

International Association of Virtual Office Assistants, www.iavoa.com
Rt. 1 Box 275
Red Oak, OK 74563
918-753-2716

International Virtual Assistants Association (IVAA), www.ivaa.org
17939 Chatsworth Street
Suite 102
Los Angeles, CA 91344
877-440-2750

Staffcentrix, www.staffcentrix.com

Virtual Planners

Back Office Solutions, www.backofficesolutions.net
P.O. Box 307
Georgetown, TX 78267
512-863-0883
Naomi Y. Scrivener, CFP, nscrivener@backofficesolutions.net

Secure Financial Management, Inc., www.sfmfinancial.com
44200 Tippecanoe Terrace
Ashburn, VA 20147
866-723-2332
Barbara Clark, CFP, bclark@sfmfinancial.com
Roron Wisniewski, CFP, rwisniewski@sfmfinancial.com

Virtual Reporting Services

Asset Management Solutions, www.assetsolutions.com
550 West Vista Way
Suite 301
Vista, CA 92083
760-643-3838
Mike Kelly, mkelly@assetsolutions.com
Centerpiece and TechFi (Portfolio 2001)

Krisan's BackOffice, Inc., www.krisan.com
804-977-3019
Krisan Marotta, krisan@stanfordalumni.org
Centerpiece

Planners Consulting Group, Inc., www.plannersconsulting.com
3327 Old Morgantown Road East
Accident, MD 21520
301-746-8899
Sandy Derato, sandy@plannersconsulting.com
Centerpiece, TechFi (Portfolio 2001), and dbCAMS+

Voice Recognition Software

If you hate to type, these programs can help. Be prepared to invest a little time training the software.

Dragon Naturally Speaking, www.scansoft.com/naturallyspeaking/
Scansoft, Inc.
9 Centennial Drive
Peabody, MA 01960
978-977-2000

IBM's ViaVoice, www.3.ibm.com/software/speech/desktop
Shop IBM
Dept. YES98
P.O. Box 2690
Atlanta, GA 30301
888-Shop-IBM

Web Collaboration

Save travel time—work with clients and other professionals one-on-one over the Web.

AfterOffice, www.afteroffice.com

Collaborate! Financial, www.collaboratefinancial.com
6029 East Grant Road
Tucson, AZ 85712
888-737-5580

GoToMyPC, www.gotomypc.com

Intranets.com, Inc., www.intranets.com
18 Commerce Way
Suite 2050
Woburn, MA 01801
888-932-2600

Thruport HotOffice Intranet Office Suite, www.hotoffice.com
5440 Cherokee Avenue
Alexandria, VA 22312
703-914-9700

Web Conferencing

Using these services, you can offer virtual client seminars, prospect for new business, and conduct virtual meetings.

Centra, www.centra.com
430 Bedford Street
Lexington, MA 02420
781-861-7000

Genesys Conferencing, www.genesys.com
32 Crosby Drive
Bedford, MA 01730
888-584-2564

iMeet, www.imeet.com
5001 Baum Boulevard
Suite 650
Pittsburgh, PA 15213
877-24-iMeet

Placeware, www.placeware.com
295 N. Bernardo Avenue
Mountain View, CA 94043
888-526-6170

WebEx, www.webex.com
307 West Tasman Drive
San Jose, CA 95134
408-435-7000

Web Site Design

There are loads of companies that can create your website, but there's only one catering to financial professionals that we can recommend with confidence:

AdvisorSites, www.advisorsites.com
Advisor Products, Inc.
115 Eileen Way
Suite 104
Syosset, NY 11791
888-274-5755

I n d e x

ABOUT BLOOMBERG

Bloomberg L.P., founded in 1981, is a global information services, news, and media company. Headquartered in New York, the company has sales and news operations worldwide.

Serving customers on six continents, Bloomberg, through its wholly-owned subsidiary Bloomberg Finance L.P., holds a unique position within the financial services industry by providing an unparalleled range of features in a single package known as the Bloomberg Professional® service. By addressing the demand for investment performance and efficiency through an exceptional combination of information, analytic, electronic trading, and straight-through-processing tools, Bloomberg has built a worldwide customer base of corporations, issuers, financial intermediaries, and institutional investors.

Bloomberg News, founded in 1990, provides stories and columns on business, general news, politics, and sports to leading newspapers and magazines throughout the world. Bloomberg Television, a 24-hour business and financial news network, is produced and distributed globally in seven languages. Bloomberg Radio is an international radio network anchored by flagship station Bloomberg 1130 (WBBR-AM) in New York.

In addition to the Bloomberg Press line of books, Bloomberg publishes *Bloomberg Markets* magazine.

London: ....+44-20-7330-7500
New York: ....+1-212-318-2000
Tokyo: ....+81-3-3201-8900

ABOUT THE AUTHORS

David J. Drucker, M.B.A., CFP, started his fee-only financial advisory firm in 1981 after working as a financial analyst in government and private industry for more than ten years. *Worth* magazine has named him one of the Best Financial Advisors in the United States every year from the 1994 inception of the survey through 2001, and in 1996 he received the NAPFA Distinguished Service Award for his contributions to the fee-only financial planning community. Drucker is a regular columnist or contributor to *Financial Planning, Financial Advisor,* and *Research* magazines, MorningstarAdvisor.com, and *NAPFA Advisor,* the monthly membership publication of the National Association of Personal Financial Advisors. He is also editor of the monthly practice management/technology newsletter for financial advisers, *Virtual Office News.*

Freelance magazine writer, book author, and virtual office consultant **Joel P. Bruckenstein**, CFP, is senior technology editor at Morningstar Advisor.com and publisher of *Virtual Office News* (www.virtualoffice news.com). He writes a monthly technology column for *Financial Advisor* magazine, and he frequently contributes articles to *Financial Planning* magazine and other industry publications. The readers of *Financial Planning* magazine named Bruckenstein to its 2006 list of Movers & Shakers. His expert opinions have appeared in the *Wall Street Journal,* the *New York Times, Investment Advisor, Investment News,* the *New York Daily News, Kiplinger's Retirement Report,* and other publications. He can be reached through his website, www.joelbruckenstein.com.

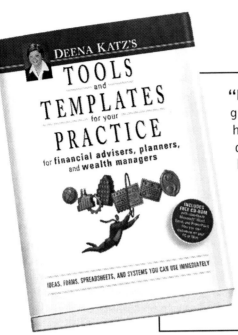

This valuable reference, packed with ideas, forms, spreadsheets, and systems from many of America's leading planners, also includes a free CD-ROM with user-ready Microsoft® Word, Excel, and PowerPoint files you can customize on your PC or Mac.

MorningstarAdvisor.com called this book **"The best, most useful volume ever written on the topic of practice management."** And Bill Bachrach, author of *Values-Based Financial Planning*, said, **"If you can't find ideas that help you serve your clients better and make more money, you aren't paying attention!"**

fuss is about and enhance your practice!

ALSO AVAILABLE

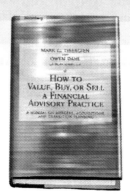

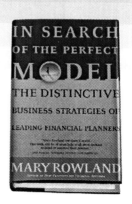

Printed in the United States
200955BV00001BA/105-262/A